Urban Rhythms: Mobilities, Space and Interaction in the Contemporary City

The Sociological Review Monographs

Since 1958, *The Sociological Review* has established a tradition of publishing one or two Monographs a year on issues of general sociological interest. The Monograph is an edited book length collection of refereed research papers which is published and distributed in association with Wiley Blackwell. We are keen to receive innovative collections of work in sociology and related disciplines with a particular emphasis on exploring empirical materials and theoretical frameworks which are currently under-developed.

If you wish to discuss ideas for a Monograph then please contact the Monographs Editor, Chris Shilling, School of Social Policy, Sociology and Social Research, Cornwallis North East, University of Kent, Canterbury, Kent CT2 7NF, C.Shilling@kent.ac.uk

Our latest Monographs include:

Waste Matters (edited by David Evans, Hugh Campbell and Anne Murcott)
Live Methods (edited by Les Back and Nirmal Puwar)
Measure and Value (edited by Lisa Adkins and Celia Lury)
Norbert Elias and Figurational Research: Processual Thinking in Sociology (edited by Norman Gabriel and Stephen Mennell)
Sociological Routes and Political Roots (edited by Michaela Benson and Rolland Munro)
Nature, Society and Environmental Crisis (edited by Bob Carter and Nickie Charles)
Space Travel & Culture: From Apollo to Space Tourism (edited by David Bell and Martin Parker)
Un/Knowing Bodies (edited by Joanna Latimer and Michael Schillmeier)
Remembering Elites (edited by Mike Savage and Karel Williams)
Market Devices (edited by Michel Callon, Yuval Millo and Fabian Muniesa)
Embodying Sociology: Retrospect, Progress and Prospects (edited by Chris Shilling)
Sports Mega-Events: Social Scientific Analyses of a Global Phenomenon (edited by John Horne and Wolfram Manzenreiter)
Against Automobility (edited by Steffen Böhm, Campbell Jones, Chris Land and Matthew Paterson)
A New Sociology of Work (edited by Lynne Pettinger, Jane Parry, Rebecca Taylor and Miriam Glucksmann)
Contemporary Organization Theory (edited by Campbell Jones and Rolland Munro)

Other Monographs have been published on consumption; museums; culture and computing; death; gender and bureaucracy; sport plus many other areas. For further information on Monograph Series, please visit: http://www.wiley.com/WileyCDA/Section/id-324292.html

Urban Rhythms: Mobilities, Space and Interaction in the Contemporary City

edited by Robin James Smith and Kevin Hetherington

Wiley Blackwell/The Sociological Review

Registered Office
John Wiley & Sons Ltd, The Atrium, Southern Gate, Chichester, West Sussex, PO19 8SQ, UK

Editorial Offices
350 Main Street, Malden, MA 02148-5020, USA
9600 Garsington Road, Oxford, OX4 2DQ, UK
The Atrium, Southern Gate, Chichester, West Sussex, PO19 8SQ, UK

For details of our global editorial offices, for customer services, and for information about how to apply for permission to reuse the copyright material in this book please see our website at www.wiley.com/wiley-blackwell.

The right of Robin James Smith and Kevin Hetherington to be identified as the editors of this work has been asserted in accordance with the UK Copyright, Designs and Patents Act 1988.

First published in 2013 by John Wiley & Sons

Library of Congress Cataloging-in-Publication Data

Urban rhythms : mobilities, space and interaction in the contemporary city / edited by Robin James Smith and Kevin Hetherington.
      pages cm. – (Wiley Blackwell/The sociological review)
    Includes bibliographical references and index.
    ISBN 978-1-118-54054-1 (alk. paper)
1. Sociology, Urban.   2. Urban transportation.   3. Public spaces–Social aspects.   4. Social interaction.   I. Smith, Robin James.
II. Hetherington, Kevin.
  HT119.U697 2013
  307.76–dc23

                                                                                          013024149

A catalogue record for this title is available from the British Library

Set in TimesNRMT 10/12pt by Toppan Best-set Premedia Limited

Printed and bound in the United Kingdom

1   2013

Contents

Series editor's introduction

Chris Shilling

The publication of a *Sociological Review* Monograph on urban issues and processes is timely, both sociologically and politically. With the global recession of 2008 placing cities near the top of policy-making agendas, urban environments came to represent an ideal medium through which to explore the conjunction of 'public issues' and 'private troubles' that had exercised the discipline since its inception (Mills, 2000 [1959]).

There are several reasons for this. Economic crisis has prompted a growing concern about the capacity of cities to retain, attract and command new sources of capital. Just as important for sociologists, however, is that the organization and lived experience of urban life appears to be associated increasingly with renewed waves of social unrest and protest. Such conflict has been generated in significant part by systems of governmentality in which the proliferation of 'gated communities' and repressively policed 'red zones' of exclusion, characterized by an enforcement of law requiring a suspension of democratic rights for some (Agamben, 2005), exist uneasily alongside the exacerbation of inequalities and rising levels of poverty.

This focus on the city is not, of course, entirely new: sociology has long recognized the importance of urban centres to those social, economic and cultural issues that lie at the heart of its disciplinary purview. Contemporary studies may be yielding new insights into the modern functioning of major cities as command and control hubs in the global economy (Sassen, 2001), the deleterious effects of city life on social capital (Putnam, 2000), racial separation and urban abandonment in the US (Wacquant, 2007), moral issues associated with cultivating sympathy for 'those who are other' in metropolitan contexts (Sennett, 1994: 18, 376), and a wide range of other issues. Nevertheless, these analyses continued to resonate with the significance placed on city life by the founding figures and early developers of the discipline.

Engels's (2009 [1845]) explorations of urban industrial life in the 1840s, for example, provided an early and still influential study of the physically damaging and spiritually dehumanizing conditions of life for working people living in urban enclaves characterized by overcrowding and lacking basic amenities. Weber (1966 [1921]) explored the differences between contrasting types of cities, and distinctive ways of city living, and located urban forms as integral to wider social, political and religious developments. Simmel (1971 [1903]) had earlier

The Sociological Review, 61:S1, pp. 1–3 (2013), DOI: 10.1111/1467-954X.12059

identified the metropolis as both liberating individuals from traditional ties, but as also threatening to dominate life through its existence as the ecological matrix of the money economy wherein qualitative values were reduced to quantitative measures. Influenced profoundly by the sociology of Simmel, the most influential department in the history of sociology, the Chicago School, sponsored a series of studies focused upon the city as an 'urban laboratory'. These covered a huge range of issues, with Park and Burgess (1967 [1925]) highlighting the importance of the city as a spatial structure and ecological organism, and identifying the significance of urban milieu for the potential creation of intelligent, self-directing publics.

The mention of Simmel is of particular relevance to our contemporary general concern with the city, and for the specific concerns of this volume on *Urban Rhythms*. Simmel's (1971 [1903]) essay, 'The metropolis and mental life' represented a watershed in terms of the manner in which sociology analysed the inter- and intra-actions between the affectual character of the materiality of cities, the development of monetary exchange and calculation, and the acceleration of modern forms of embodiment. At the centre of his analysis, moreover, is a concern with how metropolitan stimuli, individuals and media of exchange contribute to a '*rhythm of events*' that encompass 'conflicting life embracing currents' (Simmel, 1971 [1903]: 326, 339). Developing through their entanglements with each other, Simmel argued that the built environment threatened sensory overload on those accustomed to the slower rhythms of rural existence, prompting in them an emotional armouring against, and a subsequent reserve to, the stimuli with which they were faced. This resulted in a rational, calculative orientation to the 'complications and extensiveness' of metropolitan life; an orientation that not only displayed an affinity with, but also *stimulated further* the extension of monetary transactions and the treatment of people, as well as the built environment, as *means* towards ends (Simmel, 1971 [1903]: 328).

There is still much to be said for Wirth's (1967 [1925]: 218) judgement that Simmel's analysis of the city has been the single most important sociological article on the subject. Emerging from a very different tradition of analysis, however, it is Lefebvre's (1990, 2004) writings on embodiment, cities and the production of space that have arguably done most to extend Simmel's concern with rhythm. Recognizing the coexistence and co-production of social and biological rhythms, Lefebvre (2004: 21) explores the multiple possibilities of existence that characterize city life, insists on the 'lived temporality' of any valid social analysis that seeks to capture these conditions, and provides a major source of inspiration for the articles that constitute this collection on *Urban Rhythms*.

Lefebvre is a controversial figure within urban studies, with some questioning the continued theoretical utility of his writings, but Smith's and Hetherington's introduction demonstrates how his work can be used to connect long-standing problems within sociology (such as the problem of order) to new studies concerned with how the multiplicity of rhythms produced within and outside of urban areas can exert a profound effect on how cities are viewed, experienced and organized. The individual contributors to this volume develop these insights further in a series of valuable and interdisciplinary papers that insist on the generative, rather than simply reproductive, capacity of rhythm in urban life. These range from investigations that engage in a sensory elaboration and analysis of rhythms, and that explore 'red zones' and the nature of political exceptionality, to analyses of the affective, reflexive and relational character of contemporary mobility experiences, of the co-constitution of space and place through symbolic classifications and communal living, and of the multiple ways in which modern cities are layered, patterned and processed by influences from East and West, modernity and postmodernity.

The *Sociological Review Monograph* series publishes special supplements of the journal in collections of original refereed papers and could not continue without the goodwill, advice and guidance of members of the board of *The Sociological Review*, and of those anonymous referees who assess and report on each of the papers submitted for consideration for these collections. I would like to thank all of those involved in this process, especially Dave Clarke, for his very considerable input into the collection, Phil Hubbard, Rolland Munro, Carolyn Baggaley, and also the editors of *Urban Rhythms* for having produced a stimulating and timely volume.

References

Agamben, G., (2005), *State of Exception*, Chicago: Chicago University Press.
Engels, F., (2009 [1845]), *The Condition of the Working Class in England*, Oxford: Oxford World Classics.
Lefebvre, H., (1990), *The Production of Space*, Oxford: Blackwell.
Lefebvre, H., (2004), *Rhythmanalysis: Space, Time and Everyday Life*, London: Continuum.
Mills, C. W., (2000 [1959]), *The Sociological Imagination*, New York: Oxford University Press.
Park, R. and Burgess, E., (1967 [1925]), *The City*, Chicago: Chicago University Press.
Putnam, R. D., (2000), *Bowling Alone: The Collapse and Revival of American Community*, New York: Simon & Schuster.
Sassen, S., (2001), *The Global City*, 2nd edn, Princeton, NJ: Princeton University Press.
Sennett, R., (1994), *Flesh and Stone: The Body and the City in Western Civilization*, London: Faber & Faber.
Simmel, G., (1971 [1903]), 'The metropolis and mental life', in D. Levine (ed.), *Georg Simmel: On Individuality and Social Forms*, Chicago: Chicago University Press.
Wacquant, L., (2007), *Urban Outcasts: A Comparative Sociology of Advanced Marginality*, Oxford: Polity Press.
Weber, M., (1966 [1921]), *The City*, New York: The Free Press.
Wirth, L., (1967 [1925]), 'A bibliography of the urban community', in R. Park and E. W. Burgess (eds), *The City*, Chicago: Chicago University Press.

Urban rhythms: mobilities, space and interaction in the contemporary city

Robin James Smith and Kevin Hetherington

The post-industrial city of the global urban era is seen to be defined by increasingly complex social, spatial and temporal relations, characterized by conditions of change and uncertainty, exception and opportunity. This book seeks to explore and critique such conditions, both as the current state of the urban and with regards to claims of current urban theory and research. The various contributions gathered here represent contrasting approaches to understanding the city, drawing as they do from multiple, and inter, disciplinary perspectives. They also draw from a global range of cities, some which might be considered global cities too. Each paper shares a commitment to elucidating and exploring the complexity of the contemporary metropolis via a (re)consideration of the rhythmic and, increasingly, polyrhythmic nature of everyday urban life. In introducing the papers of this collection, we offer something of a contextualization of the emergence and transformation of the (poly)rhythmicities which underscore the post-industrial city.

In considering the complexity of the contemporary city, one might consider the urban as possessing something akin to a fractal organization; certainly, the closer one inspects the metropolis, the more complex the picture. To approach urban life in this manner is to suggest a possibility of holding the myriad parts of the city in view, whilst apprehending it, distally, as a coherent, patterned, logical whole. A tempting proposition in theory, but, in practice, a misleading one. Even attempting to apprehend more immediate and intimate locations, the parts constituting the whole – the street, the square, the plaza – finds the diversity and fluidity of encounters and passings-by, of seemingly patterned movements and divergent undulations, leaving one wondering how the city hangs together at all. The question of how the 'whole crazy fabric still hangs together' is, of course, not a new one. This was the very question asked by Engels (1993 [1845]) upon his first arrival in London, before his well known investigations in industrial Manchester. It was asked again in Chicago of the early 20th century by Robert Park and colleagues (Park, 1984 [1925]), in New York by Jane Jacobs (1961) and, more recently, Sharon Zukin (2010). Time has proven the troubled question of the possibility of urban social organization to be an enduring one. Indeed, given that the urban is both subject to and source of global(ized) shifts in governance, forces of integration and regulation, and the

The Sociological Review, 61:S1, pp. 4–16 (2013), DOI: 10.1111/1467-954X.12050
© 2013 The Authors. Editorial organisation © 2013 The Editorial Board of the Sociological Review. Published by John Wiley & Sons Ltd, 9600 Garsington Road, Oxford OX4 2DQ, UK and 350 Main Street, Malden, MA 02148, USA

reconfiguration and reordering of relations of space, citizenship and rights played out in localized contexts, the opportunity and challenge presented by the city for understanding human life at its most intense is perhaps more vital for the social sciences now than ever before. The question of the contemporary conditions of urban social and spatio-temporal organization is variously addressed by the works collected in this volume which explore, critique and develop an attention to urban rhythms as a coming together, an entanglement, of space, interaction and mobility.

Faced with an increasing complexity and the accelerating degree of change and flux that cities are subject to, it is, perhaps, little wonder that the social sciences have paid increased attention to the sketches of a theory and method provided by Henri Lefebvre (2004) in *Rhythmanalysis*. One might also, however, question whether such unexamined claims of urban complexity warrant their current commonality and currency? Is it not reasonable to suggest that the burgeoning industrial Manchester of the 19th century or the shifting patterns of immigration and residence in Chicago of the early 20th century exhibited dynamics of flux, flow and change that are equal to the post-industrial cities of the 21st century? Cities have always been defined by complexity. Is urban life really more complex than previously? As will be described in more detail below, the various papers gathered in this collection contribute to an examination of the grounds upon which such claims of increasing urban complexity might stand. They go on to demonstrate a range of means of thinking and researching such complexity which interrogate and critique the conditions of contemporary urban life. Collectively the papers demonstrate that a critical consideration of rhythm allows for an understanding of the contemporary urban era that distinguishes it from those of the past. Cities have always been complex and have long been sites, and products, of upheaval, social change and spatio-temporal reconfiguration. What is distinct about the contemporary era, as this book illustrates, is the way in which rhythms that emerged from and drove change in Engel's Manchester and Park's Chicago – mass industry and the State – have not simply accelerated but, rather, have dissipated. Rhythms now emerge from a syncopation of multiple, conflicting and competing sources, tensions and relations of mobilities, space and interactions.

In considering intersections of the social, spatial and temporal in cities from around the world, this volume applies, extends and critiques the insights offered by Lefebvre, among others, in investigating – theoretically and empirically – the ways in which the urban everyday is made, re-made and may, potentially, be transformed and transformative. This is a project given measure and measured by the pervasiveness of rhythm throughout urban life. As conceived by Lefebvre, an attention to rhythm offers a means with which to (attempt to) grasp something of the complexity of the contemporary city whilst resisting abstraction, fragmentation or reduction. Whilst all areas of social life – all life, indeed – are rhythmic, the work collected here makes visible distinctly urban everyday rhythms and the ways in which such rhythms are productive of the urban experience itself. That is to say, the urban has an intrinsically rhythmic organization which, in turn, gives rise to specific forms, configurations and relations of space, time, interaction and mobility. These are *urban rhythms*. And here, then, we find rhythm as means of connecting part with whole and the particular and universal; the side-walk ballet, to give a familiar example, a synecdoche of city life. Yet, whilst the pedestrian rhythm of the urban crowd – be they commuters, consumers or urban outcasts – might be understood as a signature of dominating city rhythms, rigid, restrained and repetitive, the works in this collection also stress an aspect of rhythm that is often underplayed or misunderstood; that rhythmic repetition is productive of difference. Rhythm, distinct from the metronomic, is a generative and creative force, rather than simply a reproductive one. Here, then, the machinic and generalized, dominating and resisting, rhythms of the industrial city are seen to give way to emergent and competing rhythms which are at once more closely tied to specific sites whilst being increasingly intertwined with global flows of ideas, people and objects. This view of the rhythmic organization and (re)making of the urban is not an attempt to simply locate an abstract or generalized notion of the city in the global era but, rather, draws from a global range of urban contexts – from Manchester to Rio, Jakarta to Amsterdam – in recognizing particularities and similarities, repetition and difference, rupture and continuities in and of space, mobility and interaction in the contemporary city.

Rhythm-cities

If any aspect can be said to render a given city at once unique and yet alike all others it is the characteristic ways in which daily, weekly and annual routines overlap, enmesh and are organized at a distinct pace and in a multiplicity not found in other settings. Indeed, cities become known in and described by their pace, their tempo. Stepping out and walking a newly encountered city is enough to quickly gauge its meter. One might feel to have fallen into step upon arrival or remain disturbingly out of sync; never quite catching up or sufficiently slowing down. The apparent leisure of citizens in public squares, teams of acquaintances stood on streets talking, or conversely, the crowd of strangers, moving quickly, heads down, rushing toward the centre, offer an immediate and some-way-toward-intimate 'feel' for the everyday city. In other instances, the quotidian order is disrupted, obscured or amplified, overwritten by large-scale rhythmic events – Mardi Gras in New Orleans, Carnival in Rio – which, in turn, become synonymous with the city itself; a story about the city, told by the city.

Despite the abundance of form, all cities have and exhibit a social and spatio-temporal organization. And they can be known in this way. Accessing entanglements of time, space and movement is easy enough. They are sensible in the clustering of pedestrians creating crowded and deserted spaces, the comings and goings at transport hubs, times of preparation, of opening and of closing; day rhythms and night rhythms, and in that which the city chooses to memorialize and to forget. Formations of space, time and movement give rise to,

The Sociological Review, 61:S1, pp. 4–16 (2013), DOI: 10.1111/1467-954X.12050
© 2013 The Authors. Editorial organisation © 2013 The Editorial Board of the Sociological Review

solidify in, the city and it is in this sense – to paraphrase James Joyce – that within the particulars of a given city are contained the universals of urban life. This, after all, is the thrill and the comfort, the risk and the reliability of experiencing an as yet unknown city. In the quotidian city, and the experience of the urban citizen, such order(ing)s are not always the stuff of excitement nor, necessarily, a source of comfort. Consider that most rhythmic of movements, walking (Solnit, 2001). Walking the city streets is not always a pleasurable experience. Nor is 'public space' equally accessible to all. And this without yet speaking of how borders and thresholds of urban space change with broader cycles of rupture, decay and renewal.

The city has, of course, always been a force and product of attraction and repulsion (Mumford, 1938). The force of attraction which first established the city of modernity was industry and the opportunity of employment; the associated causes of repulsion, of the coming together of strangers, of urban inequalities and divisions visible still, just as they were to Engels (1993 [1845]) walking through Victorian Manchester. In the 20th century and the combined pressures of space and time, mobility and interaction in the industrialized urban context gave cause for an early analogy with natural processes of competition in the form of the human ecology of the Chicago School:

> the study of the spatial and temporal relations of human beings as affected by the selective distributive and accommodative forces of the environment. Human ecology is fundamentally interested in the effect of position in both time and space, upon human institutions and human behaviour. (McKenzie, 1984 [1925]: 63–64)

This can, perhaps, be read as an early glimpse of the elements of a critical attention to rhythm, albeit from a 'sedentary' perspective.[1] The focus of the Chicago School scholars on competition for city space, the consequences of rapid and easy mobility and the resultant implications for social (dis)order were, of course, accompanied by a concern with the reorganization of the human psyche, of the mental life of the city and of the subordination of the spiritual and emotional to the economic and the rational (Simmel, 1950 [1903]). Indeed, the city of industrial modernity was seen to threaten the stability and sanctity of both internal and social orders and rhythms. The overwhelming pace of life in the industrial conurbation, the increasing economic rationalization of associations, were signatures of the reconfiguration of space, time and interaction. The driving force of such changes accelerating further, 'steadily multiplying, and incidentally complicating, social relations' (Park, 1984 [1925]: 8). Again, these are enduring and abiding themes for urbanists and the social sciences.

The impact of the amplification of connection, of networks and flows, has been profound in the previous decade, prompting a reconfiguration of ways of living and thinking the urban. The so-called global city of late modernity is increasingly understood as a consolidation of networks, flows and mobilities of information, goods and, of course, people; a perspective which finds a 'connected city', a node in larger-scale spatial and temporal patterns (see Neal, 2012). The ease and affordability of international travel not only results in the compression of time-space but a transformation of the local as cities are re-formed and re-imaged in reciprocal relation to the tourist gaze (Urry, 2011). Cities are not only connected communicatively, in the ways that Park described and, in some ways, foresaw, but are also connected to others in and through the circulation and proliferation of models of urban design, security and (re)development. Concerns for the authenticity and identity of cities and the death of the local abound. Representations of a fast and fluid urban are certainly appealing, yet cities are equally defined by crises, ruptures and processes of decay. The seemingly enduring global economic recession and turmoil since 2008 has certainly manifested in highly visible form at street level; whether in the form of stalled building sites, empty stores on high streets or disruption in the form of intense social and political unrest and the occupation (reclamation?) of urban public spaces. We are yet to see the degree to which the current geo-political and economic situation will continue to reconfigure the urban and whether the impact will be as dramatic and as far reaching as that which spawned the 'post-industrial' city. If the city streets in the two decades preceding 2008 had become a site for protesting global issues of a somewhat generalized rhythmic nature (more indicative of a capitalist modernity than specific to the question of locale) then, since the crisis, protest has become much more local again, more concrete and more specific to the rhythms of the here and now. It remains the case, though, that many of the processes of renewal, redistribution and regeneration initiated in the 1980s and early 1990s are still in train.

The 'themeing' of urban space and the increased attention devoted to the design of the public realm – driven by paradoxical discourses of inclusion and securitization – is concerned with the production of profitable forms of everyday inhabitation of urban space. The corporatization of city space, and the subsequent threat to authentic urban spaces and experience (Sennet, 1976; Zukin, 2010), finds extension in the colonization of the temporal frontiers of the city (see, for example, Hadfield, 2006). A seamless transition from diurnal to nocturnal economies, played out across a terrain of smooth surfaces (De Josselin de Jong, 2004). Any optimism for the possibilities of urban life and, indeed, for the realization of utopian visions of the 'good city' (Amin, 2006) is tempered within a secured, sanitized and 'safe' public realm. And whilst these generic processes have been subject to a good deal of, perhaps equally generic, critique there have been fewer attempts to attend and attune to the ways in which urban social and spatial organization is accomplished in the everyday interactions and practices of its citizens; practices and formations found reflected in and as shaped by the organization of a city's infrastructure and built environment. Whilst this level of urban social organization can be dismissed as local, lowly and particular it is at this scale which the relations producing these versions of urban life are accessible to both empirical observation and to critical scrutiny. And it is in this sense that the analysis of urban rhythms, far from tending toward individualization, offers a lens by which to access both the interaction order (Goffman, 1983) and wider frames of urban social, spatial and temporal organization in which the quotidian is realized and (re)produced.

The Sociological Review, 61:S1, pp. 4–16 (2013), DOI: 10.1111/1467-954X.12050

Returning to Lefebvre's original exposition and the well-known essay in which he surveys the city from the vantage point of his Parisian balcony, an alternative perspective – 'simultaneously inside and outside' – is offered, proposing an alternative way of engaging with the ways each of us knows, and comes to know and experience the city. We all immerse ourselves, are enrolled in, and contribute to the production of a city's rhythmic organization. Remaining somehow outside is a tall order, one which reflects the challenge of rhythmanalysis as method and as critique. To give one's self, one's body, over to the rhythms of the city but not to lose oneself, to remain at once inside and outside of a city's tempo. Why outside? For much of the time rhythms are not visible, audible, or felt by us in the course of our daily round. Even the fact that our movements – walking, breathing, talking – are rhythmic can escape our attention until, that is, they stutter or become difficult in absence or amplification, or when we rely directly upon our ability to perceive rhythm as, for example, we measure our steps in crossing the road in traffic (Lefebvre, 2004). A position simultaneously inside and outside allows an appreciation of the rhythms of internal (biological, psychological) and public rhythms of mobility, circulation and interaction in dialogue. Recognizing, recovering, the body, practice and perception within the urban environment was an important act of resistance for Lefebvre, viewing a Paris in which the metronomic march of progress had seen the mechanic replace the organic; the possible pleasures Benjamin described in giving oneself over to the spectacle of the city, contrasted with the timetabled commute and the routine plod from transport terminal to work and back; the body reduced to little more than functional carriage, the surrounding city a distraction, an inconvenience. The project of recovering the organic, the human in the contemporary global, digitally connected city, is still an important one. Yet, as argued across a number of papers in this volume, we can no longer think of rhythm in dualistic terms of the human and the organic opposed to the mechanic and the technological. The contemporary city is not that of industrial modernity. We find, instead, new assemblages of rhythmic practices, new spatio-temporal arrangement and disconnections demanding new forms of urban citizenship, use and, indeed, critical engagement. So, whilst it is attractive to do so, there is danger in simply applying or 'using' Lefebvre's discussion of rhythm when theorizing or studying contemporary urban life. In Lefebvre's words (2004: 5):

> Is there a general concept of rhythm?' Answer: yes, and everyone possesses it; but nearly all those who use this word believe themselves to master and possess its content, its meaning. Yet the meanings of the term remain obscure. We easily confuse *rhythm* with *movement*, speed, a sequence of movements or objects (machines for example). Following this we tend to attribute to rhythms a mechanical overtone, brushing aside the organic aspect of rhythmed movements.

Whilst rhythmanalysis might well be applied in a range of contexts – perhaps universally so – the locus, inspiration and target of Lefebvre's original explorations remains the city of ('so called') modernity. Put another way, to attend to the rhythm of the contemporary city is not to simply mirror the patterns of time and movement in which it presents itself but, rather, to go beyond such representations and to consider the energies, priorities and relations in which the urban is realized, reproduced and remade. In short, one must not only *find* rhythm (if you look for it you will, of course, find rhythm in all things) but think, critically, with that which an attention to rhythm reveals. In this sense, it is not the intention of this book to simply provide a testing ground for, or homage to, the work of Lefebvre. Rather, the various papers gathered herein seek to extend the methodological inspiration offered by *Rhythmanalysis* in experiencing, listening to and revealing and critically engaging the polyrhythmicity of the contemporary urban.

Each paper differently reflects the way in which an attention to the rhythmic organization of the urban is also, necessarily, an attention to and an attempt to preserve the complexity of the city. Alternate modes of knowing the city recurrently find the urban segmented, fragmented and dismantled so that it might be understood. Conversely, other modes of knowledge find the city as an impossibly frozen, immobile whole; the city known, all at once and once for all, the city of the map (see Hall and Smith, 2013a). As Lefebvre (2004: 33) has it:

> Opacity and horizons, obstacles and perspectives implicate one another because they complicate one another, imbricate one another to the point of allowing the Unknown, the giant city, to be glimpsed or guessed at. With its diverse spaces affected by diverse times: rhythms.

Rhythm is thus an apposite concept and approach for the contemporary social sciences, enabling relations of time and space and society to be made visible. Not as an apprehension of a singular relation from a singular position – as 'triangulation' perhaps – but rather to advance an understanding of (urban) social life in its full complexity, as processual, and as an emergent property of a time-space-energy dialectic. As Lefebvre (2004: 12) describes; 'the analysis does not isolate an object, or subject, or a relation. It seeks to grasp a moving but determinate complexity (determination not entailing determinism)'. An attention to and an analysis of rhythm must, then, also be resistant to the dominating rhythms of the urban which it documents in order to uncover alternate, submerged rhythms of change and possibility; 'the visible moving parts hide the machinery'. This volume seeks to extend these ideas not in simply revealing underlying, structuring, rhythms of the contemporary urban but, rather, in theorizing, describing and documenting everyday rhythms as productive, as emergent and as phenomena in their own right. Furthermore, the papers here do not arrive at rhythm via another starting point – mobility, the body, space – rather, rhythm is taken as a point of departure from which we might find such elements in relation.

Here, then, we propose and demonstrate rhythm as an important concept and mode of engagement for contemporary, interdisciplinary understandings of the urban. In many ways Lefebvre's call to rhythm has only been taken up implicitly within the social sciences. A notable exception includes work identifying the

The Sociological Review, 61:S1, pp. 4–16 (2013), DOI: 10.1111/1467-954X.12050

rhythmic organization of bodies, spaces and movement (Edensor, 2010), and other recent engagements and discussions of space and affect (eg Thrift, 2004, 2008). Yet, it remains mobility, rather than rhythm, that has caught the contemporary social scientific imagination. And the organization of contemporary urban life has certainly provided a rich seam for research and theory seeking to identify reconfigured socio-temporal and spatial relations in an era which finds 'an entire world on the move' (Cresswell, 2006: 265). Of course, in the context of the urban, any enthusiasm for mobility is tempered by the acknowledgement of interruptions, breakdowns, pauses and stillness (Hannam *et al.*, 2006; Bissell and Fuller, 2010) and a move toward the recognition of a politics of (im)mobility (Cresswell, 2010; Hall and Smith, 2013b). Mobilities research and theory has, then, done much to elucidate current relations between space, time and movement, proposing both a marked reorganization of the social and a commensurate reorganization of the way in which the social sciences must approach its topic. This volume contributes to this broader project – one which leaves behind notions of the city as either background or container to urban social life – in proposing a revalidation of rhythm as critical lens on urban life. And, again, not simply as a means of uncovering or making explicit the 'hidden' structures of urban life but, rather, as an attention to the everyday entanglements of the motion of bodies and objects, space and time which both shape and emerge from the urban quotidian. In addressing such issues, the various critiques and observations collected here demonstrate a nuanced, relational, 'moving but determinate' politics of urban space, interaction and mobility. The papers thus describe not only the ways in which the conditions of possibility for the city and its citizens exhibit a (poly)rhythmic organization but, equally, ways in which to think the future of the metropolis in terms of the right to the city, the realization of cosmopolitan urban space and the remaking of a sustainable, viable and humanistic notion of the public realm.

Polychronicities: noise, creativity and commoning

The opening section of the book proposes alternative approaches to understanding the rhythmic organization of the urban and, furthermore, the possibilities of a new critique, politics and emergent forms of urban social organization. In moving beyond structural understandings of rhythm as organizing frame, the papers seek to not only extend but revise Lefebvre's original insights in seeking to capture something of the post-industrial city; if only we knew how to look and listen.

Hetherington's paper seeks to supplement the notion of rhythm with that of noise from which patterns emerge not only within the spatio-temporal quotidian order of the city and its routines but also within the time of urban history too. Principally concerned with understanding what we are to make of the relationship between the city and its heritage, he engages with Lefebvre's understanding of rhythm through its relationship to a pre-figuring notion of noise that he draws from the work of Michel Serres (1995). He takes the city as a historical archive whose principle is to order such noise as rhythm and give account for its forms – an archive of heritage stories, for example. And yet within that store of memories, materials, accounts and lived practices that evoke a sense of past within the present are movements and shifts from the soundings and movements out of noise that subtly disrupt the very principle on which a notion of order is established. Out of the archive emerge not only voices but footprints too whose rhythms sound and dance a story to and of the noise of the city emerging from within but also counter to an archive principle.

The next paper, written by Stavrides, complements the temporal perspective of the former in tracing the development of dominant and resistive rhythms in the industrial city of modernity before moving to demonstrate the ways in which we must now rethink our understandings of rhythm, space and time in the urban archipelago. Moving beyond dualistic understandings of organic (human) rhythms dominated by or resisting mechanic rhythms of industry, Stavrides analyses the case of the 'red zone' as characteristic of an established form of contemporary governance and of the city of enclaves. Events such as the Olympic Games and the G20 summits produce 'red zones', spaces of exception in which the usual and expected rights of the citizen are suspended. These are paradoxical spaces; an exceptional disruption of the ordinary justified in preventing the exceptional (an act of terrorism, violence, protest or dissidence) occurring. Such sites are not isolated in time or space; they have a legacy in the everyday spaces of the urban archipelago; the mall, the airport, the resort. Stavrides does not, however, present a dystopian future for the urban. In considering the occupation of public squares during the summer of 2012, he points to an emergent form of spatio-temporal organization in which spaces appearing as exclusionary, as traps, can become sites of creativity, of an organic, polyrhythmic creative commoning.

Stavrides' paper asks us to look again at our understandings of rhythmicity and city space. The following paper asks us to listen again to the everyday rhythms of a familiar setting. Revill's case is the railway station and the train, spaces more readily conceived as defined by a rigid rhythmicity of the timetable. Revill moves to develop a re-reading and critique of Lefebvre's conceptualization of listening which seeks to emphasize the creative and productive qualities of rhythmicity, underplayed in Lefebvre's original discussion, where this aspect tends to cede ground to formal understandings of rhythm as frame. The paper thus utilizes rhythm as a point of departure and coalescence in developing a more affective, reflexive and relational view of contemporary mobility experiences. Here, we find rhythm as both signature and means of accessing mobility in the fullest sense, pointing to a deeper significance, distinguishing movement (as the conquering of spatial distance) from a dynamic mobility (embodied, and culturally and socially meaningful). Thought of in this way, railway stations are not just nodal points managing processes of pulse, flow and switch, but rather are sites of amplification, elaboration and transformation. The case serves as a direction to listen to such sites, and indeed, the city; to

The Sociological Review, 61:S1, pp. 4–16 (2013), DOI: 10.1111/1467-954X.12050

hear and experience them anew, as sites of imaginative resonance, creative interjection and cultural production.

In her paper on the history of the rhythmic phenomenon of the carnival crowd in Rio de Janeiro, Jaguaribe explores the historical relationship between the excesses of carnival and understandings of the city in various forms of writing and media representation. She shows, in the context of a changing society in the century after the abolition of slavery in the 1880s, how an urban, tropical modernity was articulated around notions of the festive that became part of the representation not just of carnival but also of that city; itself sometimes emblematic of Brazil as a whole. Through the heteroglossia associated with crowd and its place on the streets during carnival the struggle between the voices of different social classes was articulated. Such a dialogue expressed a relationship between the extraordinary and the mundane that is at the heart of urban experience and she charts how our understanding of the city comes to be voiced through the rhythms of that dialogue.

Margin and centre: the management of time and space

The first four papers outline a number of the challenges that face the student of the contemporary city. The insights offered each point to a need for a critical reconceptualization of our understandings of the rhythmic organization of the post-industrial city, of the selective enfolding of the past-as-noise into the present, of the potentialities of simultaneously affective and reflexive mobility experience and of the spaces of opportunity for an emergent, organic organization. In turn, such reconceptualizations propose new modes of looking at, hearing, moving in, experiencing and perceiving the public spaces of the polychronic city. An attention and an attitude toward the ways in which rhythm and repetition not only dominate, regulate or reproduce urban space but, moreover, can themselves be productive of difference and distinction. In the following section, two papers, by Hall and Smith and Simone and Fauzan, consider the rhythmic organization of city streets, public spaces, and urban economies as relational aspects of street-level city life. Central to these two papers, grounded in ethnographic fieldwork, is an attention to the ways in which an empirical engagement with the polyrhythmic city might point to a nuanced politics, tracing new lines of entanglement, of overlap and of resistance, and of conflicting patterns of social and spatial marginality. In keeping with the previous section the papers here consider the quotidian in the context of wider socio-temporal frames in relation to processes of urban remake and regeneration, local economic organization resistive to integration into that of larger spatial orders, and of the rhythms produced in and through the management and provision of welfare to marginal groups found entangled in central spaces.

The everyday management of urban public space is explored, rather literally, by Smith and Hall in a paper describing a full twenty-four hours on patrol in the city centre of Cardiff, UK. The authors trace and describe the pedestrian mobilities of various practitioners – street sweepers, Police Community Support Officers, outreach workers, and church volunteers – who, in related yet distinct ways, all contribute to the maintenance of the city centre. The circulations of the various practitioners trace connections between the central spaces and times of the city centre and the movements of those experiencing vulnerability and need. In moving beyond the confines of the 24-Hour city and the night-time economy, the authors point to a nuanced, ambivalent, politics where the various practitioners are equally involved in practices of care and maintenance, regulation and monitoring. A street-level politics made visible in tracing the lines along which moral geographies of care, regulation and management of troubled and troublesome urban populations are routinely accomplished and negotiated.

In their theoretically informed ethnography of the local organization of economic life in Jakarta, Simone and Fauzan carefully illustrate the ways in which people manage their relations with time, space and social structure in ways which give rise to new forms of association and activity. Via the stories of a number of characters and settings the authors eloquently demonstrate the ways in which time and, more specifically, *timing* plays a pivotal part in collective organization. Timing here relates to people's organization of their practical affairs and how the pacing of local economic life and affiliations enables a particular understanding of how they affect the city and how the city affects them. Simone and Fauzan's ethnography points to the ways in which considerations of timing reveals a politics of anticipation, enabling people to operate 'under the radar', to experiment with various initiatives and developments without commitment and, in a wider sense, to manage the very conditions of urban life.

Everyday entanglements: placing and planning the urban

The final section consists of two papers which differently consider the quotidian and the everyday in relation to the rhythmic accomplishment of place (Edensor, 2010). Lehtovuori and Koskela's paper takes a specific street – Calçada de Sant'Ana, Lisbon – as a case through which to explore the local ways in which space and place are co-constituted in and through symbolic meanings and the everyday communal use of the street. In focusing on the everyday rhythms of this co-constituency (Casey, 2001; Massey, 2005) – through the repetitive chopping of the butcher's cleaver, the perception of atmosphere and thresholds, visible displays of community – Lehtovuori and Koskela illustrate an inclusive and open public space, moving out beyond the setting to point to new tools of analysis and activism which have the potential to inform the creation of inclusive spaces elsewhere. Key here are, of course, Lefebvre's discussions of an approach to analysis and theory which finds spatiality and temporality together, as they are, of course, found in everyday life. And it is within this understanding that the everyday is seen as both the unit of analysis for the production of place and as the site in which change becomes possible. In this sense, Lehtovuori and

The Sociological Review, 61:S1, pp. 4–16 (2013), DOI: 10.1111/1467-954X.12050
© 2013 The Authors. Editorial organisation © 2013 The Editorial Board of the Sociological Review

Koskela seek to advance understandings of urban malleability and stability and of the city as oeuvre.

In the final paper of this collection, Lagerkvist takes us on a tour of contemporary Shanghai. The city provides an ideal case for the application of rhythmanalysis whilst also offering a serious test of the claims made in relation to the analysis and 'grasping' of contemporary urban complexity. In keeping with the attempts to develop and extend the insights offered by Lefebvre (2004), Lagerkvist attends to both the 'patterned particularities of place' and to the 'ripples' on the surface of the technocratic, official, layout of an urban heterochrony in which East and West, modernity and postmodernity meet in a 'chaotic incompatibility'. In describing the experiences of tourists taking a guided tour which deliberately constructs Shanghai as a city of difference, contrast and contradiction, and change, Lagerkvist captures something of the way in which a critical rhythmanalysis enables one to beyond 'themed perplexity' to glimpse alternative trajectories of memory and future in this globally significant locale.

Taken as a whole, this collection attends to the social, spatial and temporal organization of the contemporary city. It mobilizes rhythm in a revitalization of classic questions of the conditions of possibility, organization and (re)production of the city as a human environment offering to reconnect with the organic, the embodied, the creative and the transformative. In all its complexity – a complexity approaching the seemingly disorganized – the cacophonous and chaotic contemporary city poses new challenges for understandings of what we understand by the 'urban', 'metropolis' and 'city'; a challenge taken up by the various papers in this volume. The strongly contrasting approaches collected here – compare, for example, the ethnography of Smith and Hall and Simone and Fauzan with the theoretically orientated papers of Hetherington and Stavrides – reveal independently developed yet common themes and connections. These connections point to the power of rhythmanalysis as critical thought and movement, as an open, reflexive and exploratory critical engagement with the contemporary city. In sum, the various glimpses of cities from around the globe do much to move beyond static and divided, regulatory and resistive understandings of mobility, interaction and urban space and, instead, offer a reconsideration of the city as a polyrhythmic accomplishment in elucidating the conditions of the contemporary urban and signalling the possibilities for a creatively contested, polychronic urban.

Note

1 See Jensen (2009) for an insightful critique of, and a number of moves beyond, the 'sedentary' and 'nomadic' dichotomy of urban mobilities thinking and research.

References

Amin, A., (2006), 'The good city', *Urban Studies*, 43: 1009–1023.
Bissell, D. and Fuller, G. (eds), (2010), *Stillness in a Mobile World*, London: Routledge.

Casey, E., (2001), 'Between geography and philosophy: what does it mean to be in the place-world?' *Annals of the Association of American Geographers*, 91: 683–693.

Cresswell, T., (2006), *On the Move: Mobility in the Modern Western World*, Abingdon: Routledge.

Cresswell, T., (2010), 'Toward a politics of mobility', *Environment and Planning D: Society and Space*, 28: 17–31.

Edensor, T., (2010), 'Introduction: thinking about rhythm and space', in T. Edensor (ed.), *Geographies of Rhythm: Nature, Place, Mobilities and Bodies*, 1–20, Farnham: Ashgate.

Engels, F., (1993 [1845]), *The Condition of the Working Class in England*, Oxford: Oxford University Press.

Goffman, E., (1983), 'The interaction order, ASA 1982 Presidential Address', *American Sociological Review*, 48: 1–17.

Hadfield, P., (2006), *Bar Wars: Contesting the Night in Contemporary British Cities*, Oxford: Oxford University Press.

Hall, T. and Smith, R. J., (2013a), 'Knowing the city: maps, mobility and urban outreach work', *Qualitative Research*, online first, DOI: 10.1177/1468794112469623.

Hall, T. and Smith, R. J., (2013b), 'Stop and go: a field study of pedestrian practice, immobility and urban outreach work', *Mobilities*, 8 (2): 272–292.

Hannam, K., Sheller, M. and Urry, J., (2006), 'Editorial: mobilities, immobilities and moorings', *Mobilities*, 1 (1): 1–32.

Jacobs, J., (1961), *The Life and Death of Great American Cities*, New York: Random House.

Jensen, O., (2009), 'Flows of meaning, cultures of movements – urban mobility as meaningful everyday life practice', *Mobilities*, 4 (1): 139–158.

De Josselin de Jong, F., (2004), 'External space is given the Botox treatment', in *Landscape Architecture and Town Planning in the Netherlands 0-03*, 148–157. Bussum: Uitgeverij THOTH.

Lefebvre, H., (2004), *Rhythmanalysis: Space, Time and Everyday Life*, London: Continuum.

Massey, D., (2005), *For Space*, London: Sage.

McKenzie, R. D., (1984 [1925]), 'The ecological approach to the study of the human community', in R. Park and E. W. Burgess (eds), *The City: Suggestions for the Investigation of Human Behaviour in the Urban Environment*, 63–79, Chicago: University of Chicago Press.

Mumford, L., (1938), 'The culture of cities', in P. Kasinitz (ed.), *Metropolis: Centre and Symbol of our Times*, 21–29, New York: Palgrave Macmillan.

Neal, Z., (2012), *The Connected City*, London: Routledge.

Park, R., (1984 [1925]), 'The city: suggestions for the investigation of human behaviour in the urban environment', in R. Park and E. W. Burgess (eds), *The City: Suggestions for the Investigation of Human Behaviour in the Urban Environment*, 1–46. Chicago: University of Chicago Press.

Sennet, R., (1976), *The Fall of Public Man*, New York: Alfred A. Knopf.

Serres, M., (1995), *Genesis*, Ann Arbour: University of Michigan Press.

Simmel, G., (1950 [1903]), 'The Metropolis and mental life', in K. H. Woolff (ed.), *The Sociology of Georg Simmel*, 409–424, New York: The Free Press.

Solnit, R., (2001), *Wanderlust: A History of Walking*, London: Verso.

Thrift, N., (2004), 'Intensities of feeling: towards a spatial politics of affect', *Geografiska Annaler*, 86 (1): 57–78.

Thrift, N., (2008), *Non-Representational Theory: Space, Politics, Affect*, London: Routledge.

Urry, J., (2011), *The Tourist Gaze 3.0*, London: Sage.

Zukin, S., (2010), *Naked City: The Death and Life of Authentic Urban Places*, Oxford: Oxford University Press.

The Sociological Review, 61:S1, pp. 4–16 (2013), DOI: 10.1111/1467-954X.12050

Rhythm and noise: the city, memory and the archive

Kevin Hetherington

Abstract: Henri Lefebvre's *Rhythmanalysis*, while typically loose and underdeveloped as a work, offers a highly suggestive way of thinking about mobility and pattern within spatiality, and also alerts our attention to the importance of temporal rhythms. This paper is concerned with the rhythms of history within the city, notably how heritage gets made, remade and unmade within the city as a form of archive. Comparing Lefebvre's concept of rhythm to that of noise in Michel Serres (notably in his book *Genesis*), I explore the meaning of urban heritage – in which the past is made present – analysing how the past can interrupt the present within the city and how that opens up possibilities for critical reception and potential alternative urban futures.

Keywords: archive, heritage, memory, walking, noise, performance

The city as archive

Archives are not static things, not only do their contents change but the aspirations on which they are premised do too. The archive, as Derrida has argued, is an inherently problematic kind of space. It cannot be otherwise. It is one which, in practice, is forever involved in the seemingly contradictory process of conserving and containing the past as a total record of what has happened for posterity to see while at the same time allowing the Otherness of an outside of that record to come within and to unsettle that record and disrupt that guiding ambition (Derrida, 1996). This is not simply a philosophical problem; rather, this contest with Otherness is implicated, too, in the broad social terrain of cultural memory that archives help establish. The condition of possibility for the archive, if we follow Derrida's argument, is to always exist, but to exist in a state of doubt involving both endless recovery and record, but also erasure and revision at the same time. The archive promises total recall but never fully delivers on it. From time to time a multitude of possible external forces – from hostile armies, to looters, to fire, to bad cataloguers, to changing social attitudes over what is valued, to the sheer overwhelming volume of stuff (unsorted rubbish) waiting to be accorded access, threaten to change it or on occasions to tear it apart altogether (see Goudsblom, 1992; Polastron, 2007). In terms of

The Sociological Review, 61:S1, pp. 17–33 (2013), DOI: 10.1111/1467-954X.12051
© 2013 The Author. Editorial organisation © 2013 The Editorial Board of the Sociological Review. Published by John Wiley & Sons Ltd, 9600 Garsington Road, Oxford OX4 2DQ, UK and 350 Main Street, Malden, MA 02148, USA

broad cultural imaginings, then, Western society, around which the principle of cultural understanding and the archive process have always gone hand in hand, is ever thus premised on a state of mourning for the library of Alexandria and knowing that that is the fate of most archives in the longer term. As a total record, the archive in perpetuity is always a fantasy, even if a culturally compelling one (Hetherington, 2010).

There are many kinds of archive from libraries and museums to seed banks and record offices of the state. But archive speaks to a wider issue than that limited by these particular institutional forms. It is the cultural principle of the archive that I am really interested in here, rather than these official forms of site-specific archive (see also Osborne, 1999). More specifically, I am interested in the relationship between this archive principle as a basis for cultural memory and the urban. Significantly Michael Sheringham (2010) has pointed out that cities are indeed a form of archive – one where the past is conveyed through the everyday materiality and lived practice that shapes their composition (see also Benjamin, 1999; Sinclair, 2010). Not only the architecture and the street layout, the shops and offices, cafes and bars but the names of places and their association with past events are all a part of the multiple record of the city that one encounters in a variety of ways. But this is a street level form of archive rather than one filed away. Some of this is clearly visible and well known, other things are not; mere traces being all that is left of what once was. A collection of artefacts, signs, sedimented patterns of activity and practices embedded in the fabric of the built environment, the city lends itself to being read as an archive built up over time as a collection and a record of the past that continues to resonate in the present.

It is through such an archive principle that the past continues to inhabit the present within the urban setting. As Sheringham shows, this theme of the city-as-archive is a notable literary trope found in both fictional and nonfictional documentary texts (and sometimes both) on urban life. From Engels (1892) to Mayhew (1968); Benjamin (1999) to Sebald (2002); Aragon (1971) to Debord (1989), Perec (1997) to Sinclair (1997) and many more besides (see also Keiller, 1999), the city throws up its own archive effects awaiting literary exploration – sometimes revealed, sometimes hidden but available to cultural memory and its representation. In the spirit of Derrida's perspective on the archive, though, such effects also have the potential to reveal the sounding of memories (and also counter-memories) that sometimes call into question received archival understandings, place myths and place brandings within the detritus and the everyday that urban forms and processes are made from (see also Sheringham, 2006).

All of these authors recognize in their different ways the paradoxical uncertainty of the city as an archive or repository for the past and its future remembrance. They recognize the need to record and allow voices that otherwise might be lost to opportunity to be heard. In our time what also comes prominently into view in this description of the city-archive is not only material remainders from earlier times and daily practice that still persists with reference to long forgotten antecedents but also the broader question of their representation as heritage. Indeed, for the last three decades the issue of heritage has been the main archival trope for engaging with understanding the past within the present in towns and cities across the world. It has become the discourse of the archive as a record of the urban (on heritage as discourse see Smith, 2006).

After heritage came to prominence as an issue through UNESCO in the 1970s and its designation of sites as heritage sites (see Harrison, 2013), the term seemed to fit with the neo-liberal and consumerist times that developed in the 1980s leading some at the time to speak of a heritage industry and the consumerist packaging of cultural memory. In the urban context earlier post-war ways of clearing away old, unwanted (bomb) sites and redeveloping in a spirit of mod- ernist optimism slowly gave way as de-industrialization set in and many newly developed urban centres went into decline. The way out of this, it was hoped at the time, was through service sector and consumer-led redevelopment, regen- eration and gentrification (see Zukin, 1988, 1995). Attracting investment, facili- tating economic growth and encouraging new employment opportunities became the spur for urban change and that was facilitated by the move away from corporatist and towards entrepreneurial forms of urban governance (see Harvey, 1989; Hall and Hubbard, 1998; Cronin and Hetherington, 2008). Uncluttering the archive by simply disposing of unwanted bits of the past gave way, in effect, to its recataloguing under the heading of heritage.

For the last twenty years the focus for heritage has been around culture-led regeneration of towns and cities being shaped by public-private partnerships, the designation of areas in need of regeneration as hubs or cultural quarters, investment into saving the urban and industrial infrastructure and making it attractive to tourists and other visitors, tax breaks to attract investment, encour- aging the development of up-market housing, shopping and urban entertain- ment and increased competition between urban centres for capitalist functions. There have been some notable successes in which museums and heritage devel- opments have been prominent in this process of urban regeneration: the trans- formation of a derelict power station on the south bank of the River Thames in London into Tate Modern, Britain's leading gallery for modern art, the Guggenheim museum designed by Frank Gehry in Bilbao and perhaps above all the regeneration of central Berlin after German reunification (see Huyssen, 2003; Till, 2005). These all speak to the degree of success that some cities have had in this approach to redevelopment and economic prosperity. And the heritage/museum led approach to boosting economic growth and enhancing the brand of a city is no longer just confined to Europe and North America. From Shanghai to Rio to Abu Dhabi, through expos (Lai, 2004) to franchised models of leading Western museum brands to local versions, a model of museum and heritage development as central to regeneration and prosperity now seems glo- bally established (see Harrison, 2013).

But other examples of this approach of cultural redevelopment and museum or heritage branding have not fared so well. Museums such as *Urbis* in Man- chester or visitor centres like *The Public* in Walsall struggled to gather local support (Hetherington, 2007). In other contexts one only has to walk a block or two from the centre of a cultural quarter with its museums, theatres, restaurants and cafes to find the seedier side of urban life still there alongside unregulated car parking on empty land or sites of outright dereliction, overgrown with buddleia, fenced off and subject to nightly patrols by contracted private security guards. Rubbish, the detritus of the past, including the recent past of urban regeneration, accumulates in times of recession and economic uncertainty in particular (see Leslie, 2010). Yet this unrecorded outside, for that is what it is, always finds a way of returning to the archive as a principle of cultural under-standing. It is, as Sinclair (2010) has put it, like a virus that infects the settled nature of urban memory.

For some, though, the success or failure of such enterprise culture initiatives (as they used to be called) were never to be measured in terms of jobs, house price rises or the sale of cappuccino and theatre tickets, but were always seen in some way as the ever-same of capitalist boom and bust. But leaving aside the critiques of these practices as part of neo-liberal economic strategy, broader concerns have been raised around the questions of cultural memory that this approach to heritage and museum collections raises (see Smith, 2006). The questions and criticisms that have been raised around urban heritage as a means of presenting cultural memories have been varied but have tended to focus on their consumerist stance, simplification of stories about the past, partial accounts of certain versions of heritage and recognition of the importance of the politics of recognition and identity to remembrance of the past (Huyssen, 1995; Trouillot, 1995; Kirshenblatt-Gimblett, 1998).

To be more specific the main criticisms of this strategy of using heritage as a part of urban regeneration can be grouped under three themes:

1) That heritage is somehow staged and packaged as part of a regeneration and branding strategy that does not allow history to be experienced except in commodified form.
2) That heritage tells an incomplete story – one that marginalizes and excludes on such grounds of identity notably around race, class and gender.
3) That the presentation of history as heritage is part of a culture industry that rather than helping us to remember the past actually produces a form of amnesia and forgetfulness in which above all the history of practice becomes reified in monumental geographical sites.

But is this the terrain on which we still stand? At the beginning of 2013 and several years after the 2008 credit crunch, subsequent recession across much of the Western world and an expectation of more economic bad news to come for much of the rest of this decade much of this approach to regeneration may soon seem part of a different era. Since 2008 many Western countries have seen significant cuts in funding to the areas of culture and arts including to museums and the heritage sector. Many of the quasi-autonomous organizations set up to manage, regulate and fund heritage initiatives have been closed, merged or seen their budgets significantly cut. And a walk around many urban centres will reveal that the vulnerable areas the culture-led regeneration was, for sometimes 20 years or more, intended to regenerate are the first to see the closure of many businesses, economic blight and the emerging signs of a new round of dereliction and marginalization.

To date, however, it remains the case that neo-liberal responses to the current economic crisis remain hegemonic. What isn't there is the money to fund new culture-led initiatives on a grand scale – at least not in Europe and North America. China and the UAE, for example, are another matter. Whether we will simply see a return to the old ways of doing things as investments start to be made and a recovery begins to be spoken about remains to be seen. Rather than rehearsing the old criticisms of the heritage industry now might be an opportune moment to speak instead of an alternative take on questions of cultural memory and seek to make an intervention that proposes new models of thinking about the past through heritage.

These thoughts about the paradoxes of the archive, I argue, can help us to do that. Rather than focus on the city as a social space that is a container for history and through which heritage becomes realized in a site, I want to adopt a model that treats space as a set of relations that are fluid and mobile and in which uncertainty is ever present behind any narrative of place. That fluidity and relationality extends to questions about the past as much as it does to current social practice.

This is not a new argument. It is one that social and cultural geographers have been debating for some time, initially through problematizing issues of region and ideas of boundedness (Allen *et al.*, 1998), then by recognizing that space is not somehow separate from practice but is made through social relations and latterly by taking a more fluid and topological approach to traditional questions of topography, including involving such questions as the non-relational, the outside and other forms of absent presence that we encounter within cities (see Thrift, 1996; Massey, 1999, 2005; Hetherington and Law, 2000; Amin and Thrift, 2002).

Two themes stand out for me when approaching these questions of spatiality. The first is what we might call voice and the second is that of mobility. By voice I do not mean simply the spoken voice or the right to be heard around questions of memories and the urban pasts in the plural though that is certainly there. Rather, these relational approaches to space are interested in how it is made through practice and that often means incorporating the non-human or the materiality of a space into our understanding of it too (see Hetherington, 1997; Murdoch, 1998).

The materiality of ruins, the haunting material traces of the past that remain part of the urban fabric and the evocative power of the past to engage active subjects, are all issues that have been raised within recent urban studies attentive to questions of cultural memory (see Jaguaribe, 1999; Hetherington, 2002; Edensor, 2005). So too has been the issue of the sensing body and the idea of embodied spectatorship (see Pile, 1996). One does not see panoramic vistas of city life as one moves through them, sometimes at walking pace sometimes by car and sometimes via trains or other forms of public transport. One hears the city as well as sees it, smells it, can touch it and even taste it. So if we assume the materiality of the city is not a mute staging then the bodies that also help to make this space pass through it in ways that open up a range of different perspectives, understandings and memories. The moving body, then, might be considered as another outside intervention in the archival urban record.

We have seen some of this as a minor theme within discussions of heritage and cultural memory in the past. It has long been there in an interest in the evocative power of ruins (Edensor, 2005), in seeking out the uncanny and ghostly traces of the past hidden within the present of the city (Jaguaribe, 1999), in the 1960s Situationist approach to psychogeography (see Debord, 1989; Coverley, 2006), the derive or drift and other latter days forms of the Flâneur, and it is there in the Benjamin inspired approach to cities as archives of the past and dreamscapes in which surrealist inspired juxtapositions, chance encounters and shocks of recognition might produce an awakening onto a different vision of the past and what it might say to the present about the future (Breton, 1960; Aragon, 1971; Benjamin, 1985).

I want to say a little about some of these issues in what is to follow both in terms of the opportunities they suggest for approaching heritage as well as some of the problems that they generate too. My focus is on issues of materiality and movement as a way of interrogating how cultural memories are established and how this might speak to debates about heritage in a moment of crisis when things are up for grabs. The following two sections on cultural memory look at philosophical approaches to these questions, notably in the work of Henri Lefebvre and Michel Serres. I use the theme of rhythm in my title to capture something of this set of approaches, a term that also comes from leading spatial theorist Henri Lefebvre's final book, *Rhythmanalysis* (2004). This also raises questions of noise out of which rhythmic patterns emerge. I discuss Serres' work on this theme (1995) to supplement and extend some of Lefebvre's thinking around Rhythm. Rhythm suggests two types of pattern: patterns of sound and patterns of movement so what I want to do is draw some of that out in identifying a set of ways of thinking about heritage that might in time become a counter-argument to neo-liberal approaches to the issue without reverting back to a fetishism/reification/alienation model that typically lies at the centre of many of the readings of the urban that I identified in my list above. The final two sections that deal with questions of heritage do this around the themes of voice and footprint to capture both the sonorous and mobile characters of rhythm. I return to the issue of archive in the conclusion where I elaborate further on these as issues of outside disruptions and their possibilities.

Cultural memory and rhythm

In his last work on the city, Henri Lefebvre suggested we should become sensitive to its rhythms in order to develop our understanding of what cities are. In many respects he was referring to the everyday patters of the city shaped by the ways people moved around within it. Informed by a capitalist economic process, this largely developed around the working day, week, month and year. The flows of people, traffic, the ways in which the city is used differently during rush hour or on a Friday evening after work all highlight the rhythms and patterns that one witnesses within cities as shaped by their capitalist economies. They are made up, he suggests, not only of the built environment and infrastructures through which people move but through repetitions of activity that also produced ripples of difference that mean that any one time in the city is never quite the same as another.

Rhythm involves movement but for Lefebvre it is not simply the same as movement; mobile bodies and materialities help to establish rhythms but his real interest is in how pattern comes to be established out of the noise of a city which on first appearance might appear to be just a cacophony of singular acts without any relationship to each other. For Lefebvre, the dominant force in establishing such rhythm is capital. Not only does it establish working patterns and their associated flows through the city but it is engaged in a range of modes of ordering across a range of different time scales, some linear, some cyclical, some discontinuous or disrupted, many of which have patterns of overlap or interference between them. It is through these, he suggests, that we come to understand the make-up of an urban centre as a lived reality. From the rhythms associated with economic growth and decline, to the forms of measure associated with such things as clock time, to the rhythms associated with the uses of money in its various forms and speeds of transfer (see Pryke, 2011), to the rhythms of production and destruction, these all in some measure impact on the character of a city and leave behind traces as well as initiating new patterns of activity.

Lefebvre's main point is to suggest that attention to the rhythms of the build environment is one that challenges a Cartesian outlook on its spatiality as something fixed and plan/grid-like and alongside this to call into question overly dominant understandings of time as something linear and chronological. Rhythm makes space appear topological rather than topographical; a crumpled geography of social-material relations that cannot be accounted for in Euclidean terms such as scale, transitivity, singular location, discrete regions and so on. Such representational practices are themselves, Lefebvre believes, a product of capitalism's urban rhythms which function as an ideology of space and time (1991, 2004). Making rhythm visible and studying its multiple patterns of difference and repetition suggest a more complex understanding of space and time within an urban society.

Lefebvre does not have anything of real note to say in this work on how history, or indeed heritage and cultural memory, is folded into this analysis but it is certainly there. It is part of the noise out of which the rhythms of urban life emerge. Noise, for Lefebvre, is the background out of which rhythmic patterns of life and activity emerge. It has no rhythm in itself but is the substance from which rhythms are established. At one point he suggests we see history as part of the noise – something that influences and shapes the rhythms of the present but in ways that are not easily apparent. What I propose we take from this is a sense that cultural memories are established where rhythms become emergent from noise. How they resonate in the archive of the urban is something we need to consider too.

Cultural memory I see as something emergent and social, or at least as grouped in patterned ways, from individual memories – but not either reducible to them nor simply a sum of their total taken together – it is what emerges from noise (see Halbwachs, 1992). It is realized both through practice and through the materiality with which that practice is entangled. Famously in another one of his books *The Production of Space* (1991), Lefebvre once described social space as being like a mille feuille pastry – a thousand fragile layers of space that could crumble and mingle across their apparently stratified ordering. In other words, he imagines a social space like a town or city as a palimpsest of different spaces caught up with different times all found together in a complex and seemingly patterned whole in which dominant representations of space provide an interest-driven understanding of its patterns and forms.

That is a useful starting point in thinking about the past in relation to rhythm. Palimpsest, fragment and trace are not just complex orderings of space where we encounter elements, materialities of different times together in one space; they also have their own rhythmic effect within the city.

For example:

- Derelict sites are not simply derelict and then become regenerated as the planners and developers would like to hope. They can move in and out of use and disuse over different durations of time generating their own forms and shaping the potential for different types of practice and altering values associated with them – cultural as much as economic (see Thompson, 1979)
- The remains of the past take the form of a material trace that invites or affords forms of encounter that can alter the way that we experience the built environment and shift the patterns of repetition into that of difference.

Cultural memory and noise

A supplementary understanding of noise, more detailed than that provided by Lefebvre, can be found in the philosopher Michel Serres' work, notably his book *Genesis* (1995), which is concerned with developing an understanding of the making of order and the birth of forms that does not rely on a reductionist or foundationalist notion of origins or ground. Some will be familiar with Serres' work though his influence on actor-network theory, including the work of Bruno Latour and others (see Serres and Latour, 1995). Interested in questions of multiplicity and heterogeneity that challenge foundationalist understandings and the privileging of human agents as the loci for action, Serres' work recognizes agency as something distributed across multiplicities that are heterogeneous in character. Agency, for Serres, is an effect of this distribution within a

The Sociological Review, 61:S1, pp. 17–33 (2013), DOI: 10.1111/1467-954X.12051

network of elements rather than the intentional act of conscious beings alone. Noise is one of his main categories for thinking through this approach. It is, for Serres, a recognition that things are always multiple and cacophonous in character, not easy to disentangle or sound out. From this starting point (which is never in fact a point – one of Serres' chief metaphors is that of travelling up-stream to find the source of a river. When we do so, he suggests that instead of finding a single origin from which the water springs we find a multiplicity of sites from which the water seeps out of the ground), Serres suggests that our task in recognizing the multiple is not to render it visible through analysis as something singular (to black-box it) but to retain its multiple character.

Noise is a term used to think through these issues because it suggests a different sense to that of vision – hearing. In order to appreciate elements of urban social life as something multiple our analysis should not be about trying to see it, especially as a simple whole – which is what the Western perspectival tradition typically promotes – but rather to hear it as if we were listening to a complex piece of music. A recognition of the noise of the social, and in our case it would be the town or city, is to be open to it as a series of possibilities out of which a multiple understanding might come to be recognized of its multiple forms. In this philosophical approach possibilities replace origins or foundations and forms (rhythms in Lefebvre's terms) are born from noise as carriers of multiplicity and heterogeneity. To hear them rather than to see them, for Serres, is a major principle for how we should approach them.

Heritage and voice

Having spent some time outlining these philosophical approaches to rhythm and noise in the work of these two writers I want to spend the rest of this paper trying to show how this might be of use in addressing questions of urban heritage that follow on from some of the main principles that I have outlined. These principles include:

- Recognizing that city spaces have rhythms that produce patterns of repetition and difference that shape the ways in which those cities are lived.
- Recognizing that rhythm is not a simple temporal matter captured by the rhythms of the calendar imposed upon city life but that it incorporates elements from past times together in a way that is folded and complex.
- Acknowledging that rhythms incorporate not only human subjects but also the broad range of materials that make up the urban infrastructure and its cultural and economic uses.
- Seeing rhythm as emergent from the multiplicity of noise that is itself without pattern and without foundation. That process is one that occurs as a series of almost endless iterations as patterns get formed out of patterns and interference and feedback continue to challenge and make problematic settled understandings of place.

• That to make sense of the relationship between rhythm and noise requires that we listen to its soundings.

In the context of heritage I want to use the metaphor of voice to try and capture this approach. We can already find that in a simplified form in some of the early debates around heritage – for example, in Raphael Samuel's critique (1994) of writers like David Lowenthal (1985), Patrick Wright (1985) and Robert Hewison (1987). They, he suggests, see heritage as an imposed official discourse that reflects dominant interests and forms of economic and political power (at the time Thatcherism). They treat heritage as if it were part of a dominant ideology that somehow dupes people into seeing what true history is about. Samuel's counter position is a populist one that argues that there are many valid versions of heritage based on different identity positions and the memories they generate that sometimes run counter to those of a heritage industry.

People have their own life stories and memories of the places they live in and quite clearly they are able to articulate or give voice to them and communicate them to others without the aid of a museum or local authority heritage policy. Nearly twenty years on from these early heritage debates, the institutions that form part of this heritage industry have not left that unrecognized. It now often forms an important part of the ways in which people are engaged in participating in the narration and display of that past through the various heritage and museum displays that exist. In the past decade heritage has been less about consuming the past and more about producing the conditions of social inclusion. From the incorporation of people's stories, people's collections and recollections within heritage presentations to outreach work around such events as the Second World War with people who lived through it or local community developments, those engaged in heritage now typically recognize its multiple and heteroglot character.

Voice is more than this though. We should not reduce it simply to the stories that people are able to enunciate about their neighbourhoods and memories of the places they inhabit. The materiality also speaks, or can be given voice. This is a theme that we can also find in some of the recent work on urban ruins, phantasmagorias, ghosts and traces (Gordon, 1997; Jaguaribe, 1999; Hetherington, 2002; Edensor, 2005; Pile, 2005). Through a mixture of text and image, photographic image in particular, it is common to find those working in this field seeking to give voice to the materiality of the past so that it can not only speak to the present but provide an opportunity for a form of awakening to multiple possibilities (see Cadeva, 1997, 2001).

Walter Benjamin's Arcades Project (1999) is perhaps the first place, and a major influence, where such an approach to the material detritus of the past was first given the opportunity to speak. In that unfinished work, Benjamin remained within a visual rather than aural register when developing his argument believing that taking the detritus from the past out of its forgotten locations and making it visible as such would create an odd juxtaposition with its surroundings that defamiliarized them and whose shock would create an awakening from an acceptance of the ideological construction of how we see the past in relation to the present. Others, however, have taken these fragments and traces of the past and through visual depiction sought not only to make them visible but also to give them voice. Much of the work on waste on ruins and on traces is as much interested in the poetics of those remains as it is their politics or ethics. Tim Edensor, for example, in his work on industrial ruins (2005), or Melanie Van Der Hoorn in her work on unwanted buildings (2005) as well as a number of others who see the remains of the past though a spectral poetics of the ghostly and the haunted, seek to give voice to these traces by emphasizing their evocative – evoking – character (see also Jaguaribe, 1999; De Silvey, 2006). To evoke is to give voice through images rather than just make things visible (see Barthes, 1993). The belief behind this is often that evocation will help to reveal forms of counter-memory, hidden and sometimes inarticulate voices that are just as much a part of our past as the stories of regeneration and development told by those with an (in)vested interest. The assumed problem with heritage here is often that it is tied in with singular, capitalist practices of urban branding, image making and selling a sense of place through a selected reference to key elements of its past so that it might be culturally and economically developed. Allowing those voices to speak for their own sake, out of the archive and not on behalf of it, is what is typically at stake here.

This question of voice and sounding is about giving articulacy to noise. It is about hearing within that noise discernible voices either in spoken form or in material traces that would otherwise risk going unrecognized. It acknowledges, to a degree, that the composition of a city within space and time is multiple and suggests a heritage model that is about drawing out elements from that noise, often forgotten or unrecognized elements, so that they might be sounded as cultural memories that reveal a different pattern than would be the case if they went unrecognized. It acknowledges that our sense of the past is itself multiple and that there are a multitude of possible patterns – ways of understanding the past that might come to be recognized. In effect, it is about recognizing the punctum, or the disruptions that ripple though an urban archive and unsettle its sense of certainty around any notion of a singular cultural memory.

Heritage as footprint

Evoking and sounding the fragments that make up the multiplicity is about taking something from the noise by folding the aural into the visual. It is all about recognizing that the past is multiple and ready to be made through the soundings that are taken. The idea of how we might physically move though a city is one that engages more directly with questions of its rhythms of mobility. As well as through an interest in mobility in general (see Cresswell, 2006; Sheller and Urry, 2006), we also find this something Lefebvre was attentive to in his analysis (2004). But he was also associated with a tradition of moving through the city that also might form a basis of its critique or recognition of different realities to that presented by the rhythms of capitalism. Many will be familiar with Michel de Certeau's essay *Walking the City* which encapsulates this approach (1984). There, de Certeau counterposed the idea of the grand strategies of power that take a rather static approach to the city with mobile forms of resistance encapsulated by the tactics of walking. From this perspective, the God-Eye of the planner looking down from a position of stasis and authority produced strategies for urban understanding that conform to the dominant rhythms of the city and their archive principle of understanding a relationship between past and present: development/progress or regeneration/progress. Walking, in contrast, is about movement through space in a more fluid and dynamic way allowing little stories, neighbourhood stories to emerge and creating a series of tactics of resistance (on the history of walking see Solnit, 2001).

De Certeau was not the first to believe that walking through a space allowed it to be experienced differently from any representation that might be made of it, especially as a historicist record for the archive of how our urban lives now fit with the past. In the 1950s and 60s the avant-garde artists and the political radical Situationists developed a theory of psychogeography that was premised on the idea of the derive or drifting though which one could develop a feeling for the ambience of the city as well as reveal forgotten elements from the city's past that offered an alternative perspective on its history based around counter-memories of practice and revolt (see Debord, 1989; Coverley, 2006). Such a psychogeography continues today with small groups of people seeking to open up the city through drifting in an unplanned way through it. More than a trace of it is there in literary form in the novels and essays of Iain Sinclair (1997) and in the series of Robinson films by Patrick Keiller (1999). Both of these works are in that psychogeographical tradition trying to show how an intimate attention to the details of place and the chance encounters as one moves through somewhere allow new perspectives on it to be opened up that challenge or disrupt narrated and representational orthodoxies through which place myths and place branding are typically constructed.

One can, of course, go back further in time to Surrealists like Andre Breton (1960) and Louis Aragon (1971) who in their writings from the early part of the 20th century sought chance encounters with the ghostly and forgotten past in the arcades, parks and flea markets of Paris. Through that, they thought a dream-like understanding might emerge and an altogether different understanding of reality might be established. In their turn they stand in a tradition of poets and writers like Rimbaud, Baudelaire, Poe (see Ross, 1988), indeed right back to Rousseau for whom this Flâneur tradition of the leisurely, male stroller was a way of uncovering something hidden within the everyday and new revelations and new visions that might be made visible to the mobile subject (for general discussions on the history of the Flâneur and its critiques notably on the issue of its gendered assumptions see Wolff, 1990; Wilson, 1992; Friedberg, 1993; Tester, 1994; Parsons, 2000).

What this approach tacitly acknowledges is that there are different rhythms to the city's past-present composition than that found in the routine rhythms of daily urban life that are constructed around the process of work and organized and commodified leisure. Being mobile in such a way is intended not only to produce a different experience of the spaces of the city but more significantly of its time-space configuration of the relationship that the present has with the past(s). An attention to the ambience of the city as random rather than organized and rhythmic collection of signs is intended to make the seemingly inattentive walker more attentive to the possibility of other rhythms in which traces or fragments of the past show themselves in ways that would be missed if one was simply following and accepting the rhythms of any dominant spatial practice imposed on them by the capitalist workings of that city. Heritage in this sense is not so much something evoked as encountered, if not completely by chance, then at least through a susceptibility to the hidden rhythms that can be found in the historical traces of the past that are always left behind in a city. The disposal of the past – a capitalist imperative – is always incomplete. The trace and the fragment can always be found and their revenant charms revealed to the casual walker attentive to their possibility.

Voice, footprint and the archive – concluding comments

From the perspectives reviewed here rhythm promotes encounter and noise offers up the opportunity for evocation and sounding through which heritage as a multiple set of possibilities is established as a series of provisional patterns through which we might come to know a place. And yet can we fully account for this version of heritage through the trope of counter-memory and critique, notably of official forms of heritage that are seemingly imposed as a part of a commodified place imaging and place branding? In many ways these alternative versions of heritage are just as reliant on an archiving principle in understanding a place as those more official forms of heritage and museum practice. To evoke and to give voice through text or image often requires a degree of expertise and familiarity around advance knowledge of the history of the place one is traversing. In doing so it allows the materiality and the people one encounters to reveals to us what is otherwise hidden.

For my own part I once tried to apply this approach to the city to a section of Manchester around the shopping area associated with Deansgate and its cultural quarter surrounding the then hub museum Urbis (Hetherington, 2005). That stroll took me not only through the burgeoning sites of regeneration and shopping in a once declining industrial city, it also took me through the traces left behind of the housing of Engels' Irish slum dwellers revealed in his *Conditions of the Working Class in England* (1892). It also took me past a forgotten 19th-century arcade, past the site of the world's first department store Kendalls (one that actually pre-dates the Bon Marche in Paris) and on to the site of an anonymous business district crossroads that was marked as the site of the notorious 1819 Peterloo Massacre; a site where workers protesting for their rights were cut down by sabre-wielding soldiers and whose importance is that it is seen by many as a key moment in the emergence of radial socialist politics in Britain.

Did I find this counter-memory in the material surroundings and rhythms of that walk? Yes I did. There was a degree of chance encounter that was not anticipated in advance. Unexpected connections were indeed made. Certainly that stroll provided me with a different sense of the cultural memory expressed in the city than I would have found in a museum display or on an organized and signposted heritage trail. But I also found elements of those rhythms and patterns of memory because I already had a working knowledge of the historical archive of such a place and the significance of these fragments and traces even if I could not tie it into location exactly in advance. I had seen some of the pictures, read some of the books and visited some of the museums and official heritage sites too.

The issue is not, as some might like to believe, that there is a simple dichotomy between stasis, historicism, memory-as-amnesia and archive on the one hand and movement, discontinuity, memory as lived practice and unofficial recording on the other. Both memory and counter-memory rely on an archive principle. The difference is how they engage with its outsiderly Otherness. The juxtaposition of many of these interventions of Otherness and counter-memory around voice and footprint in the modern archive's apparent static and silent realism of facts and historicism of account does play with issue of movement and noise. Within the record of the official plan that marks out the space of representation of the modern city (Lefebvre, 1991), there are, it is true, forgotten corners, hidden voices (Wilson, 1992), hidden vistas, forgotten traces, broken fragments that afford the possibility of another perspective – notably a perspective that focuses eyes away from the intentions of the visible plan (on issues of stasis and movement in urban understanding, see Amin and Thrift, 2002). With good reason did Walter Benjamin choose the motif of the arcade, at one time the height of 19th-century urban modernity but by the early 20th century something of a forgotten remnant in which the dusty past lay all around uncatalogued, as his way of exploring such archive practices and their troubled certainties. And in such places, it was often hoped, one would encounter the past in a more affective, arresting guise: the spectral (Gordon, 1997), the phantasmagoric (Benjamin, 1999; Pile, 2005) and the uncanny (Freud, 1958) – these have also been ways in which to give a name, and a voice, to this encounter with the outside found within the city-archive and its phantasm agora.

But this is not a tradition antithetical to the archive as heritage per se. Rather, it is about ways in which the archive, challenged from without, also incorporates those challenges within its understanding opening up the notion of heritage to sound and movement. Around such an uncertain archival terrain – heterogeneous, unbounded, unfinished – the past comes to life as a contested promise of an honoured debt (see Derrida, 1994): the debt of history recognized against the grain of historicism in particular, that often goes hand in hand with the acknowledged, dominant ideological representation of urban space (Lefebvre,

The Sociological Review, 61:S1, pp. 17–33 (2013), DOI: 10.1111/1467-954X.12051

1991). But it does so in ways that still need an archive principle in its engagement with the idea of the urban but more in an endless play of uncertainty and disruption rather than order and classification. In this perspective the archive itself becomes a space of noise rather than a container of accounts out of which rhythms emerge.

One can suggest at this juncture, at a time when funding for official heritage is being withdrawn, investment is in short supply and culture-led regeneration is not as keenly available as it was just a few years ago, that approaches to heritage that recognize this element of uncertainty could be opened up within this space of doubt in such a way as to at least call into question some of the more singular and dominant narrative linked to place branding than might have been possible before. The archive always remains open to the outside, that outside as Derrida points out is disruptive but it is not altogether destructive. The issue is to recognize that as an opportunity rather than a problem. Outside and inside, city and archive, historicism and history are always folded into one another in unexpected ways. That is the basis for urban rhythm. The archive is a noisy place and out of that noise rhythms of cultural memory emerge and their soundings resonate both with and against notions of heritage.

References

Allen, J., Massey, D. and Cochrane, A., (1998), *Re-Thinking the Region*, London: Routledge.

Aragon, L., (1971), *Paris Peasant*, London: Picador.

Amin, A. and Thrift, N., (2002), *Cities: Reimagining the Urban*, Cambridge: Polity Press.

Barthes, R., (1993), *Camera Lucida*, London: Vintage Books.

Benjamin, W., (1985), *One Way Street and Other Writings*, London: Verso.

Benjamin, W., (1999), *The Arcades Project*, Cambridge, MA: The Belknap Press of Harvard University Press.

Breton, A., (1960), *Nadja*, New York: Grove Press.

Cadeva, E., (1997), *Words of Light: Theses on the Photography of History*, Princeton, NJ: Princeton University Press.

Cadeva, E., (2001), 'Lapsus imaginis: the image in ruins', *October*, 96: 35–60.

Coverley, M., (2006), *Psychogeography*, Harpenden: Pocket Essentials.

Cresswell, T., (2006), *On the Move: Mobility in the Modern Western World*, London: Routledge.

Cronin, A. and Hetherington, K. (eds), (2008), *Consuming the Entrepreneurial City: Image, Memory, Spectacle*, New York: Routledge.

De Certeau, M., (1984), *The Practice of Everyday Life*, Vol. 1, Berkeley, CA: University of California Press.

De Silvey, C., (2006), 'Observed decay: telling stories with mutable things', *Journal of Material Culture*, 11 (3): 318–338.

Debord, G., (1989), 'Report on the construction of situations and on the international situationist tendency's conditions of organization and action', in K. Knabb (ed.), *The Situationist International Anthology*, 17–25, Berkeley, CA: Bureau of Public Secrets.

Derrida, J., (1994), *Spectres of Marx: The State of the Debt, the Work of Mourning, and the New International*, New York: Routledge.

Derrida, J., (1996), *Archive Fever: A Freudian Impression*, Chicago: University of Chicago Press.

Edensor, T., (2005), *Industrial Ruins: Space, Aesthetics and Materiality*, Oxford: Berg.

Engels, F., (1892), *The Condition of the Working Class in England in 1844*, London: Swan Sonnenschein and Co.

Freud, S., (1958), 'The uncanny, in J. Strachey (ed.), *The Standard Edition of the Complete Psychological Works of Sigmund Freud*, Vol. 17, 218–252, London: Hogarth Press.

Friedberg, A., (1993), *Window Shopping: Cinema and the Postmodern*, Berkeley, CA: University of California Press.

Gordon, A., (1997), *Ghostly Matters: Haunting and the Sociological Imagination*, Minneapolis: University of Minnesota Press.

Goudsblom, J., (1992), *Fire and Civilization*, London: Allen Lane.

Halbwachs, M., (1992), *On Collective Memory*, Chicago: University of Chicago Press.

Hall, T. and Hubbard, P., (1998), *The Entrepreneurial City: Geographies of Politics, Regime and Representation*, London: John Wiley and Sons.

Harrison, R., (2013), *Heritage: Critical Approaches*, Abingdon: Routledge.

Harvey, D., (1989), 'From managerialism to entrepreneurialism: the transformation in urban governance in late capitalism', *Geografiska Annaler*, 71B: 3–17.

Hetherington, K., (1997), 'In place of geometry: the materiality of place', in K. Hetherington and R. Munro (eds), *Ideas of Difference: Social Spaces and the Labour of Division, 183–199*, Oxford: Blackwell.

Hetherington, K., (2002), 'Phantasmagoria/phantasm agora: materiality, spatiality and ghosts', *Space and Culture*, 11/12: 24–41.

Hetherington, K., (2005), 'Memories of capitalism: cities, phantasmagoria and arcades', *International Journal of Urban and Regional Research*, 29 (1): 187–200.

Hetherington, K., (2007), 'Manchester's Urbis: urban regeneration, museums and symbolic economies', *Cultural Studies*, 21 (4–5): 630–649.

Hetherington, K., (2010), 'The ruin revisited', in G. Pye (ed.), *Trash Cultures: Objects and Obsolescence in Cultural Perspective*, Cultural Interactions: Studies in the Relationship between the Arts, 11, 15–37, Oxford: Peter Lang.

Hetherington, K. and Law, J., (2000), 'After networks', *Environment and Planning D: Society and Space*, 18 (2): 127–132.

Hewison, R., (1987), *The Heritage Industry*, London: Methuen.

Huyssen, A., (1995), *Twilight Memories: Marking Time in a Culture of Amnesia*, New York: Routledge.

Huyssen, A., (2003), *Present Pasts: Urban Palimpsests and the Politics of Memory*, Stanford, CA: Stanford University Press.

Jaguaribe, B., (1999), 'Modernist ruins: national narratives and architectural forms', *Public Culture*, 11 (1): 295–312.

Keiller, P., (1999), *Robinson in Space*, London: Reaktion Press.

Kirshenblatt-Gimblett, B., (1998), *Destination Culture: Tourism, Museums and Heritage*, Berkeley, CA: University of California Press.

Lai, C.-L., (2004), 'Museums in motion', unpublished PhD thesis, Lancaster University.

Lefebvre, H., (1991), *The Production of Space*, Oxford: Blackwell.

Lefebvre, H., (2004), *Rhythmanalysis: Space, Time and Everyday Life*, London: Athlone.

Leslie, E., (2010), 'Recycling', in M. Beaumont and G. Dart (eds), *Restless Cities*, 233–254, London Verso.

Lowenthal, D., (1985), *The Past Is a Foreign Country*, Cambridge: Cambridge University Press.

Massey, D., (1999), *Power-Geometries and the Politics of Space-Time, Hettner-Lecture, 1998*, Heidelberg: Department of Geography, University of Heidelberg.

Massey, D., (2005), *For Space*, London: Sage.

Mayhew, H., (1968), *London Labour and the London Poor*, New York: Dover.

Murdoch, J., (1998), 'The spaces of actor-network theory', *Geoforum*, 29 (4): 357–374.

Osborne, T., (1999), 'The ordinariness of the archive', *History of the Human Sciences*, 12 (2): 51–64.

Parsons, D., (2000), *Streetwalking the Metropolis: Women, the City and Modernity*, Oxford: Oxford University Press.

Perec, G., (1997), *Species of Spaces and Other Pieces*, London: Penguin.

Pile, S., (1996), *The Body and the City: Psychoanalysis, Space and the City*, London: Routledge.

Pile, S., (2005), *Real Cities: Modernity, Space and the Phantasmagorias of City Life*, London: Sage.

Polastron, L., (2007), *Books on Fire: The Tumultuous Story of the World's Great Libraries*, London: Thames and Hudson.

Pryke, M., (2011), 'Money's eyes: the visual preparation of financial markets', *Economy and Society*, 39 (4): 427–459.

Ross, K., (1988), *The Emergence of Social Space*, Basingstoke: Macmillan.

Samuel, R., (1994), *Theatres of Memory: Past and Present in Contemporary Culture*, London: Verso.

Sebald, W. G., (2002), *Austerlitz*, London: Penguin.

Serres, M., (1995), *Genesis*, Ann Arbour, MI: University of Michigan Press.

Serres, M. and Latour, B., (1995), *Conversations on Science, Culture and Time*, Ann Arbour, MI: University of Michigan Press.

Sheller, M. and Urry, J., (2006), 'The new mobilities paradigm', *Environment and Planning A*: Vol. 38: 207–226.

Sheringham, M., (2006), *Everyday Life: Theories and Practices from Surrealism to the Present*, Oxford: Oxford University Press.

Sheringham, M., (2010), 'Archiving', in M. Beaumont and G. Dart (eds), *Restless Cities*, 1–17, London Verso.

Sinclair, I., (1997), *Lights Out for the Territory*, London: Granta.

Sinclair, I., (2010), 'Sickening', in M. Beaumont and G. Dart (eds), *Restless Cities*, 257–276, London Verso.

Smith, L., (2006), *Uses of Heritage*, London: Routledge.

Solnit, R., (2001), *Wanderlust: A History of Walking*, London: Verso.

Tester, K., (1994), *The Flâneur*, London: Routledge.

Thompson, M., (1979), *Rubbish Theory: The Creation and Destruction of Value*, Oxford: Oxford University Press.

Thrift, N., (1996), *Spatial Formations*, London: Sage.

Till, K., (2005), *The New Berlin: Memory, Politics, Place*, Minneapolis: University of Minnesota Press.

Trouillot, M., (1995), *Silencing the Past: Power and the Production of History*, Boston, MA: Beacon Press.

Van der Hoorn, M., (2005), *Indispensable Eyesores: An Anthropology of Undesired Buildings*, Utrecht: University of Utrecht.

Wilson, E., (1992), *The Sphinx in the City: Urban Life, The Control of Disorder, and Women*, London: Virago.

Wolff, J., (1990), 'The invisible flaneuse: women and the literature of modernity', in *Feminine Sentences: Essays on Women and Culture*, 34–50, Cambridge: Polity Press.

Wright, P., (1985), *On Living in an Old Country*, London: Verso.

Zukin, S., (1988), *Loft Living: Culture and Capital in Urban Change*, London: Radius.

Zukin, S., (1995), *Cultures of Cities*, Oxford: Blackwell.

Contested urban rhythms: from the industrial city to the post-industrial urban archipelago

Stavros Stavrides

Abstract: In industrial societies, dominant mechanic rhythmicalities were treated by critical thinkers and artists as forces of dehumanization and alienation. Organic rhythmicalities (bodily or cosmic ones) were alternatively explored in an effort to create a possible harmonious synthesis of nature and machine civilization. Rehumanizing the city-machine has, however, ceased to be a meaningful venture in post-industrial societies. Contemporary post-industrial cities are characterized by site-specific rhythms which create a multifaceted urban normality. Each urban enclave has its specific rules and rhythms of use, and is controlled through a localized 'state of exception' in which certain general laws and rights are suspended. Contesting contemporary rhythmicalities might thus mean contesting the rhythmicalities of exception which establish spatiotemporal separations and discriminations. Profiting from an ongoing discussion about the inventive tactics of the weak and the dispossessed, this paper focuses on the 'squares movement' in order to discover exemplary acts of such a possible 'polyrhythmical' resistance. In the occupied squares people have devised ways to escape the imposed normality of urban 'enclavism' in search of polyrhythmical spaces and practices of commoning.

Keywords: organic, polyrhythmicity, resistance, enclavism, thresholds, commoning

Rehumanizing the city machine

Industrial society was, as we know, heavily criticized as anti-human. Both its opponents and its supporters considered mechanized production as this society's core characteristic. The image and idea of the 'machine' thus became emblematic. For the supporters, machines were connected to limitless transformative power, to the proliferation of goods and novelties, to progress. For the opponents, machines were replacing humans, destroying man-nature relations, alienating producers from their products.

Part of this dispute was focused on a very distinctive characteristic of the producing machines. Their rhythm. Rhythm, for some, meant power and speed, thus emblematizing the dynamic continuity of production and progress (or,

The Sociological Review, 61:S1, pp. 34–50 (2013), DOI: 10.1111/1467-954X.12052
© 2013 The Author. Editorial organisation © 2013 The Editorial Board of the Sociological Review. Published by John Wiley & Sons Ltd, 9600 Garsington Road, Oxford OX4 2DQ, UK and 350 Main Street, Malden, MA 02148, USA

rather, production as a prerequisite of progress) while for others rhythm symbolized a ruthless anti-human rationality.

W. Ruttmann's emblematic film *Berlin: Symphony of a Great City* (1927) begins with a sequence of wave images in rhythmic movement, continuing with alternating images of electricity poles and train rails intended to depict the tempo of a train's movement. These sequences seem to epitomize a characteristic attempt to compare the rhythmicalities of the industrial city with those of nature (Natter, 1994). It is not absolutely certain that Ruttmann chose to film so many instances of urban mechanical rhythms in order to praise the modern city's image as a well-functioning urban machine. He clearly inserts images in the film which show machine-like working rhythms as inhuman and full of anxiety (Natter, 1994). Ruttmann, however, does explicitly aim to present the city as a kind of synthesis of different rhythmicalities; mechanic, but also human or natural. This symphonic reading of the industrial city can be taken to represent a form of criticism that does not simply oppose dominant mechanic urban rhythms with an organic rhythmicality which can be used as an antidote to alienation. We can possibly understand this kind of criticism as a form of overcoming the organic versus mechanic antithesis through the power of the artist's/composer's gaze. Establishing a comparison between those two rhythmic domains, *Berlin* attempts a heroic synthesis comparable to that presented in Fritz Lang's *Metropolis* in the form of a final compromise between human aspirations and mechanical power. Ruttmann's 'montage mapping of Berlin' in a film characterized by 'the rhythmic principles of its editing' (Donald, 1999: 77) and Lang's attempt 'to imagine motion pictures as a form for mediating between technological and organic rhythms' (Cowan, 2007: 239), hint towards a possible reconciliation between mechanic and natural/human rhythmicalities in modern metropolis. Rutmann explicitly expresses this aim when referring to his film as a 'film symphony' created 'from the million-fold actual energies of the great city organism' (in Gaughan, 2003: 43). The choice of the word is crucial: an organism may have discrete parts (each one with distinct function/rhythms) but all of them belong to a coordinated and coordinating 'whole'.

In a different context, humanizing rhythms has been thought of as a means to tame time as created and controlled by machines. This was explored by the vitalist theories at the beginning of the 20th century, which are especially focused on the workings of human body as a whole. E. Jaques Dalcroze's system of 'eurhythmical gymnastics' (May and Thrift, 2001: 30) gained an unprecedented fame because it proposed a kind of cure through body training for the alienating experience of industrial society's mechanic rhythms. There is a long history of analogous attempts to reactivate bodily organic rhythmicalities in order to discover a new balance with the outer world. What is important, however, is that organic rhythms were projected to specified repeatable acts and gestures bordering a complete geometrization of the human body. Strangely, gymnastics imitated the precision of machines in the coordination of human bodies. Organic rhythmicality was both a means to express the natural rhythms of human body and a means to educate bodies for a new life in a society characterized, in

Simmel's famous formulation, by an 'intensification of emotional life' (Simmel, 1997: 70). The idea of depicting the 'choreographed' movement of the masses, in an effort to exalt the power modern society had to create the 'new man', is an idea which characterizes both critical art (as in Ruttmann's and Vertov's films) and Nazi (Strathausen, 2003: 34) as well as proto-fascist art (Herf, 1993). Elevated to an emblematic depiction of the collective power of the 'people' or the 'Volk', the image of a disciplined group that executes coordinated movements permeated the modernist imaginary. Coordinated bodies seem to have been considered as the locus of the only power that could possibly tame machine's dangerous dynamism (in direct contrast to impotent and alienated individuals).

Kracauer's criticism of the anti-human elements of a production system based on the intensification of mechanic rhythms is not based on a longing for a lost organic unity between man and nature. He does, however, explicitly seek to recuperate the emancipating potential of human reason trapped in the instrumental rationality of mechanic civilization (Reeh, 2004: 97).

His approach to the 'Tiller girls' mass culture phenomenon (Allen, 2007: 23) is illuminating. For him, the girls, by coordinating their bodies in highly geometrical 'dance' formations, were actually expressing a kind of abstract rationalization of human movement. As in the experience of the chain of production, 'organization stands above the mass' and 'community and personality perish when what is demanded is calculability' (Kracauer, 1995: 78). What he terms as 'mass ornament' becomes a kind of empty abstraction which cannot express a humanizing attitude towards nature (human nature included). Tiller girls are bodies without meaning, bodies synchronized as useless machines. 'Mass ornament' becomes in this context an abstract imitation of machine, a mythologizing of machine rhythmicality which subtracts from machine civilization its only possible legitimization (the transformation and appropriation of nature through production). Eurhythmics is both perfected and hollowed out from its originating intention in the Tiller girls 'gymnastics': perfectly coordinated bodies and no-bodies at the same time.

Rhythmicality appears both in the form of a social illness and in the form of this illness's cure during a period in which the industrial model of production was dominant. Rhythms could express and become the battlefield of an ongoing struggle between man and machine. It is likely that the actual experience of the city's modern inhabitants was a mixed experience of diverse rhythmicalities overlapping and sometimes clashing with each other (May and Thrift, 2001; Amin and Thrift, 2002). What made mechanic rhythmicalities dominant was a prevailing hegemonic belief in technological progress which had projected an understanding of urban rhythms as instantiations of the ever-accelerating tempo of progress on to urban life.

Contesting urban rhythms in modernity's urban machine meant bringing natural rhythms (bodily or cosmic ones) into comparison with mechanical ones. Whether in search of a lost organic rhythmicality or in search of a creative synchronization with nature (emblematized in eurhythmics and symphonic interpretations of the city correspondingly), acts of contestation seem to estab-

The Sociological Review, 61:S1, pp. 34–50 (2013), DOI: 10.1111/1467-954X.12052

lish a necessary common ground: the city considered as the locus of an unavoidable encounter between natural and mechanic rhythmicalities. Rehumanizing the city machine meant – for both perspectives – reinstituting this encounter, this comparison, in hope of a possible harmonious synthesis.

What has changed in post-industrial societies is (among other things of course) both the hegemonic belief in social time's accelerating tempo as well as the kind of criticism which attempts to appropriate rhythm as a means to rehumanize time that had become instrumental in machine production.

A new form of segmented time seems to have emerged in these societies. Diverse rhythmicalities organized in different spatiotemporal enclaves have imposed a dominant experience of discontinuous and dismantled time. It is not that the rhythmicalities of the modern metropolis have ceased to exist. It is that such rhythmicalities are now increasingly organized and separated into distinct urban settings, and defined as characteristic of those settings, rather than existing as part of an intense, machine-centred production of overarching urban rhythms. Contemporary urban rhythms appear as enclave-bound rhythms. And a crucial element for both their production as well as for their criticism, is their dependence on a mechanism which suspends the continuity of social time: the mechanism of exception.

The mechanism of exception and the city of spatiotemporal enclaves

As we will see, exception punctuates social time in the form of a temporary suspension of established rhythms. Exception is thus connected to some form of emergency, to some kind of need that justifies it, since social reproduction is, and always was, a form of control of the future through repetition. For exception to be imposed and to become recognized as necessary, a threat to social reproduction must appear to be imminent. Exception is, or at least promises to be, a temporary break in social time's continuity.

Let us consider an example: in contemporary cities temporary measures of control are imposed in urban space supposedly necessary to ensure 'public safety'. Parts of the city are closed and people are not allowed to approach. 'Red zones', as they are called, mark those areas of exception.

> Red zones appear to belong to these kinds of spatial formations that have nothing to do with the rhythms that organize public spaces. No cyclical rhythm seems to govern their emergence, no linearity calculates their presence in the modern city. Red zones instantiate a form of temporal conception which is not based on repetition, i.e. rhythmicality, but on exception. Red zones are erected in exceptional cases and represent the 'state of emergency'. Red zones though, are not as exceptional as they seem. Rather they constitute 'exceptional' cases of a whole category of metropolitan rhythms that tend to define the characteristics of today's urban public spaces (Stavrides, 2010: 37).

Red zones define an area of a city in which access is temporarily either completely restricted or allowed for certain categories of inhabitants under specific terms explicitly defined through relevant special legislation or imposed *ad hoc* by the police. In the case of major meetings of world leaders (WTO and IMF meetings, EU Ministers' or Leaders' meetings, APEC meetings etc.) red zones supposedly protect potential targets of terrorist attacks but also attempt to keep protesters as far away as possible from the place of the meeting. Epstein and Iveson (2009: 274) show how the practice of defining a 'Declared Area' through a specific 'APEC Meeting (Police Powers) Act 2007' in Sydney essentially meant a 'quarantining of dissent' (2009: 277).

Official rhetoric presents red zones as a necessary curtailment of the rights of a city's inhabitants, justified by presenting a potential threat to the city's peace as omnipresent; a threat which comes from people allegedly waiting for opportunities to destroy normal urban rhythms. Depending on each country's political situation and the corresponding form of social consensus those intruding 'others' can be presented as terrorists, violent and organized protesters, or simply villains. An attributed characteristic that all such 'others' share, however, is the will to upset the city's normality. Ironically, although red zones constitute spatiotemporal constructions which explicitly upset urban rhythms, they are legitimized by a security praising rhetoric which accuses 'others' as aiming to upset those very urban rhythms which define urban 'normality'. Exception is justified by recourse to a normality threatened by possible exceptional acts.

Red zones do not, however, simply evaporate after the end of a meeting or a highly securitized mega-event such as the Olympics. In most cases, extra measures remain effective for an undefined period; supposedly having proven themselves necessary for the protection of a city's life from ongoing threats (Horne and Whannel, 2012). In Athens, for example, measures such as the installation of surveillance cameras and the closing of the street in front of the Presidential Mansion every day after 21:00, although imposed as extra security measures during the Athens 2004 Olympics, were never suspended afterwards. In Athens too, the monument of the Unknown Soldier in front of the Hellenic Parliament is, this year (2012), still routinely cordoned with fences when a demonstration takes place; a measure imposed after the violent clashes with the police during the massive anti-austerity demonstrations last year.

'Security zones' seem to have become normalized in major cities, as in the case of New York after 9/11. As Németh and Hollander (2010: 29–30) explicitly show, in this city there is not only an expanding 'fortressing of public or civic structures' but also a 'clustering around high-value private buildings' too (as, for example, around Goldman Sach's global headquarters). Security zones engulf public space by limiting and monitoring access. Wire mesh or wrought iron fences often mark those closed spaces which explicitly define 'public' and private buildings as highly controlled urban enclaves. Everyday urban rhythms (as, for example, everyday trajectories of people going to work) are readjusted according to these measures which, although they have the appearance of temporariness, become permanent. 'Shrinkage of public space' (Németh and Hollander, 2010) brings about a redistribution of public and private rhythmicalities.

Similarly, Jon Coaffee describes how a 'ring of steel' has been developed around London's 'City' area. At first, measures were taken to establish a security zone in response to Provisional IRA threats. But after 9/11, the 'City' gradually became an area characterized in 'excluding itself from the rest of central London, through its territorial boundedness, surveillance and fortification strategies' (2004: 294). It is highly indicative that many exceptional measures were gradually routinized by being renamed (and thus justified) as necessary and efficient traffic control measures (Coaffee, 2004). Once again the city's normality appears to be protected through explicit deviations from the very normality invoked!

The spatiotemporal definition of a 'forbidden city' in the form of an area declared as in need of extra protection measures, has something of a very old urban strategy. Borrowing Foucault's (1995) image of a plague-infected city which becomes an object of surveillance and scrupulous study by the authorities, Agamben (2001) describes the dominant logic of urban disinfection. Using the example of Genova during the anti-G8 protests in 2001, he shows how governing urban elites in cases of an urban threat attempt to control the areas of the city which are crucial for the reproduction of dominant urban habits and values. Thus, they define areas to be sealed off and disinfected from plague (the contemporary form of 'plague' being dissident acts and demands) by securing the enclaves of the rich and the powerful while abandoning other parts of the city to potential 'unrest'. As the recent case of the police and army military operations in Rio's favelas proves, threats to the city's normalized order cannot be tolerated when the city (or the corresponding state) attempts to build a marketable global image of peaceful development. In the case of Rio, the Brazilian state obviously intends to showcase a peaceful urban environment (that may attract visitors and investment partners) ahead of the upcoming 2016 Olympic Games. UPP, the so-called favela 'pacification' programme, explicitly presents favelas as normalized through exceptional police forces' acts and measures. Normalization in those city areas which are literally occupied by the UPP special forces is imposed as a state of exception which authorities seem willing to extend well beyond 2016.

Red zones and security zones define areas of exception, areas which are cut from the rest of the city and are specifically controlled by forces allegedly devoted to ensuring public safety and security. These acts of defining separated and secluded areas necessarily demonize those who are to be kept 'outside'. Those 'others' are defined as threatening potential trespassers, as sources of anomaly in a city which should remain peaceful and well ordered through its spatiotemporal routines if it is to remain 'safe'.

Prototypical red zones, 'designed to create and reinforce a distinction between 'virtuous' citizens and 'unruly' protesters' (Epstein and Iveson, 2009: 278), gradually evolve into spatiotemporal constructions which, by regulating urban rhythms, actually come to define an emerging model of citizenship. It is as if red zones 'ceremonially describe the new citizen' (Stavrides, 2010: 38) who inhabits a city in a permanent state of emergency. Curiously, law-abiding citizens are considered those who willingly abandon their allegedly universal rights (these very rights that constitutions and laws define) in exchange for a feeling of security. Their 'right to the city' is curtailed and defined according to enclave embedded regulations: lawful citizens are those who only know how to follow site-specific rules.

Perhaps the most extreme case of a red zone becoming a permanent construction, although still presented as the result of an ongoing state of emergency, is the wall erected by the Israeli government in Palestine. Palestinians are defined by this wall as a captive population of second-class citizens living in a discontinuous territory of 'nonviable Bantustans' (Sorkin, 2005: xix).

We need, here, to pause for a moment and discuss the phenomenon described as a 'state of exception'. If we take as a starting point Agamben's relevant theorizations (Agamben, 1998, 2005), we discover in the state of exception two important moments. First, a period in which society is under threat and the state (or any other kind of sovereign authority) appears as the protector of society. Second, a period which is presented as temporary, during which certain important laws are suspended so as the state can effectively face the threat. This procedure has a very important prerequisite, however: only sovereign power has the 'lawful right' to suspend the law (Agamben, 1998: 21 and 28). Suspending the law proves power. But precisely because law is suspended, and not violated or eliminated, the 'force of law' prevails. What the mechanism of the state of exception ensures is that the promise of law (the force of law) remains, even though law is temporarily suspended (Agamben, 2005: 39). A state of exception, then, does not simply correspond to a state of anomie, it is not the opposite of law, it is a state in which law (*ius*) and concrete acts (*factum*) 'fade into each other' creating a 'threshold of undecidability' (2005: 29). When exception is prolonged, when exception becomes the rule, exceptional measures are turned into rules which completely obliterate any possible distinction between act and law (Agamben, 1998: 170). Normalized exception does not thus take the form of a set of new laws but rather that of a set of new routines; new habits which are justified by administrative reasoning alone. In a state of normalized exception, rules have the form of protocols which define patterns of behaviour without recourse to rights.

Controlling the city in modern metropolitan conditions increasingly poses new problems for the governing elites. Large, global cities are extremely complex mechanisms of social and economic relations. An emerging model of urban governance understands the city as an archipelago of urban enclaves, each one secluded and defined by a recognizable spatial perimeter. In those enclaves, administrative protocols direct people how to work, live and consume under defined and repeatable conditions.

The city of enclaves (Stavrides, 2010; Marcuse and Van Kempen, 2002), is 'an archipelago of "normalized enclosures" ' (Soja, 2000: 299). In this city, spaces are defined and secured by specified use protocols which mould citizens as enclave users. In every enclave, as in a mall, an airport, a big stadium, a corporate tower, a recreation area or resort, a gated community or condo-

The Sociological Review, 61:S1, pp. 34–50 (2013), DOI: 10.1111/1467-954X.12052

minium, specific general rights supposedly guaranteed by law are suspended. 'An urban enclave is usually a carefully planned system of human relations regulated by protocols of use. While such protocols have the appearance of administrative or functional directions for use, they essentially constitute a localized legal system in place of a suspended general law' (Stavrides, 2010: 35).

Face-control in clubs, automated security control in large department stores and sophisticated entrance controls in gated neighbourhoods and big office buildings ask you to abandon the right to move freely in public or quasi-public space, the right to be anonymous or to choose your dress and expression codes, the right to work under generalized protection measures (a right brutally suspended in labour enclaves as in malls, fancy restaurants and various inner city sweatshops). To paraphrase Augé, entering an enclave obliges you to prove your innocence in advance (Augé, 1995: 102).

New urban rhythms and the tactics of the weak

As people experience nowadays a period during which an enormous economic crisis directly affects the rules and forms of social reproduction, they are forced to accept that their society is under constant threat, and to live their lives in a constant search for protection and predictability. Sometimes control points assume an apotropaic character, exorcizing through their everyday metastatic presence the 'evils' of instability and unpredictability. Everyday 'prophylactic rituals' (Turner, 1977: 168–169 and 1982: 109–110), performed in order to allegedly protect from imminent 'outside' threats, ceremonially normalize exception: As in the case of traditional societies, 'prophylactic rituals' are practices meant to keep away exceptional threats (as natural disasters) and to ensure that arhythmical events will not destroy social spatiotemporal order.

In contemporary metropolises citizens are enclave-bound users, quasi-citizens enjoying suspensible rights. And a large number of people live even below this line of formal citizenship. People with no rights at all, such as 'illegal' immigrants, have to live either secluded in stigmatized enclaves of misery and exploitation or in constant movement, chased by metastatic mobile control points. Those non-citizens present the limit of a process of advanced 'enclavism' (Atkinson and Blandy, 2005) in which urban form represents and enforces social hierarchical organization. Urban enclavism, thus, culminates in 'advanced marginality', to use Wacquant's term (2008) or, rather, advanced marginalization. The normalization of a state of exception is already part of the everyday practices of contemporary urban citizens who spend most of their lives in urban enclaves.

The mechanism of normalized exception increasingly dominates the production of contemporary urban rhythms. If the industrial modern city was the generator and locus of alienating mechanical rhythms, contemporary post-industrial cities seem to generate and sustain localized, site-specific rhythms which for many create predictable and thus relieving life conditions. The city of enclaves presents itself to most people as a city of opportunities, a city of fantasized choices, even though enclave rhythms are very strictly controlled and constantly checked.

Criticizing contemporary rhythmicalities cannot thus mean choosing organic or human rhythms in place of mechanic ones. If social reproduction is essentially rhythmical, that is canonizing, in today's societies this rhythmicality seems to have dispersed in a wide variety of social rhythms, space-bound rhythms which are separated and differentiated. The urban archipelago is not the locus of an existing or even fantasized rhythmical coordination, a coordination that once fuelled the dreams of Futurists (the city as a factory or arsenal) and the practices of constructivists (as in Arseny Avraamov's 'Symphony of Factory Sirens' and El Lissitzky's electromechanical show 'Victory over the Sun'). The modernist imaginary, epitomized in the image of a man-creator who orchestrates urban symphonies by managing to tame and control natural and mechanical rhythms alike, has completely lost its power. What has replaced it is perhaps a post-modernist (or anti-modernist) imaginary which celebrates the post-industrial city's alleged polyrhythmicality and attempts to present it as a source of indi-vidualized pleasure and freedom. P. Marcuse convincingly warns us that this imaginary supports acts which veil existing patterns of hierarchical relationships among people with a 'cloak of calculated randomness' (Marcuse, 1995: 243). What appears as the freedom to choose, the freedom to enter or abandon an urban rhythm considered as a specific life-setting, is essentially a new form of partitioned and controlled urban order which assigns to people the urban rhythms which define them. Such defining rhythms can guarantee the privileges of some, securing their microcosms of secluded urban affluence. Many others, however, are threatened and chased by different urban rhythms, and are forced to devise ways to escape their regulating spatiotemporal perimeters.

Learning to inhabit exception is an important task for those who are in danger of being trapped in the rhythmicality of specific urban enclaves. For those for whom exception is meant to control and contain them, inhabiting exception indeed means finding ways to insert hidden rhythmicalities of survival, based on disguised and protected habits, into exception's closed spatiotemporal universe.

The way such vulnerable people inhabit urban rhythms can be understood through the model of everyday practices suggested by de Certeau. His idea of a distinction between strategies and tactics can provide ground to conceptualize urban rhythms as a field of asymmetrical contestation. Strategy describes the form of calculus which characterizes 'a subject of will and power (a proprietor, an enterprise, a city, a scientific institution) which can be isolated from an environment' (de Certeau, 1984: xvii). Strategy has a rationality which effec-tively measures space-time. Strategy seems to be a form of practice which controls predictability by transforming time into space, by spatializing time.

Tactics characterize those 'others' (as opposed to the 'proper') who cannot count on controlling neither space nor time. What they can do, however, is to attempt to take advantage of opportunities opened in time: 'A tactic depends on

The Sociological Review, 61:S1, pp. 34–50 (2013), DOI: 10.1111/1467-954X.12052

time – it is always in the watch for opportunities that must be seized "on the wing" ' (de Certeau, 1984: xvii). Tactics is not, however, a random set of 'opportunistic' activities. The weak devise ways to calculate too, to predict and to establish habits. Their rhythmicalities have therefore to 'insinuate' themselves into the dominant rhythms, not simply destroying or suspending them, but taking advantage of the opportunities created by them.

In all major metropolises 'informal networks of communication, mobility, employment, exchange, and cooperation' (Hardt and Negri, 2009: 254) sustain an everyday inventiveness of the poor, of the dispossessed and of those who live in marginal and precarious conditions. Through 'expansive circuits of encounter' (Hardt and Negri, 2009: 254) those people regularly manage to avoid control points, to devise ways to escape from the urban enclaves meant to contain their life, and to take advantage of urban rhythmicalities meant to regulate uses of public space. Informal traders, illegal workers and those who by need learn to travel without money, are inventive appropriators and trespassers who often occupy the interstices of the urban archipelago's spatiotemporal order.

An informal petit-merchant knows how to insinuate his or her selling habits into the dominant rhythms of urban public space. She knows where and how to stand, she knows which places can be used repeatedly, as they are less controlled, less prominent and so on (Brown, 2006, 2010). In informal trade a lot of learned tactics become important in establishing routines that can be both effective and, at the same time, keep people alert so as to be able to escape from sudden invasions (of racist militants, for example, who at times attack coloured informal traders in certain urban neighbourhoods). This kind of everyday wisdom is based both on the ability to read and recognize dominant rhythmicalities and on the ability to insert temporary rhythms into those spaces left open by dominant rhythms.

Lefebvre was hinting towards the idea of people being able to divert dominant rhythmicalities. He claims that 'rhythms play a major role' in 'a struggle for appropriation', as 'the citizen resists the state'. Furthermore, 'civil, therefore social time, seeks to and succeeds in withdrawing itself from linear, unirhythmic, measuring/measured state time' (Lefebvre, 2004: 96). Lefebvre attributes a 'nonpolitical manner' to these acts of space appropriation and he mentions diverse relevant practices: walks, encounters, intrigues, diplomacy, deals, negotiations (2004: 96).

Lefebvre's ideas can acquire new meaning in the context of the city of enclaves. Instead of a centrality (epitomized in the modern state's regulatory power) which organized the urban order and maintained its rhythms, we now experience an archipelago of centralities organized in the form of ordered spatiotemporal enclaves. People now have to resist not simply a unirhythmic dominant order but, rather, a set of disconnected rhythmicalities.

'A tactic is an art of the weak', de Certeau (1984: 37) tells us. There is a long discussion as to whether this art actually creates forms of resistance (see Bennett, 1998; Buchanan, 2000; Frow, 1991; Hetherington, 1998; Pile and Keith, 1997). But in terms of the reasoning developed in this essay, a tactic can be problematized as a possible locus of criticism thus: can the described tactics of the weak indicate a way of inhabiting exception not as a trap but as a place in which fugitive rhythmicalities may emerge? Urban enclaves of normalized exception strategically trap people in rhythms which reproduce defined roles (thus perpetuating stigma or privilege). But life in the sea of the urban archipelago, considered as a 'public' area punctuated by control and surveillance rhythms, can never be reduced to the order of those rhythms. People's tactics insinuate themselves in this order. People 'invent livelihoods' (Robinson, 2006: 86) and inhabit the world's cities as sites 'for the constant reinvention of (already inventive) traditional practices' (2006: 90). Lots of people live in this way, and, sometimes, they even find the courage to overtly challenge hegemonic rhythms.

The squares movement: Towards a polyrhythmical urban democracy?

What kind of rhythmicalities emerge in explicit acts of defying dominant rhythms in public space? A widely referred to and diversely interpreted passage of W. Benjamin seems to provide an interesting entrance to the question. He maintains that, 'the tradition of the oppressed teaches us that the state of emergency in which we live is not the exception but the rule . . . [i]t is our true task to bring about a real state of emergency and this will improve our position in the struggle against fascism' (Benjamin, 1973: 248–249).

What can a real state of emergency mean in this context? Is this another term for the well-known radical break with normality, revolution? Is this one more way to conceptualize in terms of time and space a radical otherness, a radical exteriority? Probably it is something more than that. In Benjamin's thought, interest for the past is always indicative of a sense of danger (1973: 247). Continuous time, either in the form of unstoppable progress or in the form of a narrative explanation of the present, is mythological time (1973: 254). Time that conceals opportunities, time that traps people and inhibits human emancipation.

To be able to go beyond these forms of time closure, people have to experience and value time discontinuity. People have to see past and present as each revealing the potentialities of the other. Instead of exception (considered as a rupture in social time's continuity) becoming the trap which contains new ways to impose dominant rhythms, instead of exception becoming the source and legitimization of localized rules, exception could become the testing ground of new rhythmicalities. This new 'state of emergency', urgently needed in order to create opportunities for a different future is thus an opening in time's closure. Virno (2008: 92) describes 'innovative action' as 'urgent action'. 'Those who accomplish it are always in a state of emergency' (2008: 92).

Could we possibly understand the recent squares movement as an emergent form of such a contestation of dominant urban rhythms? Can we find in the collective appropriation of public spaces in square occupations which took place in certain European, Arabian and American cities, examples of new spatiotemporal rhythms?

The Sociological Review, 61:S1, pp. 34–50 (2013), DOI: 10.1111/1467-954X.12052
© 2013 The Author. Editorial organisation © 2013 The Editorial Board of the Sociological Review

We can approach the squares movement as a form of reinvention of public space (Miraftab, 2004). Authorities do not simply control public space but effectively impose the rules of its use. Use of public space is, thus, 'authorized' use (Hénaff and Strong, 2001). Through the explicit or implicit implementation of civic behaviour rules, authorities create relevant 'urban imaginaries', 'mental and cognitive mappings of urban reality' (Soja, 2000: 324) through which people learn to interpret city-space as public or private. Unauthorized uses are banned and often directly confronted by 'security' forces. In the contemporary urban archipelago public space is space moulded through rhythmicalities which sustain a state of normalized exception. Public space is thus inhabited and interpreted, under the influence of dominant urban imaginaries, as necessarily fragmented, secluded, use-specific and partitioned. This is why a growing critical discussion on the meaning of urban public space is focused more and more not simply on the idea of the erosion of public space but on the transformation of such spaces through which 'publicness' and 'civility' are destroyed or distorted (Low and Smith, 2005; Mitchell, 2003; Hou, 2010).

The squares movement has created a different kind of space: 'common space' (Angelis and Stavrides, 2010). Crafting new spaces of solidarity and communication was absolutely important for this movement. Not only because this made people more able to demand social and economic justice but because common space became a kind of performative representation of justice and equality.

Let us look at a concrete example: the Syntagma square occupation in Athens. Space was from the beginning organized in ways that greatly differed from the everyday routines which characterize *the* central square of Athens. Syntagma is not simply a very important circulation node in Athens centre. It also carries dense symbolic meaning, being situated in front of the Parliament building and containing a ceremonial focus point, the Unknown Soldier's Monument.

Greek 'aganaktismeni' ('indignados', rightfully angry) chose this square to express their rage against devastating and unjust austerity measures and to cry their discontent for politicians and corrupt state (Giovanopoulos and Mitropoulos, 2011). By doing so, however, they have transformed the square to an area in which a temporary occupation gradually formed a new model of publicness. Protesting in common for many days has produced spaces of thinking in common, spaces of living in common, spaces of exploring alternative values in common.

In a way, the new uses of the square were invented in exceptional circumstances. Everyday rhythms were not, however, abolished but reintegrated to a new polyrhythmical urban environment in the making. What can be described as a decentralization recentralization dialectics (Stavrides, 2012: 589) can capture the dynamics of this polyrhythmicality. People were involved in various coexisting initiatives.

Each micro-square had its own group of people who lived there for some days, in their tents, people who focused their actions and their micro-urban environment to a specific task: a children playground, a free reading and meditation area, a homeless campaign meeting point, a 'time bank' (a place where services are exchanged eliminating money and profit), a 'we don't pay' campaign meeting point (focused on organizing an active boycott of transportation fees and road tolls), a first aid centre, a multimedia group, a translation group stand and so on. There were various levels on which those micro-communities were connected, and, of course, all of them had to follow the general assembly's rules and decisions. However, differences in space arrangement choices and in expression media (with the use of banners, placards, stickers, images, 'works of art' etc.) were more than apparent. Although they shared a common cause and a target (the Hellenic Parliament), each micro-square established different routines and aesthetics and organized different microevents during the occupation. (Stavrides, 2012: 588)

Each micro-square was thus characterized by its own space and time. Each was secreting its own urban micro-rhythms. But those micro-squares were not closed to themselves; they did not develop into alternative micro-enclaves. Remaining connected to the General Assembly – the centre of decisions taken in common – those micro-squares were more like passages than defined places. They were spaces in the making, spaces in which social roles were questioned and opened. In-between spaces are not spaces of a situated identity but spaces in which identities are negotiated and tested (Stavrides, 2010). Micro-squares, thus, as in-between spaces, participated in the development of a network of passages. Each of them contained a micro-community which simply developed an idea or an initiative to be included in a wider common cause.

The General Assembly was not, therefore, a centre of dominance but a centre in constant remaking; a centre dependent on the loose coordination and creative autonomy of the micro-squares. This has resulted in new emergent forms of urban rhythms. The General Assembly was meant to provide the canvas of rules on which dispersed initiatives would flourish. Coordination was not a simple technical task but the most prominent representation of collective solidarity. No dominant rhythms could be imposed in this process. Polyrhythmicality did not, however, result in a chaotic dissonance. The decentralization–recentralization dialectics ensured that certain motives of actions were regularized in ways that expressed and corroborated shared values. The taking care of, for example, the collection of garbage in the small tent city that developed in the square, was not organized as an 'institutionalized procedure' but was explicitly expressed in the idea of the rotation of duties. And when this task acquired a crucial importance, as the square had to be cleaned from the remains of poisonous tear gas after a brutal police charge, people were spontaneously coordinated as equals: Long chains were formed, through which water was transported hand to hand from the only available source, the square's fountains, in small bottles to be emptied on the pavement. This spontaneous rhythmicality of bodies coordinated with no coordinating centre, clearly expresses the meaning of direct democracy, so regularly debated in the square assembly. Direct democracy can, perhaps, mean not only an equality of opinions but also a self-conscious synchronization aimed at a commonly recognized cause. So different from the allegedly rehumanized

The Sociological Review, 61:S1, pp. 34–50 (2013), DOI: 10.1111/1467-954X.12052
© 2013 The Author. Editorial organisation © 2013 The Editorial Board of the Sociological Review

'eurhythmical' marionettes, the synchronized bodies of square 'commoners' possibly perform democracy as a rhythmicality of differences in coordination.

Polyrhythmical life developed in the occupied square. And this poly-rhythmicality was at times opened to new rhythms and at times was condensed in common rhythms, rhythms developed in common. This was a different way of inhabiting exception. Exception was not a trap but rather a spatiotemporal threshold.

Inside the temporary space of the occupied square, people could develop new habits and new roles, new rhythms which characterized new forms of life in common. This was only possible, however, because the square itself was never closed, never fantasized or practised as a 'liberated' enclave, as an alternative stronghold. The square was something like an urban threshold, belonging to everybody and nobody at the same time, in which different groups and individuals could negotiate their presence, their acts and their suggestions.

It was the police and the media that tried to enclose this area, to convert it to a trap, to an exception-as-trap. When the police charged (either provoked by stone-throwing or simply in an effort to 'clean' the area), the square was meant to be defined as a closed world, as a ghetto or as an illegal stronghold. People, however, remained peacefully in the square with amazing courage and determination. In one of these police charges characterized by brutal physical violence, some gathered at the centre of the square and started to dance to the music of a Cretan lyre. As if to expressly reflect the power of solidarity and direct democracy, those coordinated bodies symbolically escaped the brutal trap of an imposed state of exception. And it was this act that gave people the courage to return to the square and peacefully reoccupy it.

Conclusion

Contesting urban rhythms meant, in the context of the industrial city, attempting to think and live beyond the predominance of mechanic rhythms. Although the modern city never developed along the lines of the model envisaged by the prophets of eternal progress, understanding this city as an ordered rhythmical universe not only played a role in the dominant practices of social control but also created a shared imaginary in which machines were presented as generators of modern urban life.

Today's large cities are not anymore dominated by mechanic rhythms. Nor can they be explained by recourse to an imaginary saturated with either images of triumphant productive rhythms or nightmare images of alienating mechanization. In the contemporary urban archipelago, a different kind of canonization-through-control prevails. Normalized exception legitimizes and produces enclave-bound urban rhythms which participate in various levels of social reproduction. Attempts to contest or criticize dominant rhythmicalities have to thus change form and not simply content. It is not that a different kind of rhythm dominates now but that a different co-existence of rhythmicalities has emerged. These rhythmicalities are actually defined by the spatial boundaries of the corresponding urban enclaves and are not meant to be compared, changed or synchronized. The urban archipelago thus corresponds with an archipelago of urban rhythms, island-rhythms floating on a sea of chaotic noise (which is often marked by the metastatic rhythms of public space control points).

Contesting urban rhythms, in this context, means, perhaps, attempting to create polyrhythmical spaces of negotiation and coexistence, in which porous boundaries prevent both spatial as well as temporal closure. People forced to devise ways to inhabit exception, people who invent ways to insert their own fleeting and hidden rhythmicalities into existing urban spatiotemporal enclaves, can perhaps provide valuable examples of an art of the weak which recognizes urban rhythms as a contested terrain.

People can even cross and sometimes do cross the boundaries of everyday inventiveness to discover that their life can be shaped through practices of collective appropriation of space and time, practices of polyrhythmical commoning. Their practices can perhaps 'produce a lacuna, a hole in time, to be filled by an invention, a creation. That only happens, individually or socially, by passing through a *crisis*' (Lefebvre, 2004: 44). In a period of crisis, like the one we live in, new forms of life in common may possibly emerge. The squares movement has shown us that crisis can be connected to collective creativity. Collective action may indeed 'become irregular' (Lefebvre, 2004: 44) in search of new, collectively produced and controlled rhythms of social coexistence. Collective action has not, however, simply added new rhythms or, even, new kinds of rhythm to the dispersed polyrhythmicality of the post-industrial enclave city. Collective creativity has expanded and enriched potential encounters thus establishing the ground of comparison between different collective rhythms. Emerging rhythmicalities of mutual recognition and coexistence are rhythmicalities meant to be compared, meant to be coordinated in gestures of solidarity with no orchestrating centres (real or fantasized), meant to be always open to transformations through exchanges. In light of this prospect, can we possibly understand and experience direct democracy as polyrhythmical commoning?

References

Agamben, G., (1998), *Homo Sacer: Sovereign Power and Bare Life*, Stanford, CA: Stanford University Press.

Agamben, G., (2001), 'Genova e il nuovo ordine mondiale', *Il Manifesto*, 25 July.

Agamben, G., (2005), *State of Exception*, Chicago: University of Chicago Press.

Allen, J., (2007), 'The cultural spaces of Siegfried Kracauer: the many surfaces of Berlin', *New Formations*, 61: 20–33.

Amin, A. and Thrift, N., (2002), *Cities: Reimagining the Urban*, Cambridge: Polity Press.

Angelis, M. de and Stavrides, S., (2010), 'Beyond markets or states: commoning as collective practice (a public interview)', *An Architektur*, 23 (also at http://www.e-flux.com/journal/view/150).

Atkinson, R. and Blandy, S., (2005), 'Introduction: international perspectives on the new enclavism and the rise of gated communities', *Housing Studies*, 20 (2): 177–186.

Augé, M., (1995), *Non Places: Introduction to an Anthropology of Supermodernity*, London: Verso.

The Sociological Review, 61:S1, pp. 34–50 (2013), DOI: 10.1111/1467-954X.12052

Benjamin, W., (1973), *Illuminations*, London: Collins/Fontana.

Bennett, T., (1998), *Culture: A Reformer's Science*, London: Sage.

Brown, A. (ed.), (2006), *Contested Space: Street Trading, Public Space, and Livelihoods in Developing Cities*, ITDG Publishing.

Brown, A., (2010), 'Street traders and the emerging spaces for urban voice and citizenship in African cities', *Urban Studies*, 47 (3): 666–683.

Buchanan, I., (2000), *M. De Certeau: Cultural Theorist*, London: Sage.

Coaffee, J., (2004), 'Recasting the "ring of steel": designing out terrorism in the City of London?', in S. Graham (ed.), *Cities, War and Terrorism*, Oxford: Blackwell.

Cowan, M., (2007), 'The heart machine: "rhythm" and body in Weimar Film and Fritz Lang's *Metropolis*', *Modernism/Modernity*, 14 (2): 225–248.

De Certeau, M., (1984), *The Practice of Everyday Life*, Berkeley, CA: University of California Press.

Donald, J., (1999), *Imagining the Modern City*, London: Athlone Press.

Epstein, K. and Iveson, K., (2009), 'Locking down the city (well, not quite): APEC 2007 and Urban Citizenship in Sydney', *Australian Geographer*, 40 (3): 271–295.

Foucault, M., (1995), *Discipline and Punish: The Birth of the Prison*, New York: Vintage Books.

Frow, J., (1991), 'Michel de Certeau and the practice of representation', *Cultural Studies*, 5 (1): 52–60.

Gaughan, M., (2003), 'Ruttmann's Berlin: filming in a "hollow space"?' in M. Shiel and T. Fitzmaurice (eds), *Screening the City*, London: Verso.

Giovanopoulos, C. and Mitropoulos, D. (eds), (2011), *Democracy under Construction*, Athens: A/synexeia Editions (in Greek).

Hardt, M. and Negri, A., (2009), *Commonwealth*, Cambridge, MA: Belknap Press.

Hénaff, M. and Strong, T. (eds), (2001), *Public Space and Democracy*, Minneapolis: University of Minnesota Press.

Herf, J., (1993), *Reactionary Modernism – Technology, Culture and Politics in Weimar and the Third Reich*, Cambridge: Cambridge University Press.

Hetherington, K., (1998), *Expressions of Identity: Space Performance and Politics*, London: Sage.

Horne, J. and Whannel, G., (2012), *Understanding the Olympics*, London: Routledge.

Hou, J. (ed.), (2010), *Insurgent Public Space. Guerilla Urbanism and the Remaking of Contemporary Cities*, London: Routledge.

Kracauer, S., (1995), *The Mass Ornament*, Cambridge, MA: Harvard University Press.

Lefebvre, H., (2004), *Rhythmanalysis: Space, Time and Everyday Life*. London: Continuum.

Low, S. and Smith, N. (eds), (2005), *The Politics of Public Space*, New York: Routledge.

May, J. and Thrift, N., (2001), *Timespace: Geographies of Temporality*, London: Routledge.

Marcuse, P., (1995), 'Not chaos but walls: postmodernism and the partitioned city', in K. Gibson and S. Watson (eds), *Postmodern Cities and Spaces*, Cambridge, MA: Blackwell.

Marcuse, P. and Van Kempen, R. (eds), (2002), *Of States and Cities: The Partitioning of Urban Space*, Oxford: Oxford University Press.

Miraftab, F., (2004), 'Invented and invited spaces of participation: neoliberal citizenship and feminists' expanded notion of politics', *Wagadu: Journal of Transnational Women's and Gender Studies*, 1: 1–7.

Mitchell, D., (2003), *The Right to the City: Social Justice and the Fight for Public Space*, New York: Guilford Press.

Natter, W., (1994), 'The city as cinematic space: modernism and place in *Berlin, Symphony of a City*', in S. Aitken and L. Zonn (eds), *Place, Power, Situation, and Spectacle: A Geography of Film*, London: Rowman and Littlefield.

Németh, J. and Hollander, J., (2010), 'Security zones and New York City's shrinking public space', *International Journal of Urban and Regional Research*, 34 (1): 20–34.

Pile, S. and Keith, M. (eds), (1997), *Geographies of Resistance*, London: Routledge.

Reeh, H., (2004), *Ornaments of the Metropolis: Siegfried Kracauer and Modern Urban Culture*, Cambridge, MA: MIT Press.

Robinson, J., (2006), *Ordinary Cities: Between Modernity and Development*, London: Routledge.

Simmel, G., (1997), 'The metropolis and mental life', in N. Leach (ed.), *Rethinking Architecture*, London: Routledge.

Soja, E. W., (2000), *Postmetropolis: Critical Studies of Cities and Regions*, Malden, MA: Blackwell.

Sorkin, M., (2005), 'Introduction: up against the wall', in M. Sorkin (ed.), *Against the Wall*, New York: The New Press.

Stavrides, S., (2010), *Towards the City of Thresholds*, Trento: Professionaldreamers (available at http://www.professionaldreamers.net/_prowp/wp-content/uploads/978-88-904295-3-8.pdf)

Stavrides, S., (2012), 'Squares in movement', *South Atlantic Quarterly*, 111 (3): 585–596.

Strathausen, C., (2003), 'Uncanny spaces: the city in Ruttmann and Vertov', in M. Shiel and T. Fitzmaurice (eds), *Screening the City*, London: Verso.

Turner, V., (1977), *The Ritual Process*, Ithaca, NY: Cornell University Press.

Turner, V., (1982), *From Ritual to Theatre*, New York: PAJ.

Virno, P., (2008), *Multitude: Between Innovation and Negation*, Los Angeles: Semiotext(e).

Wacquant, L., (2008), *Urban Outcasts: A Comparative Sociology of Advanced Marginality*, Cambridge: Polity Press.

The Sociological Review, 61:S1, pp. 34–50 (2013), DOI: 10.1111/1467-954X.12052

Points of departure: listening to rhythm in the sonoric spaces of the railway station

George Revill

Abstract: This paper argues that rather than simply enabling studies of regulation and embodiment, rhythm can facilitate reintegration of the apparently separate dimensions of mobile experience enabling them, as Cresswell says, to 'make sense together'. Taking a critical lead from Lefebvre's engagement with Lacan, it argues that in order for this to happen a more active and reflexive sense of listening to rhythm is needed than that provided by Lefebvre. Drawing on a conception of listening developed by Ihde, Nancy and LaBelle the paper concludes by exploring some ways in which the rhythms of the railway station produce experiences which are simultaneously affectively embodied and deeply socially and culturally meaningful.

Keywords: mobility, rhythm, listening, acoustic space, transport infrastructure

Introduction

Railway stations have been characterized as one of the rhythmic hubs of urban life. The diurnal flows of commuters cut across the episodic surge of long-distance passengers and the intermittent movements of leisure travellers. Together these provide compliment and counterpoint to the rhythms of street life beyond the station as people move in out and through the city. As nodal sites within networks of linear routeways radiating out from towns and cities, stations constitute key sites for understanding the rhythms of urban life based on mobility. The mobilities studies literature has frequently drawn on ideas of rhythm in order to understand the nature and experience of movement itself and a key text for many is Henri Lefebvre's (2004) short book *Rhythmanalysis: Space, Time and Everyday Life*. Typically within this literature rhythmanalysis has been a starting point for studies concerned with both the regulation of mobility and the affective flow and flux of embodied mobile experience (Binnie *et al.*, 2007; Edensor, 2009; Fincham *et al.*, 2010). Yet the infrastructures and technologies of mobility such as railway stations also have cultural meanings which inform our use and experience of them, as car drivers, cyclists or passengers on trains and buses. In his pioneering work on the cultures of travel and mobility Cresswell (2006, 2010, 2011) has adopted a formulation based on

The Sociological Review, 61:S1, pp. 51–68 (2013), DOI: 10.1111/1467-954X.12053
© 2013 The Author. Editorial organisation © 2013 The Editorial Board of the Sociological Review. Published by John Wiley & Sons Ltd, 9600 Garsington Road, Oxford OX4 2DQ, UK and 350 Main Street, Malden, MA 02148, USA

Lefebvre's (1991) tripartite division of conceived, perceived and lived space in order to recognize this multidimensional nature of mobile experience which is simultaneously both affective and reflexive. This paper argues that rhythm can contribute to such an inclusive approach to mobility providing a productive means of reintegrating the apparently separate dimensions of mobile experience enabling them, as Cresswell (2010) says, to 'make sense together'. Taking a critical lead from Lefebvre's engagement with Lacan, this paper argues that in order for this to happen, a more active and reflexive sense of listening to rhythm is required than that provided by Lefebvre. Thought of this way, rhythm instigates and informs culturally rich and historically situated meaningful experience and the railway station becomes a place of imaginative resonance and creative interjection rather than simply a site of regulation and embodied routine. The paper begins by considering Lefebvre's rhythmanalysis in relation to themes within the mobilities literature as these apply to the specificities of the railway station. It then considers rhythmanalysis in relation to Cresswell's call for an approach to mobilities able to engage simultaneously with affective and reflective experience, habitual routine and cultural meaning. Drawing on a conception of listening developed by Ihde, Nancy and LaBelle, the paper concludes by exploring some ways in which the rhythms of the railway station produce experiences which are simultaneously affectively embodied and deeply socially and culturally meaningful.

Mobility, rhythm and the railway station

Studies of mobility within social science have increasingly drawn on the experience of rhythm as a means of engaging with the experience of mobility. Studies of walking, cycling and public transport have stressed the ways in which the polyrhythms of motion, stasis, engagement and detachment forge specific embodied experiences of movement (Hein *et al.*, 2008; Bissell, 2009a, 2009b; Fincham *et al.*, 2010). Edensor has usefully highlighted three major themes in Lefebvre's rhythmanalysis which inform mobilities studies within social science. The first common characteristic, according to Edensor, is a concern with rhythm as a modality of regulation and governance. This is couched in terms of both conformity and opposition to dominant rhythms (Edensor, 2009). Railways have clearly played an important part making the rhythmic patterns which govern and regulate modernity. As Kern and others have shown, railways played a central role in the making of a modern time sensibility resulting in the regional, national and ultimately global integration and coordination of time zones, working patterns and economic activity (Kern, 1983; Schivelbusch, 1986; Tsuji, 2006). The importance of the timetable to the safe and efficient functioning of railways as spatially extensive 'machine ensembles' (Schivelbusch, 1986) and the strict time discipline placed upon workers and travellers has been key to the inculcation of time discipline as a key component in the collective and individualized responsibilities of industrial capitalism. In the 19th century, 'railway time' was more than just a practical reality, it was a moral imperative calling for self-discipline and respectability. The ways in which railways played a central role in the establishment of unified time zones across Britain, Europe, North America and eventually the world was clearly central to the development of temporally and spatially coordinated commercial and social activity. Ultimately this resulted in the integration of local, regional and national economies, and social and cultural systems within networks of global reach. Perhaps it is no coincidence, for example, that Richard Sears (founder of Sears, Roebuck and Co., the giant US mail order company) began his career as a railway station agent in Minnesota where he sold timber, coal and – most importantly for both his developing business and a growing sense of time consciousness – watches (Revill, 2012). Sears, Roebuck pioneered scientific salesmanship which in turn helped to define the modern consumer at the same time as making the latest and most fashionable consumer goods available to people living in remote rural places. Thus the railway station as a point of rhythmically ordered coordination and exchange participated in the construction of nationally based markets. These resulted in the increasing orientation of consumers towards national and international trends and fashions, leading to the greater coordination of patterns and styles in the purchase and consumption of goods and services (Chandler, 1977; Cronon, 1991). In this way the rhythmic scheduling of railways helped produce both markets and consumers.

A second area of shared concern for the mobilities literature is the body as a rhythmically permeable and responsive entity. Rhythm-based studies of travelling by public transport, waiting at railway stations and sitting on trains, have frequently been couched in terms of the passivity and boredom generated by habitual routine and the civil inattention developed to cope with crowding and social uncertainty (Bissell, 2009c). Lefebvre foregrounds bodily rhythms, emphasizing that the rhythmanalyst must draw on 'his [*sic*] breathing, the circulation of his blood, the beatings of his heart and the delivery of his speech as landmarks' (2004: 21). According to Lefebvre, rhythmanalysts must take their own body – 'its respirations, pulses, circulations, assimilations . . . duration and phases of durations' – as the measure of other rhythms (Edensor, 2009: 4). It is certainly the case that the regular scheduling of trains, the visceral experience of mechanical energy, rhythmical counterpoint of stillness and motion, interruption and connectivity feed senses of presence and absence, excess and lack, belonging and loss, boredom and engagement, which are deeply seated in our bodily experience of the railway. Sigmund Freud (2001) couched his thoughts on the embodied experience of railway travel primarily in terms of rhythms of repetition and interruption. He entertained lifelong fears about missing trains, and about being caught up in railway accidents. His earliest thinking concerned with railways focused on the psychopathology of shock, what we might call today post-traumatic stress disorder. Cultural historian Wolfgang Schivelbusch (1986) has most usefully explored this in his discussion of 'railway spine', the condition elaborated by doctors during the 19th century to explain human reactions to the experience of technologically mediated accidents and catastrophes. However, Freud's more long-term interest is demonstrated in the case of 'Little Hans' and the study in infant sexuality. Here the train's psychological significance lies in the rhythmical experience of bodily motion. Dread for railway travel here signifies repression, that blockage on the psychological journey to satisfactory adult sexuality in the modern human subject (Freud, 2001; Carter, 2001).

As Kirby (1997) shows in her study of the depiction of railways in early cinema, both the experience of rail travel and that of cinema the spectator can be understood as constitutive of a new urban subjectivity through a series of rhythmic correspondences, analogies and equivalences. Following Freud and Schivelbusch she argues that key to this experience was the shock and trauma manifest in relation to speed, acceleration and simultaneity. This was exemplified in film by rapid point-of-view shifts within the frame and jump cuts across different shots. On the one hand these new 'spectator passengers', were psychically habituated to anticipate and be immune to shock. Whilst on the other hand they were:

> jostled by forces that destabilized and unnerved the individual, creating a hysterical or, in nineteenth-century terms, 'neurasthenic' subject. In the urban railway films of early, classical, and avant-garde cinema, the power of disruption and discontinuity as expressed doubly by the train and the cinema contributed either directly or indirectly to the creation and re-creation of such an unstable subject. (Kirby, 1997: 7)

For Kirby (1997: 8–9) what mattered most in early railway films was the shock effect in and of itself, 'the thrill of instability, which addressed a new subject cut loose from its moorings in traditional culture'. Thus many early films exploited the train image for its shock potential often at the expense of narrative coherence. The fear of accidents as commonly reported in newspapers and magazines informed cinema's representation of the train as a 'terroristic creature' exemplified in the allegedly terrified response for the first spectators of the Lumière brothers' 1895 film *L'Arrivée d'un train en gare de la Coitat* (Loiperdinger, 2004). In these and other ways rail travel provides a multiplicity of embodied and associational rhythmic experiences ranging from the clickety-clack of wheels running over rails to the sound of a whistle or horn cutting through the still silence of the night.

A further key area in the engagement between mobility and rhythm identified by Edensor relates to the rhythmic production of place. In this sense rhythm informs the progressive sense of place originally outlined by Massey (1993). The enfoldings of space and time create nodal points through which pass a multiplicity of flows and practices which make place as a fluid, contingent and highly permeable formation. As Edensor (2009: 4) says '[p]lace can thus be depicted, performed and sensed through its ensemble of normative and counter rhythms, as Lefebvre suggests'. Edensor highlights the railway station as a key site:

> The obvious example of a train station reveals a very recognisable though shifting polyrhythmy composed out of separate strands, with its periodic announcements,

flows and surges of passengers, departing and arriving trains according (or not) to the timetable, the presence of newspaper sellers during rush hours, and the ongoing pulse of buying and selling in the retail outlets, as well as the interruptions, unexpected incidents and breakdowns. (Edensor, 2009: 4)

It is unsurprising that Edensor should pick on the railway station as an archetypal place made in mobility. The railway station itself has been variously figured as a conduit and collecting point for a wide range of flows, practices, biographies and narratives. Variously characterized by contemporaries as cathedrals to commerce and as kaleidoscopic 'babel towers', the railway station has been called by social historians Richards and MacKenzie (1988: 137) 'an extraordinary agent of social mixing'. As a location where heterogeneous voices and cultures interact, commune and conflict, the railway station acts as a simultaneously centrifugal and centripetal force in the production of modern urban life (Revill, 2012). From a complimentary perspective, Schivelbusch (1986) characterizes the railway station as 'the gateway to the city' both regulating and controlling its flows and announcing the point of transition and translation into the rhythms of city life. Such figurations are expressed in a wide range of cultural materials exemplified by W. P. Frith's painting of a crowded station platform at the Great Western Railway's terminus at London, Paddington (Freeman, 1999: 237) – *The Railway Station* (1862) has all the qualities of a Victorian novel with its wealth of characters and incidents, plots and subplots. John Schlesinger's documentary film *Terminus* (1961) echoes the cameos and conversations set up in Frith's painting by portraying a day in the life of London's Waterloo station. In a series of panoramas and interludes his film charts 24 hours in the life of the station as it intersects with a wide range of individual biographies, reflecting and engaging a wide range of temporal rhythms in the process. Opening and closing shots of the beehives located on the roof, figure the station and by implication the city itself in terms of the naturalized habitual coordinated pulse, flux and flow of the swarm (Revill, 2012). In Schlesinger's film the intensities of rush hour are framed by quiet cadences of morning preparation and the slow wind down of late evening closedown. In between earnest city gents, frightened lost children, irate holidaymakers and busy workers move in and through the station. The tannoy system punctuates the day with periodic announcements cutting across an infinite variety of conversations, exclamations and exchanges. In this context Richter describes the rhythmic encounter of the station as simultaneously a mode of governance and a distinctive and particularly modern experience of place. She argues that even as the social life of the railroad mirrored that of cities, train travel differed from urban life and created a distinctive milieu. Only rail travel demanded the constant and simultaneous negotiation of both urban social disorder and the systematic ordering associated with large technological systems and corporate business. Thus 'the railroad stood squarely at the crossroad of the major social, business, cultural and technological changes remaking national life during the second half of the nineteenth century' (Richter, 2005: 81).

Rhythm and the experience of mobility

Mobilities researchers are right to emphasize the regulatory role of rhythm as a key part of Lefebvre's rhythmanalysis. For Lefebvre, rhythm seems to suggest the underlying structures of city life deeply embedded in the processes and practices of capitalist reproduction. This is most evident in his well-known description of the view of Paris from the window of his apartment. Here Lefebvre looks out from the balcony of his apartment in the centre of Paris and reflects on the flux and flow of pedestrians and automobiles, the diurnal cycles of commuting, work and leisure and the long durée structurings of architectural form and ecologies of organic growth. However, it would seem that Lefebvre's major concern here is to undermine precisely the notion of spectacle suggested by the view from the window.

> The window overlooking the street is not a mental place, where the inner gaze follows abstract perspectives: a practical, space, private and concrete, the window offers views that are more than spectacles; mentally prolonged spaces. In such a way that the implication in the spectacle entails the explication of this spectacle. (Lefebvre, 2004: 36)

From Lefebvre's balcony, vision and the cultural superstructure it represents is epiphenomenal, an enticing and distracting theatre of display, a 'simulation of the real' (Lefebvre, 2004: 32). To this extent Lefebvre's concern with rhythm is grounded in fundamental regulatory processes. The visible surfaces and inter-sections of rhythmic interplay offer a mere 'glimpse', hinting or 'murmuring' the truth of underlying systems, logics and processes. Within this mind set the body seems to offer little more than a site for the realization of foundational truths. Taken as a whole, *Elements of Rhythmanalysis* is strongest on those elements of rhythm that point towards underlying economic, social and political structures, their cyclical and linear, interjections and interpolations, repetitions and flows. If as Elden (2004b: xiii) suggests, Lefebvre's writing on rhythm is influenced by Gaston Bachelard's poetics of space then there is little in the book to offer a systematic unpacking of the creative and the poetic. Even the chapter on music is most centrally concerned with metre and measure as rule governed bodily experience rather than the processes and practices of invention and elaboration (see Said, 1992).

Transport infrastructures such as railway stations are often obdurate and deeply embedded in social and material life. Our encounters with them are frequently experienced as either transitory, just in passing as we move through the ticket barrier or take the phone call; or superficial to the extent that our attention lies beyond the technology itself on the task or action it enables or facilitates. To this extent, the railway station is indeed a model for the tacit structuring of regulation and the embodied experience of flux and flow. Yet at the same time we should remember that transport technologies such as railway stations have a distinctive and sometimes high profile and iconic presence in

The Sociological Review, 61:S1, pp. 51–68 (2013), DOI: 10.1111/1467-954X.12053

popular imaginations and public histories. Transport infrastructures and related iconic machinery continue to play highly charged and richly layered symbolic roles in histories of modernity, imaginings of nation building, social, economic and cultural progress and narratives of individual self-fulfilment. Modern mobile lifestyles, tourists and travellers, career professionals and commuters, are enabled by practices, habits, expectations and norms informed by these histories. Travel decisions are rarely made through rational logic alone, the rise of the motor car no less than the reluctance of many to use public transport has grounds in the social and cultural positioning of these transport modes and especially in the public histories, social values and personal memories that inform their use. Cresswell and others have forcefully argued that writing the experiences of mobility without locating its practices within historical and geographical specificity generalizes the experiences of mobility, flattening out difference, universalizing and naturalizing inequalities in the process (Cresswell and Verstrate, 2002; Dival and Revill, 2005; Solnit, 2001). In this context Cresswell (2010: 18) has characterized mobility as 'a fragile entanglement of physical movement, representations, and practices'. For Cresswell, such 'constellations of mobility' are formed from three elements, in turn these are: particular patterns of movement, representations of movement and ways of practising movement. In concert they constitute entities or systems which 'make sense together'. Here Cresswell draws on Edward Soja's (1989) reading of Lefebvre, in a tripartite formulation which owes much to Lefebvre's theorization of conceived, perceived and lived space developed in *The Production of Space* (1991). In this way Cresswell seeks to bring together the apparently disparate components of mobility as meaningful experience, drawing together sensitivity to the affective experience of movement with a critical politics of cultural representation.

This suggests a rather more co-constructed and balanced relationship between the apparently hidden underlying rhythms of mobility, the cadences of its immediate and affective practice and the reflective social and cultural meanings through which we make sense of and come to reflexively understand these experiences. In many respects rhythm seems an ideal medium with which to address issues of co-construction and mutual dependency. Rhythmic qualities of amplitude and frequency, periodicity, recurrence and intensity direct attention, for example, to the co-constitution of space and time. An attention to rhythm ensures, as Elden (2001, 2004a) suggests, that we learn a primary lesson from Lefebvre's *The Production of Space* and recognize the relationship between time and space as no longer 'one of abstract separation coupled with an equally abstract confusion between these two different yet connected terms' (1991: 351). In this way the capacity of rhythm to produce, carry and disclose the topological enfolding of times and spaces in the making of lived experience should point directly to a range of processes which integrate and envelope. As Burgin (1996) says, the imbrication of social space and mental space within lived space is central to Lefebvre's problematic, and consequently rhythmanalysis should provide a clear route towards making these resolutions.

For the above to be fully realized rhythmanalysis would have to be as comfortable with the meaningfulness of reflexive cultural experience as it is with regulatory structurings and embodied affectivities. In this context, Burgin (1996) has forcefully argued that a major stumbling block is Lefebvre's essentially passive understanding of perception. He attributes this to Lefebvre's division of the labouring from the perceiving body:

> Lefebvre's insistence on the centrality of the body subverts the distinction he makes between 'representations of space' and 'representational space.' If as he insists, and as psychoanalysis would agree, 'The whole of (social) space proceeds from the body,' then how is he able to see such 'representations of space' as geometry as exempt from the same bodily determinations as 'representational space'? The answer to this question probably lies in Lefebvre's division of the labouring body from the perceiving body, in which perceptual processes are seen as essentially passive. (Burgin, 1996: 30)

Burgin's criticism of the theoretical separation of the labouring body from the perceiving body might also cast light on Lefebvre's insensitivity to the productively creative dynamics of rhythm. Perhaps this is the key to its underdeveloped theorization of the processes and practices of reflexively organized invention and creativity suggested above. Railway stations are clearly encountered through a range of historically resonant and culturally meaningful symbolic codings and associations in addition to a range of experientially rich sensations and stimuli. In fact, as Ihde's post-phenomenology of technology suggests, these two dimensions of experience are mutually co-constituted (Ihde, 2003, 2009). In this context, Ihde champions what he calls a relational or interrelational ontology which is sensitive to historical specificity and by implication to the reintegration of affective and reflexive experience (Langsdorf, 2006).

> Technologies transform our experience of the world and our perceptions and interpretations of our world, and we in turn become transformed in this process. Transformations are non-neutral. And it is here that histories and any empirical turn may become *ontologically* important, which will lead us to the pragmatist insight that histories are also important in any philosophical analysis as such. (Ihde, 2009: 44)

Listening to rhythm

In one important sense Lefebvre is well aware of the active qualities of perception. An often neglected aspect of Lefebvre's rhythmanalysis project is its engagement with the work of Jacques Lacan and its formulation as a sort of 'listening cure' in contradistinction to psychoanalysis (Gregory, 1995: 41, 1997). In this respect the idea of listening as an active practice is contrasted with the more passive physiological sense of hearing. It suggests an active engagement with a speaking subject, an openness and sensitivity to positionality, intention and meaning. Listening is thus a hermeneutical disposition made possible in conjunction with recognitions of historical and geographical context, sequence and situatedness. Though Lefebvre is keen to assert the attentiveness of the social scientist as rhythmanalyst he seems to have neglected this as a mode of being in the world which extends also to the subjects of his study. Listening is not just the preserve of the analyst or the social scientist; rather it is fundamental to social relations and reciprocities. To this extent these aspects of Lefebvre's rhythmanalysis remain underdeveloped and require further expansion and explanation.

By championing the place of the social scientist as a listener, Lefebvre usefully shares common ground with recent writing in sociology and cultural studies. Back (2007), for example, promotes a conception of the rhythmic and the sonic thought together as part of a more attentive and engaged sense of 'listening' to social practice. This is couched in terms of the multi-sensory qualities of human experience, as an ethical exercise in hermeneutical sensitivity in response to the apparently alienating distance of vision. Yet, if rhythmanalysis is to be a medium of social listening then, as Burgin suggests, Lefebvre's essentially passive understanding of perception provides something of a conceptual barrier. In contrast to Lefebvre's search for underlying truths in rhythm, more recent theorists have figured listening as a much more active engaged and co-constructed set of practices. Thus listening becomes a site for the processes and practices of invention and creativity in terms of both reflexively organized poesis and self-organizing autopoesis. In this context Jean-Luc Nancy questions the foundational ontology of rhythm as underlying reality whilst usefully echoing Lefebvre's concern with the rhythmic body:

> . . . shouldn't truth 'itself,' as transitivity and incessant transition of a continual coming and going, be listened to rather than seen? But isn't it also in the way that it stops being 'itself' and identifiable, and becomes no longer the naked figure emerging from the cistern but the resonance of that cistern – or, if it were possible to express it thus, the echo of the naked figure in the open depths? (Nancy, 2007: 3–4)

For Nancy, the resonance of the cistern not only provides a container, a ground on which the meaningful truth of the body is presented to the world but its echoing cavernous volume transforms and remakes truth in the process. For Nancy, the sense of reverberation, the interference patterns created by the interaction between body and cistern actively produce rather than simply reflect. In fact Nancy (2007: 5) argues that hearing and listening, activities most closely associated with rhythm, have 'a special relationship with *sense* in the intellectual or intelligible acceptance of the word (with "perceived" meaning)'. In this case to sense is to make sense. It is an active conscious process of ontological making in a manner which resonates with Ihde's interrelational ontology. Perhaps it is not surprising that Ihde's relational ontology is also informed by his earlier work on listening (Ihde, 1976). Here one has to turn to more recent theorists informed by these sorts of ideas and concerned with rhythm as an expression of meaningful experience to find work which might carry the task of rhythmanalysis forward if it is to embrace the experience of mobility in terms of Cresswell's fragile entanglements. As with Nancy and Ihde many of these authors engage with rhythm as part of a broader sense of the sonic (see also Attali, 1977; Schwarz, 1997; Erlmann, 2004).

Brandon LaBelle's (2010) work on acoustic territories begins to suggest some of the potential for a broader conception of rhythm which is often embodied and experienced in sound and expressed through acoustic and resonant spaces of reverberation, repetition, diffusion, interference and echo. For LaBelle, the qualities of sound produce distinctive spatial experiences, sounds are diffuse and pervasive, they reverberate, resound, echo and decay in complex and unexpected ways. The substantially passive receptivity of hearing and the active interpretative processes of listening encourage sounds to encompass us whilst at the same time seeming to reverberate deep inside our heads, engaging and questioning senses of self and other. Thus sound brings us into intimate contact with activities, actions and events which lie well outside the reach of other senses, round the corner, over the next hill or in an adjacent room (Revill, 2013). The meanings created, communicated and translated through sound are associative:

> The *associative* dynamics of sound lends greatly to triggering *associative* forms of discourse and knowledge. This is both participant within physics and phenomenological behaviour of sound, as well as forming the conceptual and psychodynamic frame for recognizing how hearing is already an associative act. For what we hear is not mostly what we seem nor can it strictly be pinned down to a given source, or brought into language. Often sound is what lends to directing our visual focus – we hear something and this tells us where to look; it eases around us in a flow of energy to which we unconsciously respond. Sounds are associated with their original source, while also becoming their own thing, separate and constantly blending with other sounds, thereby continually moving in and out of focus and clarity. (LaBelle, 2010: xix)

Where for Lefebvre the view from the balcony is merely an image simulating the real and requiring rhythm to engage its deeper reality, for LaBelle the rhythmic and the sonic shape vision, structuring social experience as complex and contingent. Thus LaBelle argues that sound and by implication rhythm is simultaneously a sense of feeling and a considered reflection on experience, it wraps together that which is affective and that which is representational in contingent topological formations. It is multisensory always in dialogue with vision, touch and language and to this extent his account is sympathetic to Serres' (2008) understanding of the semiotic importance of touch, contact and connection as moments of decision making and differentiation in which meanings are made and conveyed. It is also congruent with the sense of rhythm developed in Karen Barad's (2003, 2007) adaptation of diffraction as a way of figuring difference within phenomena rather than between oppositional terms.

Barad asserts (2003: 817) contra Lefebvre that reality is not composed of things-in-themselves or things-behind-phenomena but 'things'-in-phenomena. Here her work intersects with Ihde's relational ontology of technology and Nancy's conception of listening. It is through specific intra-actions that a differential sense of being is enacted in the ongoing ebb and flow of agency. Thus, according to Barad (2003: 818), '[t]emporality and spatiality emerge in this

The Sociological Review, 61:S1, pp. 51–68 (2013), DOI: 10.1111/1467-954X.12053

processual historicity. Relations of exteriority, connectivity, and exclusion are reconfigured'. In this way she argues that 'the primary ontological units are not 'things' but phenomena – dynamic topological reconfigurings/entanglements/relationalities/(re)articulations' (Barad, 2003: 817). Rhythm and particularly for her the interference patterns created in diffraction might be thought of as key to such a figural and processual sense of ontology able to weave together a heterogeneous range of socio-material textures (Crang, 2001: 200). LaBelle also draws on this sort of processual ontology; sounds are spatio-temporal events, arcs of rhythmical movement linking two points in time (Revill, 2013). Thus:

> Auditory knowledge is a radical epistemological thrust that unfolds as a spatiotemporal event: sound opens up a field of interaction, to become a channel, a fluid, a flux of voice and urgency, a play of drama, of mutuality and sharing, to ultimately carve out a micro-geography of the moment, while always already disappearing, as a distributive and sensitive propagation. (LaBelle, 2010: xvii)

Such a conception of sound seems in sympathy with the idea of rhythm as the means of connection between disparate milieus suggested by Deleuze and Guattari for whom rhythm exists whenever a passage is 'transcoded' from one milieu to another. Thought of in this way, communication between milieus is thus a coordination between heterogeneous space-times. In describing such lines of flight, refrains organize territories, register and inscribe understandings of the world and open up a 'virtual' world of possibility and becoming (Thrift and Dewsbury, 2005: 105; see Deleuze and Guattari, 1988: 315–317). In these ways rhythm may be seen to connect apparently separate realms of existence not merely as the epiphenomena of underlying processes but as a set of ontologically generative processes creating a relational ontology which connects the affective and reflective, the material and the imaginal.

In this sense rhythm can be thought of as more than a cipher for regimes of governance or a marker setting out the phenomenological contours of the flow of unreflected sensory experience through the body. Rather it is a key medium through which Cresswell's fragile entanglement of physical movement, representations and practices might be understood as making sense together. In this context, following Nancy and Barad, 'making sense together' is itself productive of phenomenological reality rather than merely an assemblage of parts resting within an underlying ontological realm. Thus, if the railway station is an archetypal site for the examination of urban rhythms then it may prove instructive to revisit the themes of governance and the body highlighted by Edensor. The following section returns to the railway station in order to explore a few of the possibilities for a rhythmanalysis better able to embrace the reflexivity and cultural creativity of rhythm in light of the above discussion.

Governance and body: interruption and repetition

As Law (2003) has shown in his discussion of the Ladbrooke Grove train crash, though infrastructures often appear almost transparent as they run unnoticed in the background, system failure brings us up sharp with their existence and our dependence on them. At such moments infrastructures take on a phenomenological presence which may shape experience in creative and reflexive ways well beyond the affordances of habit. In this context the interruption of rhythm may not only alert us to the presence of underlying cyclical patterns of regulation but also to its creative capacity to reverberate, resound, gather momentum, amplify and actively transform. Take, for example, that most evocative of poems written about a train stopping in a station – Edward Thomas's poem *Addlestrop*, written in 1915 after he had signed up for military service in the army and published posthumously in his collected works (Thomas, 1920; see also Lucas, 1997; Longley, 2009). It tells of an unscheduled stop at a rural station during a hot summer's day. Window open in the pause after the train has come to rest and before the signal drops and the train moves off again, the author's attention is drawn beyond the railway in the stillness and heat of the afternoon. The sound of a single blackbird punctuating the silence catches his attention. As its sound resonates out across the landscape so the author becomes sensitized to the natural sounds of the day and he becomes increasingly aware of a world beyond the tracks. Resounding at greater and greater distance bird song transforms the dull silence of the moment created by the train's unscheduled stop. The detachment initially felt by the author is soon transformed into an intimate and connected sense of a landscape full of life, vitality and hope.

> And for that minute a blackbird sang
> Close by, and round him, mistier,
> Farther and farther, all the birds
> Of Oxfordshire and Gloucestershire.
> (Thomas, 1920: 52)

In this example the rhythm of the train journey, the way it is structured by timetable, signalling and safety systems, is not just revealed by the unscheduled station stop, rather it is creatively transformed. Interruption of the predictable routine of the journey initiates an expansive rhythmically induced sonoric resonance which opens out from the traveller in ways which heighten perception and activate an imaginative reflexivity (Revill, 2013).

Thought of in this way, railway stations are not just nodal points managing processes of pulse, flow and switch, but rather are sites of amplification, elaboration and transformation. In this context railway stations can be understood, for example, as participating in the life of national communications as much more than points of arrival and departure for passengers and goods. Rather, they act as resonant and lively conduits for political messaging. Interruptions to station routine have thus instigated a wide range of temporary and contingent political spaces. As Lisa Mitchell (2009) has shown in her study of language and regional politics in southern India since the 1950s, railways continue to act as a powerful and informal conduit for political communication. They are sites for protests, violence and graffiti feeding back local and regional complaints and objections to the centre of power. Such extraordinary means of political com-

The Sociological Review, 61:S1, pp. 51–68 (2013), DOI: 10.1111/1467-954X.12053

munication continue to be important for the poor, and those who believe themselves to be otherwise unheard or disenfranchised. Perhaps in this way we can come to better understand a range of incidents from the Dutch train hostage crisis in 1975 involving a group claiming independence for the south-east Asian islands of South Molucca, to the Madrid train bombings of 2004, often attributed to al-Qaeda inspired terrorists. In May 2007, for example, full-scale riots broke out when services were interrupted during the evening rush hour at Constitución station, Buenos Aires, one of the largest stations in South America. One hundred police attended the incident, firing rubber bullets and tear gas as rioters pelted them with rocks, smashed windows, set fire to the ticket sales area, looted shops and ripped payphones from the walls as the protest spilt out on to the street. The riot was the second outbreak of violence within a year. The previous September cancelled trains resulted in three train carriages being set alight and police making seven arrests (*Guardian*, 2008; *Daily Telegraph*, 2008). Such behaviour was indicative of a complex array of otherwise pent-up frustrations relating to Argentina's recent history, especially its serious economic problems and the subsequent widespread unemployment, welfare cuts, raging inflation and neoliberal reforms. Passengers had complained for years about poor commuter rail services on lines leading from Constitución station in downtown Buenos Aires to the capital's poor southern suburbs. Privatized in the 1990s, failure of the Buenos Aires commuter lines to provide punctual services on overcrowded routes provoked commuters from poor suburbs to give voice to a range of long-standing social concerns amplified through the nation and beyond by the railway station (Revill, 2012). In these examples the rhythmic counterpoint of routine, system failure, pent-up anger and spontaneous protest produces and reshapes the civic sphere, creating direct connections between local, national and international concern. Thus rhythm intentionally and unintentionally becomes an active and reflexive part of governance enabling people to participate in political processes in complex, informal and unexpected ways. Such rhythmic elaborations invited and enabled by failures in regulatory rhythmic structuring not only reflect public concerns but actively promote the construction of publics as more or less informal, contingent and temporary formations.

Like the inventive elaborations of interruption, the rhythmic interplay of repetition and routine, arrival and departure, transfer and embarkation can also be creative. Lefebvre readily admits that repetition is never exact and always embraces the sort of contingency which produces social and material difference. The repetitive moments of expectation, loss and excess which exceed and inform the habituation of routine at the railway station also form starting points for complex cultural imaginings. Such rhythmically founded imaginings are evident in a wide range of well-known cultural materials from Tolstoy's *Anna Karenina* (1873–1877) to David Lean's film *Brief Encounter* (1945). Meeting and parting, separation and union, desire, yearning and fulfilment are central to an experience of personal mobility in which the railway station is both a space of routine and simultaneously highly charged with imaginative expectations. Films, songs and novels portray lovers meeting and fugitives escaping by train; wracked with guilt and despair heroes and villains commit suicide under advancing locomotives, whilst chance meetings result in life-changing encounters on platforms and in station waiting rooms. Thus routine repetition is not just a vehicle for a retreat into reactive passivity, rather it is also a medium for inventive rich and culturally complex day dreams, imaginative flights of fancy and bodily desires.

The experience of individualized social proximity is familiar for many who use public transport and frequent railway stations. Yet rather than simply marking underlying rhythmic alienation, such rhythms produce social interaction with deep social and cultural resonance, characterized in, for example, Simmel's (1903) idea of the 'proximate stranger'. Take, for instance, this newspaper report from the 19th century:

> I was a passenger on an excursion train to Melbourne last Saturday, and upon returning witnessed at that station a disgraceful proceeding on the part of several railway clerks . . . This young gentleman was drunk . . . on the platform he threatened if he did not actually molest a minister who had in no way interfered with him, he attacked and forced a man onto the railway and directly commenced a free fight. . . .

> He dared a porter to touch him, stating he was a clerk with a first class pass, which he frequently exhibited, and there is no doubt whatever that if it had not been for this – if he had been an ordinary passenger, unconnected with the company, who had thus acted, he would surely have been arrested. . . . (Letter to the *Derby Mercury,* 24 July 1872)

This minor altercation between a drunken railway clerk and a platform full of day trippers must have been echoed in countless encounters and at many times and places. Yet in spite of its trivial nature, it seems so highly suggestive of the social relationships forged by the experience of railway travel. The anonymity of the crowd on the platform, the mixing of ages, genders and classes, the vagaries and incivilities of the random encounters produced by such coincidence, all seem to suggest those anxieties and intensities by which late 19th-century sociologists distinguished modern mobile urban life from what they perceived as its sedentary rural predecessor. It is not without significance that the drunken railway clerk flaunts his first-class pass, as a talisman protecting him from the sanction of those around him. A corporate perk for higher status administrative staff allowing free first-class rail travel, the first-class pass signifies both social and physical mobility in bodily terms. Waving his pass in front of fellow travellers and railway workers alike he tells the world as both a privileged passenger and a career bureaucrat 'you cannot touch me, I am going places'. For Simmel (1903), the stranger represents a synthesis between 'freedom' (mobility) and 'fixation' (stability), between near and far, somebody who is connected yet disconnected. Thus the stranger met on trains and station platforms disturbs expectations of physical and emotional distance, bringing into intimate presence the kind of difference and otherness anticipated and tolerated only at a distance. The stranger challenges individualized senses of self at the same time that the response to this presence both encourages assertions of individuality and objectifies the generalized presence of

The Sociological Review, 61:S1, pp. 51–68 (2013), DOI: 10.1111/1467-954X.12053
© 2013 The Author. Editorial organisation © 2013 The Editorial Board of the Sociological Review

the crowd. Coding the body within encounters generated by polyrhythmic pulse and flow on the crowded station platform thus forms a point of departure for culturally charged social positioning in terms of both self and other.

Conclusion

In these brief examples rhythm is a medium of elaboration rather than just habituation. The sound of bird song beyond the carriage window no less than the gathering voice of protest on the station platform produce rhythmic arcs of sound in the sense suggested by LaBelle. They bridge material and social realms moving out beyond the immediate and the local, gathering and generating energies, alliances and social meanings embedded in and embodied by patterns of sympathetic resonance and semiotic association. Whilst the routine rhythms of habit form a ground from which a range of imaginative excursions proceed, repetition is itself a maker of difference in which even minor variations produce loss and excess which is socially and culturally as well as materially generative. As the example of the clerk with a first-class travel pass shows, random initial encounters develop in contingent ways drawing on a wide range of social and culturally situated understandings and expectations. Interruption almost by definition produces a moment of reflexivity in the break or space between iterations raising awareness of relationships based on situations of presence and absence involving self and other. Whilst the imperfections and context dependence of repetition encourage configurations of interruption, refraction and diffraction generating difference as rhythms contingently overlap and reinforce each other. In this context listening is an active and always to some extent reflexively organized practice not only for social scientists as researchers but for all social actors. The conception of listening developed by Ihde, Nancy, Back and LaBelle takes this as a starting point when considering rhythm as a medium of social organization and communication which moves between and brings together material and imaginal, affective and reflexive realms. From this position rhythm does not so much reveal underlying realities in the sense Lefebvre might have thought of it. Rather rhythm is an active producer of realities as contingent ontological couplings of complimentary, divergent and disparate dimensions of experience. From such a starting point, this paper has argued that rhythm can contribute more fully to an inclusive approach to understanding experiences of mobility. This may provide a productive means of reintegrating the apparently separate dimensions of mobile experience enabling them, as Cresswell (2010) says, to 'make sense together'.

For Ferrarini (2005) the contemporary conception of the railway station based on the maximization of its income-generating capacity is envisaged as a junction for different kinds of traffic, a 'fulcrum for the reorganization of the surrounding area itself'. For her, this marks a 'transformation in the very conception of the railway station'. The regeneration of the Kings Cross/St Pancras area of London related to new high speed and regional rail links is an iconic example. Relevant here is the conception of 'terminal' present in the work of architectural critic Martin Pawley (1998) and deriving both from the transport hub and the computer. In this conception a terminal is a nodal point for the access and exchange of a heterogeneous mix of information, flows and services. It is significant that Steven Connor (1997: 212) positions such a nodal networked conception of experience as central to 'the switch-board experience' of modern life found in early telephone systems, radiophonic broadcasting, and the cinema. The juxtaposition of 'switchboard' and 'broadcasting' suggests a complex combination of directed and arbitrary flows, gatherings and dispersals which have direct relevance to networked infrastructures such as railways. Together these suggest on the one hand processes of channelling and exchange, and on the other to emit, transmit, shed, throw, shine, radiate and spread. Thus for Connor (1997: 212) these means of communication perform a new shuffling between the 'rapture and capture' of sight and sound. There are echoes in this formulation of LaBelle's (2010: xix) notion of rhythmic associational 'promiscuity' and the trajectory of spatio-temporal events, arcs of rhythmical movement linking two points in time. Like the computer terminal the station has become a junction point within a territorial system, of mixed traffic flow, a place in which movement is translated into millions of individual lifestyle choices, acquisitions and purchases. Thus, as makers of place, stations as terminals are culturally generative and exemplify the points where objects or actions are translated from one mode or register of circulation to another. The act of translation or transhipment is a point of creative elaboration. It marks cultural location and value as tradable commodities at once remaking and elaborating social meaning. The rhythmic interplay of lack and excess, movement and stasis constitute the station as a place where multiple points of departure, fulfil and generate desires, wants, needs and expectations.

References

Attali, J., (1977), *Noise: The Political Economy of Music*, trans. 1985, Manchester: Manchester University Press.

Back, L., (2007), *The Art of Listening*, Oxford: Berg.

Barad, K., (2003), 'Posthumanist performativity: how matter comes to matter', *Signs: Journal of Women in Culture*, 28 (3): 801–831.

Barad, K., (2007), *Meeting the Universe Halfway: Quantum Physics and the Entanglement of Matter and Meaning*, Durham, NC and London: Duke University Press.

Binnie, J., Edensor, T., Holloway, J., Millington, S. and Young, C., (2007), 'Mundane mobilities, banal travels', *Social and Cultural Geography*, 8 (2): 165–174.

Bissell, D., (2009a), 'Travelling vulnerabilities: mobile timespaces of quiescence', *Cultural Geographies*, 16: 427–445.

Bissell, D., (2009b), 'Visualising everyday geographies: practices of vision through travel-time', *Transactions of the Institute of British Geographers*, 34: 42–60.

Bissell, D., (2009c), 'Conceptualising differently-mobile passengers: geographies of everyday encumbrance in the railway station', *Social and Cultural Geography*, 10: 173–195.

Burgin, V., (1996), *In/different Spaces: Place and Memory in Visual Culture*, Berkeley, CA and London: University of California Press.

The Sociological Review, 61:S1, pp. 51–68 (2013), DOI: 10.1111/1467-954X.12053

Carter, I., (2001), *Railways and Culture in Britain: The Epitome of Modernity*, Manchester: Manchester University Press.

Chandler, A., (1977). *The Visible Hand: The Managerial Revolution in American Business*, Cambridge, MA: MIT Press.

Connor, S., (1997), 'The modern auditory I', in R. Porter (ed.), *Rewriting the Self: Histories from the Renaissance to the Present*, 203–223, London: Routledge.

Crang, M., (2001), 'Rhythms of the city: temporalised space and motion', in J. May and N. Thrift (eds), *Timespace: Geographies of Temporality*, London: Routledge.

Cresswell, T., (2006), *On the Move: Mobility in the Modern Western World*, New York: Routledge.

Cresswell, T., (2010), 'Towards a politics of mobility', *Environment and Planning D: Society and Space*, 28 (1): 17–31.

Cresswell, T., (2011), 'Mobilities 1: catching up', *Progress in Human Geography*, 35 (4): 550–558.

Cresswell, T. and Verstraete, G. (eds), (2002), *Mobilizing Place, Placing Mobility: The Politics of Representation in a Globalized World*, Amsterdam: Rodopi.

Cronon, W., (1991), *Nature's Metropolis: Chicago and the Great West*, New York: Norton.

Daily Telegraph, (2008), 'Argentinians Torch Train Over Delays', *Daily Telegraph*, 5 September, http://www.telegraph.co.uk/news/worldnews/southamerica/argentina/2686366/Argentina (accessed 7 November 2009).

Deleuze, G. and Guattari, F., (1988), *A Thousand Plateaus: Capitalism and Schizophrenia*, London: Athlone Press.

Divall, C. and Revill, G., (2005), 'Cultures of transport: representation, practice and technology', *Transport History*, 26 (1): 99–111.

Edensor, T. (ed.), (2009) *Geographies of Rhythm: Nature, Place, Mobilities and Bodies*, Farnham: Ashgate.

Elden, S., (2001), 'Politics, philosophy, geography: Henri Lefebvre in recent Anglo-American scholarship', *Antipode*, 33 (5): 809–825.

Elden, S., (2004a), 'Between Marx and Heidegger: politics, philosophy and Lefebvre's "The Production of Space" ', *Antipode*, 36 (1): 86–105.

Elden, S., (2004b), 'Introduction', in H. Lefebvre, *Rhythmanalysis: Space, Time and Everyday Life* (trans. S. Elden and G. Moore), London: Continuum.

Erlmann, V., (2004), *Hearing Cultures: Essays on Sound, Listening and Modernity*, Oxford: Berg.

Ferrarini, A., (2005), *Railway Stations: From the Gare de L'Est to Penn Station*, Milan: Electa Architecture.

Fincham, B., McGuiness, M. and Murray, L. (eds), (2010), *Mobile Methodologies*, Basingstoke: Palgrave Macmillan.

Freeman, M., (1999), *Railways and the Victorian Imagination*, New Haven and London: Yale University Press.

Freud, S., (2001), *Standard Edition of the Complete Psychological Works of Sigmund Freud* (eds A. Strachey and A. Tyson), London: Hogarth Press and the Institute of Psycho-analysis.

Gregory, D., (1995), 'Lefebvre, Lacan and the production of space', in G. B. Benko and U. Strohmayer (eds), *Geography, History and Social Sciences*, 15–44, Amsterdam: Kluwer Academic.

Gregory, D., (1997), 'Lacan and geography: the production of space revisited', in G. Benko and U. Strohmayer (eds), *Space and Social Theory: Interpreting Modernity and Postmodernity*, 203–231, Oxford: Blackwell.

Guardian, (2008), 'Buenos Aires hit by rush hour rail riot', *Guardian.co.uk* 6 May, http://www.guardian.co.uk/world/2007/may/16/argentina/print (accessed 7 November 2009).

Hein, J. R., Evans, J. and Jones, P., (2008), 'Mobile methodologies: theory, technology and practice', *Geography Compass*, 2 (5): 1266–1285.

Ihde, D., (1976), *Listening and Voice: A Phenomenology of Sound*, Athens, OH: Ohio University Press.

Ihde, D., (2003), 'If phenomenology is an albatross is postphenomenology possible?' in D. Ihde and E. Selinger (eds), *Chasing Technoscience: Matrix of Materiality*, 117–130, Bloomington, IN: Indiana University Press.

Ihde, D., (2009), *Postphenomenology and Technoscience: The Peking Lectures*, Albany, NY: SUNY Press.

Kern, S., (1983), *The Culture of Time and Space*, London: Weidenfeld and Nicolson.

Kirby, L., (1997), *Parallel Tracks: The Railroad and Silent Cinema*, Exeter: University of Exeter Press.

LaBelle, B., (2010), *Acoustic Territories/Sound Culture and Everyday Life*, New York: Continuum.

Langsdorf, L., (2006), 'The primacy of listening: towards a metaphysics of communicative interaction', in E. Selinger (ed.), *Postphenomenology: A Critical Companion to Ihde*, 37–47, Albany, NY: SUNY Press.

Law, J., (2003), 'Ladbroke Grove, or how to think about failing systems', published by the Centre for Science Studies, Lancaster University, Lancaster LA1 4YN, UK, at http://www.comp.lancs .ac.uk/sociology/papers/Law-Ladbroke-Grove-Failing-Systems.pdf.

Lefebvre, H., (1991), *The Production of Space*, Oxford: Blackwell.

Lefebvre, H., (2004), *Rhythmanalysis: Space, Time and Everyday Life* (trans. S. Elden and G. Moore), London: Continuum.

Loiperdinger, M., (2004), 'Lumiere's arrival of the train: cinema's founding myth', *The Moving Image*, 4 (1): 89–118.

Longley, E., (2009), 'Thomas, (Philip) Edward (1878–1917)', Oxford Dictionary of National Biography, 2004; online edn, October 2009), http://www.oxforddnb.com/view/article/36480 (accessed 6 July 2010).

Lucas, J., (1997), 'Discovering England: the view from the train', *Literature and History*, 6 (2): 43–47.

Massey, D., (1993), 'Power-geometry and a progressive sense of place', in J. Bird, B. Curtis, T. Putnam, G. Robertson and L. Tickner (eds), *Mapping the Futures: Local Cultures, Global Changes*, 59–69, London: Routledge.

Mitchell, L., (2009), *Language, Emotion and Politics in South India*, Bloomington, IN: Indiana University Press.

Nancy, J-L., (2007), *Listening*, New York: Fordham University Press.

Pawley, M., (1998), *Terminal Architecture*, London: Reaktion.

Revill, G., (2012), *Railway*, London: Reaktion Books.

Revill, G., (2013), '*El Tren Fantasma:* arcs of sound and the acoustic spaces of landscape', *Transactions of the Institute of British Geographers* (in press).

Richards, J. and MacKenzie, J. M., (1988), *The Railway Station: A Social History*, Oxford: Oxford University Press.

Richter, A., (2005), *Home on the Rails: Women, the Railroad, and the Rise of Public Domesticity*, Chapel Hill, NC: University of North Carolina Press.

Said, E. W., (1992), *Musical Elaborations*, London: Vintage Books.

Schivelbusch, W., (1986), *The Railway Journey: The Industrialization of Time and Space in the 19th Century*, Leamington Spa: Berg.

Schwarz, D., (1997), *Listening Subjects: Music, Psychoanalysis, Culture*, Durham, NC: Duke University Press.

Serres, M., (2008): *The Five Senses: A Philosophy of Mingled Bodies*, London and New York: Continuum.

Simmel, G., (1903), 'The metropolis and mental life', in D. Frisby and M. Featherstone (eds), *Simmel on Culture: Selected Writings*, 174–186, London: Sage.

Soja, E. W., (1989), *Postmodern Geographies: The Reassertion of Space in Critical Social Theory*, London: Verso.

Solnit, R., (2001), *Wanderlust: A History of Walking*, London: Verso.

Thomas, E., (1920), *Collected Works*, London: Selwyn & Blaunt.

Thrift, N. and Dewsbury, J. D., (2005), ' "Genesis eternal": after Paul Klee', in *Deleuze and Space*, 89–108, Edinburgh: Edinburgh University Press.

Tsuji, Y., (2006), 'Railway time and rubber time: the paradox in the Japanese conception of time', *Time and Society*, 15 (2–3): 177–195.

The Sociological Review, 61:S1, pp. 51–68 (2013), DOI: 10.1111/1467-954X.12053

Carnival crowds

Beatriz Jaguaribe

Abstract: Through selective readings of literary chronicles, artistic and media representations, this paper explores how a particular kind of crowd – the carnival crowd –
has been interpreted and represented in key periods of Rio de Janeiro's history. I
argue that the temporal, spatial and aesthetic configurations of the carnival crowd
express the bodily dimensions of a profane collective celebration that mirrors the
distinct cultural negotiations of the city. In contemporary Rio de Janeiro, the return
of the carnival crowd also highlights old and new forms of public interaction. The
presence of partying multitudes in the streets of the city posits considerable organizational and social challenges. But the carnival crowd is endorsed by the media, the
municipal authorities and the tourist industry because it represents a major source of
commercial profit, it promotes a mythical image of the hedonistic city and it also
expresses an ultimate celebratory occupation of public space.

Keywords: carnival, crowds, city, media

Caught in the crowd

In 2011, the carnival took place in early March. Under the blazing summer sun,
I stood with a couple of friends in an old colonial square in downtown Rio. The
live carnival band was playing full blast, street vendors were plying wares of
masks, drinks and trinkets. The crowd kept getting thicker and thicker. Soon my
carnival mask was glued to my face and the tinsel and serpentine coils streaking
my hair were soaked with sweat. The crowd swayed and sang. My body was
sandwiched between other bodies. I had no choice but to follow the rhythm and
relax with the flow. As the band changed tunes, people moved accordingly and
brief blanks of empty space emerged. After many hours, we broke loose from the
crowd. Crossing the street and perching myself on the stone steps of a baroque
church, I could see from afar the dense mass of pulsating, compacted people. I had
been a part of the variegated, anonymous, sweat drenched, loud, carnival crowd.

My carnival experience was far from unique. The year 2011 established Rio
de Janeiro as the main city of street carnival in all of Brazil. The municipality
authorized the partying of 425 *blocos*. Varying in size and sophistication, the
blocos are associations of friends, residents of the same neighbourhood, or
amateur and professional lovers of carnival that gather together and form a

The Sociological Review, 61:S1, pp. 69–88 (2013), DOI: 10.1111/1467-954X.12054
© 2013 The Author. Editorial organisation © 2013 The Editorial Board of the Sociological Review. Published by
John Wiley & Sons Ltd, 9600 Garsington Road, Oxford OX4 2DQ, UK and 350 Main Street, Malden, MA 02148,
USA

samba group. Famous *blocos* such as *Simpatia é Quase Amor, Monobloco, Escravos da Mauá, Suvaco do Cristo, Carmelitas, Cordão do Boitatá, Cordão do Bola Preta,* among others, congregate with thousands of followers who either samba through the streets or gather as dancing multitudes in public squares. The recent revival of street carnival in Rio is largely due to their impetus and animation.[1] Although all *blocos* feature musical percussion and the presence of partying crowds in the streets, they differ considerably in regards to the type of music played, the forms of sponsorship and their historical existence. Some *blocos* have existed for decades, while others are merely sporadic media or business events that emerge due to sponsorship of beer brands or through the allure of a pop singer or celebrity figure. The oldest and by far the largest *bloco* is the *Cordão do Bola Preta* that dates back to 1918 and its participants wear the black and white colours of the association. The *bloco Cacique de Ramos* (1961), whose participants wear costumes of native American Indians, is one of the most powerful *blocos* of the north zone of Rio and it continued to occupy the street of the city even during the most repressive years of the military dictatorship. The *Banda de Ipanema* founded in the 1960s has become renowned for its exuberant drag queen revellers, whereas the *Cordão do Boi Tatá* is celebrated for its masqueraded crowds and the excellence of its percussion. The sporadic *blocos* fabricated by commercial sponsors and media celebrities usually manifest a different modality of crowd participation that features a greater similarity to the partying of the audiences in pop music concerts or the gatherings of fans celebrating a sports event. In these media or commercial *blocos* the carnival costumes practically disappear and are substituted by a T-shirt with a brand name. The greatest number of people gather in downtown Rio. In 2011, the famous *Cordão do Bola Preta,* brought together two million revellers as it paraded in downtown Rio. The gigantic crowd surpassed in numbers even the famous street carnival group the *Galo da Manhã* from the north-eastern city of Recife.

Days after the carnival had ended, the streets of the neighbourhoods of Ipanema and Copacabana and also downtown Rio were still reeking from the urine of thousands of people who had used the public sidewalks as toilets.[2] The urine-soaked sidewalks and the revellers who had freely urinated in the public thoroughfare were the subject of intense press coverage, debates and outrage from the neighbourhood associations. In a city that is notoriously disrespectful of sound pollution; in a city where garbage collectors gather tons of trash carelessly tossed on the sands of beaches, public sidewalks, parks and squares; and in a city that is quite lax in its public decorum, the stench from the urine of the carnival revellers was nonetheless considered to be a form of 'barbaric' incivility.[3] Aside from this specific issue, the masses of compacted people, the millions that followed the carnival bands, the rowdy partying, and the daily merrymaking were largely greeted by the press with celebratory enthusiasm. After all, the carnival is the iconic moment of the city. Nevertheless, letters from outraged citizens protesting against the tumult, the drunkenness and the overall lack of decorum also featured in the daily press. In either celebration or dispar-

The Sociological Review, 61:S1, pp. 69–88 (2013), DOI: 10.1111/1467-954X.12054

agement, the issue at stake was the overwhelming impact of the crowd and the bombastic occupation of the streets by the partying multitude.

In this paper I will explore through selective readings of literary chronicles, artistic representations, and media productions, how a particular kind of crowd – the carnival crowd – has been interpreted and represented at key periods of Rio de Janeiro's history. Although individual people may have varied motives for assembling together, the presence of the carnival crowd in the contemporary metropolis may also be interpreted as a celebration of collective belonging, as a desire for bodily contact, and as a manifestation of a playful performative engagement amongst city dwellers. The carnival crowd in the streets reinforces bodily presence and negates the spectral quality of mass media audiences. This is not to endorse a disjunction between the public crowd and media communication. Similar to many contemporary crowd formations, the crowds that gather together at the carnival *blocos* also rely on digital communications, cell phones and other media as a source of information and exchange. Indeed, many contemporary crowd formations begin as individual nodes in digital space and gain concrete presence in the streets. But the call of the streets reinforces the need of bodily contact. It speaks of energies that are both domesticated and unleashed as ecstasy, the visitation of the marvellous, the rupture of the bland, and as the transformative passion of the festive body. Or conversely, the experience of being entangled in the crowd, albeit a carnival crowd, may produce panic, nausea, impatience, and fear. In either its celebratory or dystopian version, the feeling of being in the crowd can be overwhelming precisely because it frays the boundaries between the self and the other.

The presence of the modern crowd in urban spaces has – since the urban gatherings of the late 18th century – elicited a vast array of responses from municipal and government authorities, artists, intellectuals, politicians, religious leaders and anonymous dwellers, among others.[4] The anxieties about the mob, the crowd or the rabble evoke fears of disarray, the uprising of the unruly populace, the orgy of inverted hierarchies, and the breakdown of norms and public decorum. Conversely, the crowd is also celebrated as a possible form of revolutionary agency or as the manifestation of a collective celebratory epiphany. In the specific case of Rio de Janeiro, the carnival crowd has been a major feature of urban life since the mid 19th century (Pereira Cunha, 2001; Ferreira, 2004). If at the beginning of the 20th century, local elites sought to contain popular carnival and domesticate the public partying in the streets, by the end of the 20th century the celebration of the 'carnival crowd' became an official municipal policy.

For the contemporary urban dweller being 'caught in the festive crowd' can be a counterpoint to the fragmented sphere of consumption, to the individuality of the competitive market, and to the isolation of media spectatorship. I am suggesting, therefore, that the merging in the carnival crowd as a form of experience offers a contrast to the theories of mass alienation by the culture industry and yet it is also distinct from the notion of the individual singularities of the network multitude as formulated by Hardt and Negri (2004). The carnival experience differs from the multitude theory of Hardt and Negri because political agendas are not necessarily enacted.[5] Moreover, the singularity of each participant in the crowd is both reinforced by the dancing and costumes but it is also erased as people merge together in order to become a crowd that is physically present in the metropolitan space. Despite glaring social disparities, racial and gender discrimination, and the maintenance of social privileges, Rio de Janeiro has become – through the impact of its numerous favelas communities, the struggles of citizenship and the rise of new political agendas – a more democratic city. The appeal of carnival as a moment of truce, of inversion of hierarchies and as a form of cathartic release remains but the structures of the quotidian against which it transgressed have also been modified.

The impact of the carnival crowd, mostly in Rio de Janeiro and the northeastern cities of Salvador and Recife, is a phenomenon that obeys no designated agenda or purpose other than that of pleasure, playfulness, catharsis and the performative display of cultural identity. Although the origins of the Brazilian carnival follow the Catholic religious calendar – carnival takes place seven Sundays before Easter Sunday – the carnival parades of the samba schools, the balls in enclosed spaces, and the merrymaking in the streets are not related to transcendental religious beliefs but to carnal relish and ecstasy in the kingdom of this world. As it actively endorses an anti-puritanical sensorial engagement with the world, the carnivalesque impulse is the opposite of ascetic rectitude and meditative contemplation. It is a feast that celebrates the merging with the flesh of the world. Although many commercial motives can be ascribed to the maintenance of carnival practices, the crowds who participate are not themselves commercially motivated. Distinctly from the crowds that gather to watch music concerts and from the crowds that cheer at sporting matches, the carnival crowd is actively engaged with itself. Live music is played and appreciated but it is the dancing, the masquerade, the drinking and being part of the crowd itself that constitute the street carnival experience. While street carnival has long faded from major European cities and exists in limited choreographed forms in Venice, Nice and in New Orleans in the United States; in Brazil, carnival has Rio de Janeiro, its second largest city, as a central stage of the festivity (Moraes, 1958: 11). The Rio carnival is a testament to the coupling between contemporary urban life with a collective communal frolic.

Carioca crowds[6]

Throughout the 19th and a large part of the 20th century, the depiction of the crowd in Rio de Janeiro followed the tendencies espoused by the 'lettered city' of European social thought and artistic imagination.[7] But a crucial difference lay in the composition and nature of the metropolitan crowd. Rio de Janeiro was one of the main ports of the slave trade in the Americas (Karasch, 1987). The official abolition of slavery only occurred in 1888. Throughout the Empire from 1822 to 1889 and until the demise of the Old Republic in 1930, the society of Rio was heavily hierarchical as the upper rankings of society held control of the economy, politics and social institutions. Popular classes had little democratic expression, civil rights or direct power. Freed slaves, poor immigrants and a feeble petite bourgeoisie composed the lower and middling ranks of society. The advent of the Republic in 1889 did little to alter the conditions of the working poor and the hierarchical division of the social classes. But by all counts, the city until the 1930s presented a reduced public sphere where the 'Lettered City' composed of high-ranking officers, civil servants, politicians, lawyers, doctors, engineers and clergymen constituted the network of power. The depiction of the crowd and the popular classes in the prose of Machado de Assis (1839–1908), Aloísio de Azevedo (1857–1913), Olavo Bilac (1865–1918), João do Rio (1881–1921), Lima Barreto (1881–1922), and other writers and journalists of the late 19th and early 20th century, emphasized the divide between the poor and the ruling class in a highly undemocratic and overtly stratified society. If the abolition of slavery provoked a massive festive response from the urban poor, the same cannot be said of the proclamation of the Republic in 1889. In his book *Os bestializados* (1987), the historian José Murilo de Carvalho analysed how the press depicted popular reaction to the proclamation of the republic as that of a dumbly passive crowd. Carvalho (1987) emphasizes, however, that the muted reaction was not just the product of passivity but rather the result of popular mistrust of the political manoeuvrings of the ruling classes. But if the popular classes were cordoned off from political and economic power the same cannot be said of their cultural influence.

Already in the 19th century and throughout the 20th, the carnival crowd highlights the force of popular collective festivities and representations. Although the rallying crowd, the sporting crowd and the religious multitude make their presence felt in many moments of the city's history, it is the carnival crowd that posits the most singular aspect of the city's cultural negotiations. The persistence of the carnival motif and the various meanings that were attributed to the festivity has been a constant subject in Brazilian social sciences, media and artistic interpretations.[8] The point to be discussed is whether carnival and the revelling crowds constitute a heteroglossic space that expresses an alternative form of modernity.

Roberto DaMatta's highly influential study from the late 1970s proposed that in a hierarchical society that was, nevertheless, permeated by ambiguous social relations based on favours and patronage, carnival was the festivity of cathartic collective release (DaMatta, 1997). During the carnival time, social signs were inverted. The poor were decked out in glorious finery, men were clothed as women, impoverished black men and women were transformed into baroque courtiers of the French Court, family men shed their inhibitions, and housewives revelled in insinuating costumes. DaMatta was examining the rituals and the festivities of Brazilian carnival in their modern dimension and his analysis details not only the hierarchical element of Brazilian society but also the slippages and the ambiguous negotiation of cultural norms. Carnival thus responds to both the momentary overturning of social hierarchies and also to the anarchic individualistic element that addresses and invents forms of subversion and spaces of pleasure. DaMatta does not deny that carnival also mirrors the rules of society but instead of insisting in the unmasking of power domination or in denouncing class exploitation, he is concerned with the socially creative dimensions of the carnival celebrations. Thus he claims:

> let me aware my reader that I know very well that Carnival reproduces the world; but I am certain that this reproduction is neither direct nor automatic. The reproduction is dialectical, with many self-reflections, circuits, niches, dimensions, and levels. That is precisely why society can change and why there can be, after all, hope for the world. (DaMatta, 1991: 62)

Other scholars of carnival festivities (Pereira de Queiroz, 1992; Soihet, 1998; Ferreira, 2004; Pereira Cunha, 2001) differ in regards to the nature of the carnival crowd. Pereira de Queiroz disagrees with what she surmises to be DaMatta's notion that carnival provides a social truce and posits that carnival celebrations, even in their current configuration, are permeated by class distinctions and that one of the mythologies of the carnival ethos is the supposition that the festivities and the gathered crowd disrupt hierarchical orderings (Pereira de Queiroz, 1992: 214–223). Instead she proposes that carnival is indeed a collective form of merriment but that the popular classes are assigned specific roles and specific spaces within the overall festivity (Pereira de Queiroz, 1992: 218). In contrast, Rachel Soihet stresses her disagreement with Pereira de Queiroz affirming that – even in the new avenues reformed by Mayor Pereira Passos at the beginning of the 20th century – the carnival crowd always presented a mixing of classes where revellers of the lower classes participated in the folly (Soihet, 1998: 58). Finally, Pereira Cunha argues that the carnival celebrations oscillated between hierarchy and mingling, between the manifestations of a popular Portuguese inspired Zé Pereira banging of the drums with a more elaborate imposition of a high-class carnival imitative of Venice and Nice; between the carnival of the masked balls and the street carnival of Afro-Brazilian musicality (Pereira Cunha, 2001: 262–277). Like Pereira de Queiroz, Pereira Cunha emphasizes that carnival relies on a myth of social unity and suspension of class, racial and gender discrimination. Yet she also sustains that carnival was an inventive mode of dispute and juxtaposition between classes and cultural traditions:

> Before it became a tourist attraction and an official symbol of nationality, Carnival was the main form of expression of a society dilacerated by wounds that were difficult to heal. It seems comforting that in those years pain was expressed through laughter and mockery. Today, I doubt this would be possible. (Pereira Cunha, 2001: 314–315, author's translation).

The pessimistic note at the end of her lengthy cultural study of carnival's history was spurred by the TV coverage of the *arrastão*, the muggings perpetuated by funk youngsters from favelas and poor suburbs who, in the 1990s, had flocked to the sands of Ipanema beach and had assaulted tourists, middle-class

The Sociological Review, 61:S1, pp. 69–88 (2013), DOI: 10.1111/1467-954X.12054

residents and enemy gangs. The violence of the youngsters and the extremely violent police repression that issued in response to the assaults generated a charged atmosphere of fear and paranoia that was extensively fuelled by the media. The momentary emptying of the beach – one of Rio de Janeiro's favoured gathering grounds – seemed to endorse the portrait of a city on the brink of collapse. Yet the same demonization of the funk groups by the media was then reverted, as funk rhythms became increasingly consumed by the middle classes. Indeed, the funk beat was even introduced in the carnival percussions of some samba schools. Thus, the dialectics of inclusion/exclusion, discrimination/ contagion, violence/celebration continues to inform the daily disputes of the city as it reinvents itself.

For any native carioca, carnival is inevitable and even those who flee from the festivity know that it will take hold of the city. It is precisely the repetitive nature of the carnival event that signals that the festivity is not fuelled by a desire to produce a definitive rupture with the social structure of the city. Rather subversion, satire, the display of the grotesque/wondrous body and marvellous imaginaries may puncture normative conventions but they are instances of a yearly ritual. As a form of social release, the carnival had a varying impact according to a diversity of historical moments. Within the narrow confines of colonial society, under the strictures of the imposed bourgeois decorum of the 19th century, during the authoritarian regime of Getúlio Vargas in the 1930s, and also during the lengthy military dictatorship, carnival had distinct functions as a form of merriment, social release, subversion or affirmation of the system. In contemporary Rio, carnival is still the major collective event of the city but it is also a form of entertainment, business and consumption. The crucial aspect of the Rio carnival and indeed of the carnival manifestations all over Brazil is how they have been transformed but not vanquished by modernization as was the case with most of the carnival celebrations in Europe. And yet, as many scholars have emphasized ever since the 19th century, the lament of the loss of an 'authentic' carnival has been repeated in press accounts just as the critique of its commercialization has also been voiced by intellectuals and artists. (Moraes, 1958: 109)

The comeback of the carnival crowd, the return of the multitude of revellers to the streets of the city mitigated to a large extent the proclamations of carnival's demise as a media event. But the point to be made is that the partying crowd is also fuelled by the imaginaries of carnival wrought by the media and by a vast repertoire of artistic representations. Yet it is not the orchestrated and media aspect of carnival that renders it powerful. The force of carnival is given by a bodily experience of sensorial enticement, by the unleashing of baroque imaginaries, and by the combustion of the partying crowd.

Under the sway of Momo: carnival of masks, letters and images[9]

From its initial colonial beginnings as the Portuguese *entrudo*, consisting of a series of pranks performed during the days of carnival – amongst which featured

prominently the rough play of flinging lime-scented paraffin balls or even malo-
dorous fluids at the faces and bodies of passing pedestrians in the city; to its
highly elaborate orchestration in the carnival parade at the *sambódromo*, the
biggest popular event in the world, carnival in Rio de Janeiro became synonymous with the city itself.[10] Throughout its history, carnival has also mirrored the
negotiations between classes, cultural heritages and the tensions of crowd
control by the elite, the police and the authorities.

Widely practised in colonial Brazil by all sectors of society, including the
slaves, the *entrudo*, nevertheless, obeyed rigid class distinctions. Members of the
aristocracy or families of high rank played among themselves in the recesses of
their homes (Pereira Cunha, 2001: 57). Slaves did not throw filthy substances at
their masters and between the slaves themselves those of the highest rank were
entitled to pelt 'inferior' slaves as they wished. Ferreira (2004: 87) details that
during the days of the *entrudo*, foreign visitors were particularly favoured as the
hilarious butt of the flying balls by the Brazilian families they were visiting. The
entrudo was both a family event and a form of popular entertainment. In the
narrow streets of early colonial Rio de Janeiro, streets of uneven cobblestones,
scant illumination and pestilential stench of waste, the *entrudo* was fervently
practised by slaves and poor free men and women. After independence in 1822,
the *entrudo* was still popular but increasingly frowned upon as the local elite of
the new empire sought to emulate more elegant forms of carnival entertainment.
But it was only in the mid 19th century that the *entrudo* was subject to a decisive
campaign of disparagement in favour of the more refined and elegant masked
balls copied from the French bourgeoisie (Ferreira, 2004; Pereira de Queiroz,
1992; Pereira Cunha, 2001; Moraes, 1958; Galvão, 2009). In 1851, the first
carnival associations of the upper classes were founded. By 1855, not only were
masked balls in enclosed salons an essential part of the carnival frolic but the
upper classes themselves in sumptuous displays of allegorical floats and rich
costumes organized a parade through the streets of Rio de Janeiro (Ferreira,
2004; Pereira Cunha, 2001). The carnival parade of the *Sumidades Carnavalescas*
gathered multitudes and in the latter part of the 19th century, the *Grandes
Sociedades* (Great Societies) such as the famous *Tenentes do Diabo* (The Devil's
Lieutenants), *Os Democráticos* (The Democrats), and *Os Fenianos* (The Fenians)
organized enormous parades decked with allegorical floats. These carnival societies competed among themselves and also embraced political causes such as the
abolition of slavery and the need for a republican agenda. The competitions were
fuelled by newspaper coverage and multitudes from all areas of the city flocked
to watch the parade (Ferreira, 2004; Coutinho, 2006; Galvão, 2009).

In the early 20th century, the elite revellers also engaged in the 'Battle of
Flowers' where the participants decked their automobiles with flowers copying
the model of the contest held in Nice. The popular classes also made their
appearance in *cucumbis*, assemblages of revellers playing instruments of African
origins, in the *cordões* composed by multitudes of poor revellers with their
instruments, and in the more sophisticated *ranchos*, that had the working classes
decked out in homespun costumes. Pereira Cunha states that:

The Sociological Review, 61:S1, pp. 69–88 (2013), DOI: 10.1111/1467-954X.12054

The fear of the carnivalesque multitude in the streets, the excited and exciting reunion of people that descended from the suburbs and peripheries in packed street cars towards the downtown areas of the city during the days of festivity was made explicit in the decades of 1880–1890 in successive accounts of the press, and it increased to a loud pitch in the first years of the Republic. (Pereira Cunha, 2001: 94, author's translation)

To stress her point, Pereira Cunha quotes a press account published in the newspaper *Diário de Notícias*, on 11 February 1891:

'It is unnecessary to add that all the streets of the city regurgitated with curious people that elbowed each other in anxious despair . . . Streets filled with people . . . Masses of compact and black people agitated as if made of mercury . . . And in the midst of the blackness of the popular mass . . . echoed the laughing chimes of fair colors . . . And these fair colors, springing from the midst of the darkness of the gathered people, were like Venetian lanterns piercing in shouts of light the dark night of a sky without stars'. (Pereira Cunha, 2001: 95, author's translation).

Commenting on the discriminatory colour encoding of this passage with its elliptic metaphors, Pereira Cunha highlights the distinction made between the black crowd of the popular sectors and the superior light emanating from the Venetian lanterns associated with the Europeanized guise of the elite revellers. Elite anxieties about the contagion of the crowd and the intermingling with the popular classes are prevalent in the press accounts of the 19th century and the early decades of the 20th, thus Soihet quotes a reportage from the carnival of 1912:

because nowhere else in the world one sights a family that is bedecked in silk and that gives receptions, a family with aristocratic pretentions and stuffy pompous airs of 'don't dare to touch me' forget all the conveniences of aristocratic elegance and good taste in order to elbow each other in the public square next to such a despicable plebeian crowd like ours. (*A noite*, 3-2, Soihet, 1998: 56, author's translation)

In keeping with the anxieties concerning the mingling of the 'rude' crowd with the upper classes, Olavo Bilac (1865–1918), the celebrated academic poet and journalist states: 'There existed places where the prudent bourgeois could not go without inciting a grave scandal . . . But with the arrival of carnival, the serious man hid his seriousness inside a domino costume, tied a mask to his austere face and good-bye prudence!' (Bilac, 1997: 774). Yet the poet proclaimed, at the turn of the 20th century, that carnival had lost its punch because the laxity of morals dimmed the transgressive powers of the feast of Momo.

The mask has lost its primitive charm. In order to breathlessly sink one's teeth in the pulp of the forbidden fruit it is no longer necessary to wear a mask on one's face. The tasty fruit is there at the reach of all the hands, offering itself, giving, imposing with an impudence that no longer offends the harsh glance of morality. A new and busy society that doesn't have time for scruples has substituted the old patriarchal society; and in this manner, the mask has lost its value because it has lost its use.

Nevertheless, it is not because of this, thank God, that the people cease to have fun in these three days of noise. They say that to become a crumpled, wet, trodden, filthy, flu ridden, bruised and rheumatic man can be anything but fun. Why? Fun is everything that is new, everything that goes beyond the execrable monotony of bread earning and of eating at the proper time. (Bilac, 1997: 775, author's translation)

At the end of the 19th century and the beginnings of the 20th, Brazilian carnival was intensely disputed by the popular classes and the ruling elite precisely because more bourgeois forms of carnival partying were being imported, while the already embedded popular Afro-Brazilian and Luso-Brazilian traditions continued to exist.

In his book of 1908, *The Enchanting Soul of the Streets* (*A Alma Encantadora das Ruas*), João do Rio (1881–1921), a writer, journalist, decadent dandy and admirer of Oscar Wilde, describes the African inspired merrymaking of the *cordão* in one of the main streets of downtown Rio. I quote at length the passage because João do Rio's prose is a vivid amalgam of an aestheticized sensibility infused by literary decadentist metaphorization where ambivalences towards sexuality, the popular classes and race are also tinged by a desire to overcome repression. The exotic 'other' also offers dangerous yet fascinating possibilities of contagion, fear and release:

It was right there, in the Rua do Ouvidor. You couldn't even walk; the crush was such one could hardly breathe. There were men feverishly elbowing their way through the mob, women with flushed faces, children screaming, characters yelling jokes; every face convulsed in a plethora of merriment . . . A strange smell, a mixture of dirt, cheap perfume and the stench of sweat and alcohol, added even further to the atmosphere of promiscuity. The while street had been transformed; in its multicolored costume of streamers and confetti it seemed that Harlequin himself had come to greet the revellers as they leapt about in madness and debauchery. . . .

The cordon surged menacingly forward. In the lead, a reckless group of four or five adolescent mestizos, with shoes undone and great pointed bows, ran forward, mouths wide open, emitting rasping cries. Behind them came a tall black man bedecked with feathers, dripping with sweat, his face shinning like pitch, with his massive naked arm outstretched, holding an iron spear. Next a group in red and yellow with golden sequins blazing from their backs came rippling through, locks of bushy hair clinging to their sweating faces in a nauseous mêlée. And all around the crush, barefoot or in clogs, men were walking about, tripping over, waving torches, holding up live snakes whose teeth had been removed, lizards decked out in ornaments, terrifying turtles uttering great raucous cries. (Do Rio, 2010: 245, 247, 249)

As is usual in João do Rio's journalistic writing, the observation of the street scene is narrated in the first person and the observer, poised as a bourgeois *flâneur*, is both attracted and repelled by the manifestations of the frenzied popular carnival. Yet in order to pedagogically explain the compelling force of the *cordão*, João do Rio makes his narrator-author dialogue with a friend who extols them as the flesh and soul of carnival in contrast to the bland choreography of the elitist Europeanized masked balls and allegorical floats. Caught in the sway of the crowd, the author-narrator finally agrees and exclaims:

The cordons are Carnival, they are the last link to the pagan religions; they preserve the sacred ritual that derides religion. The cordon is the soul of Rio, passionate, lecherous, desolate, half slave, half rebel, drooling with lust for the women and longing to dazzle, blustering, meek, barbaric, pitiable. (Do Rio, 2010: 265)

For the upper classes who had deposited so many expectations on the city's embellishment, the vision of the Africanized *cordão*, its musical rhythm and totemic animals all bespoke not only of unruliness but also of projections of atavistic fantasy into the mirage of the city's cosmopolitan façade.[11] The incompatibility between bourgeois norms and notions of progress with the 'archetypal' re-emergence of unnamed deities and forces not only produced an atmosphere of estranged re-enchantment for the bourgeois observer, but it also suggested the compelling fascination of the contagion with the crowd. Despite his use of disparagement and facile caricature, João do Rio's writings on the *cordão,* as indeed most of his reportage, reveals a powerful acknowledgement of the heterogeneous experiences of the city. The *cordão* fascinates, repels and threatens not only because it does not comply with the modernizing Westernizing norms but also because it brings to the forefront forms of collective ecstasy, contagion and celebration that endure in the maze of the metropolis.

João do Rio's revelatory carnival story of 1910 'The Baby in Pink Tarlatan' (Melhores Contos, 2001) is a tale about the anxiety of mingling with the crowd, the threat of the masquerade, and the disruptive appearance of the grotesque. Narrated in the first person, the story is told by a jaded dandy, João do Rio's cynical character, Heitor de Alencar. Alencar tells his circle of friends how in a recent carnival celebration he departed from his acquaintances and mingled with the throbbing multitude. In their midst, he spots a person dressed as a baby in pink tarlatan. The baby is seductive, rosy, winsome and playful. They part company and in the following night Alencar again sights the amazing creature. They dance around each other and the Baby with surprising energy leads the Alencar away from the crowd. They exchange kisses and caresses but the odd hard resin nose attached to the Baby's face keeps getting in the way of their erotic exchange. When Alencar attempts to remove the false nose he is violently repelled by the Baby. Finally, in exasperation, he tears the nose away and the Baby wails plaintively. The Baby had no nose, its face was a skull of meat, nose-less and ghastly. The Baby pleads and says that it is only in carnival that it can 'enjoy'. The mingling with the popular crowds away from the guarded spheres of the upper classes, the tumultuous moment of carnival where inversions are enacted and norms are overturned is finally cast as a grim encounter with death personified as a dainty pink eroticized Baby.[12] Tinged by the macabre, João do Rio's carnival tale is more than an exercise in a literary genre. It makes manifest the deep anxieties of eroticism and death unleashed by the partying popular crowd and carnivalesque inversion.

By the 1930s carnival had been officially consecrated. Vargas's coup of 1930 terminated the Old Republic. The shift in power did not entail the burial of the landed gentry nor the obliteration of entrenched political oligarchies throughout Brazil. But the coup of 1930, and the subsequent dictatorship of the New State from 1937 until 1945, brought a novel approach to popular urban culture and the urban proletariat. The mayor of Rio de Janeiro, Pedro Ernesto, sponsored together with the Touring Club a carnival parade, as well as a number of other official festivities. As quoted by Ferreira *et al.* (2008), the discovery of carnival as an export product and as a source of pride and financial gain is expressed in glowing words by the journalist Berilio Neves in a piece published in *Diário de Notícias*, on 4 February 1932:

> Carnival does more to make us known abroad than our poets, our thinkers, our men of art and intellectuals. It's irritating to say it but what Dr. Pedro Ernesto is doing at this moment, together with the Touring Club do Brasil, is supremely patriotic: giving incentive and life to the Carioca Carnival. When the entire world finds out that we make the most picturesque and joyful Carnival within memory since the Babylonic splendor until now, Rio will take in hundreds of thousands of tourists. And then the Carnival will bring to us, with surplus, that which the goldmines of the XVII century could no longer provide: gold. For the first time in the history of humanity word will go out about a party spree that gives no financial loss and, yes, profit. (Ferreira *et al.*, 2008: 215)

By 1935, the samba schools were sponsored by the municipality and the nationalist agenda they themselves adopted obliged them to compose samba lyrics and thematic parades centred on themes from Brazilian history.[13] Broadcast through the National Radio, samba became the official national rhythm of the nation and, to a large extent, the popular culture of Rio de Janeiro was also promoted as the national culture of Brazil itself in a concerted effort to homogenize regional disparities under the rubric of a national identity sponsored by the state. Until 1942, the samba parades were held in the Praça Onze, a legendary neighbourhood of Afro-Brazilian culture and also a place of Jewish immigrants.[14] In 1942, the Praça Onze was demolished by the opening of a new avenue, Presidente Vargas. The samba schools then shifted and paraded either in the old Avenida Rio Branco or in the newly inaugurated Avenida Presidente Vargas. By the 1940s, Rio de Janeiro's samba school parades were a major feature of the Rio carnival and the figure of the *mulata* was enthroned as a national symbol.[15]

Ever since the late 19th century, carnival festivities had not only been the subject of press reportage but also relied on the press for the promotion of the carnival festivities (Galvão, 2009: 28–29). From the beginnings of the 20th century until the 1940s, journalists associated with the festivities formed a specific niche of carnival chroniclers (Coutinho, 2006). From 1928 until the 1970s, the illustrated magazine *O Cruzeiro*, had a crucial role in exhibiting carnival images centred either on the grandiose parade, on masked balls or in the merrymaking of anonymous revellers. The advent of television in the 1960s not only meant that the Carnival parade gained a global dimension but it also altered the spatial structure of the festivity itself. Under the military dictatorship and especially in the 1970s, street carnival in Rio de Janeiro was reduced. The 1970s and 1980s expressed the height of the controlled carnival festivities. Television coverage and the illustrated magazines *Fatos & Fotos* and *Manchete* sold to millions the visions of both a glorified grandiose parade, as well as the clichéd

The Sociological Review, 61:S1, pp. 69–88 (2013), DOI: 10.1111/1467-954X.12054

images of *mulata* Samba Shows and racy footage of enclosed carnival balls where scantily clad revellers bathed in sweat were photographed in insinuating positions. But the presence of the carnival crowd in the streets was muted. With the exception of the carnival group of the *Banda de Ipanema* (Band from Ipanema) created in the 1960s by an irreverent association of artists and intellectuals, and of the aforementioned famous *Cordão do Bola Preta* (Group of the Black Ball), the streets of the south zone of Rio de Janeiro and the downtown area were not crowded by revellers. In the north zone of the city, people dressed as *clovis*, a costume supposedly derived from the word 'clown', continued to appear but the real comeback of the *clovis* groups bouncing to the funk rhythms happened around 2006.

Carnival imaginaries: spatiality, temporality, aesthetics

Carnival features as the crucial festivity of collective invention that displays how popular culture, artistic imaginaries, media broadcasting, social relations, ritual, memory, repetition and consumption are entwined, orchestrated and essayed. Brazil is often coined the 'Pais do Carnaval', the 'Carnival Nation', and despite the variation between the different carnival festivities in the country, it is celebrated throughout the whole of the nation.

Reduced during the 1970s when the military dictatorship still held sway, undermined in the early 1980s when the media-dominated parade of the *sambódromo* eclipsed alternative forms of partying, street carnival had a resurgence in the mid 1980s and has been on the increase ever since.[16] A myriad of factors may be signalled as having contributed to the revival of Rio's street carnival. The redemocratization of civil society and the ever-increasing prestige given to manifestations of popular culture contributed to the celebration of street carnival. Commercially the tourist industry and businesses sponsoring the event envisioned, in street carnival, a lucrative form of seducing potential visitors and consumers. Media coverage of the street carnival extolled the comeback as an 'authentic' demonstration of the city's joyful spirit. The often populist political rhetoric of municipal and government authorities entailed an active endorsement of the carnival activities that is manifest in the closing of the streets for the merrymaking and in the making of guides, maps and itineraries of the party. Aside from this plethora of capitalistic, management and entrepreneurial factors, street carnival also revived as a response to the repetitiveness of the media coverage. It conveys the desire for an alternative and yet a traditional form of fun and it also complies with the bohemian ethos of reoccupying street areas and public spaces.

The need to thrust one's self in the thick of the crowd is also often coupled by the documentation of the act itself; revellers film themselves and others amid the festive throng. In certain iconic carnival *blocos* such as the Band of Ipanema, the drag queen outfits and the exuberant parading of the masqueraded body are also purposefully geared for televised consumption. Space is concretely occupied by bodily presence in the street and yet the experience of 'being there' is also vicariously registered. The *spatial configurations* of the carnival crowds address also the broader issue of how the presence of the crowd in the metropolis shaped modern contemporary experiences. The presence of the carnival crowd in the contemporary city not only varies according to the nature of the carnival manifestation and the areas of the city that are occupied by the merrymaking revellers, but also the physical crowd either in the streets, in ballrooms or in the contained space of the *sambodrómo* is shadowed by another invisible crowd represented by the multitudes of anonymous spectators that watch or read about the events through TV coverage, press reportage or the Internet. The premise here is that the existence of this mass audience of global dimensions influences and alters the nature of the physical spectacle of the carnival crowd itself.

The balance between irreverence and tradition, repetition and innovation, misrule and conformity is mirrored in the *temporal* experience of the carnival event. But crucially, the rhythm of the carnival parade and of street carnival is not the mechanical pace of the modern crowd of workers as seen in emblematic films such as *Metropolis* (1926); it is not the frenzied rush of the modern teeming city as captured in the avant-garde camera eye of Dziga Vertov. Neither is it fuelled by the fast-paced adrenaline-drenched Manhattan of jostling crowds that features in so many contemporary movies. Evidently a techno-syncopated carnival can be achieved though audio-visual manipulation. The same can be said of the fast-paced films of the modern and contemporary metropolis. But whereas the mechanical rhythm and the acceleration of time depicted in avant-garde films may not have corresponded to the actual registered temporality of lived time, they did address the shift in sensorial experience that city dwellers developed of modern existence itself. By contrast, although rhythmic, pulsating and even frenzied, carnival time is distended. The partying is prolonged and the duration of the samba parades are extremely lengthy. The revellers participate individually as each person dances, sways, plays and blends according to their own dictums, desires, abilities and physical resistance. But the collective rituals and energies of the crowd also shape the merging of the individual in the bodily maze. The tourist appeal of such manifestations is indicative of a desire to tap into the feeling of a collective celebration and to partake of an experience that may be erotic, exotic, novel or ritualistic. But while this belonging to the carnival crowd is sporadic for many tourists and even for the natives of Rio, for the favela communities that gave birth to so many samba schools, and for the poor suburbs of the periphery, the carnival experience is an engrained manifestation of cultural identity.

Carnival time is *profane time* in Agamben's sense of the return to common usage of that which had been secluded within the domains of the Gods (Agamben, 2007). Carnival's profanity, its fleshy, bombastic, excessive, destructive and creative impulses cast the sacred into the impure soil of the mundane. But it also dialogues with enchantment by instilling a collective moment of make believe and fantasy. Through rituals of masquerade, excess and inversion, car-

The Sociological Review, 61:S1, pp. 69–88 (2013), DOI: 10.1111/1467-954X.12054
© 2013 The Author. Editorial organisation © 2013 The Editorial Board of the Sociological Review

nival seeks to erase the banal calendar-time of everydayness and instil a different temporality of suspension that is, nevertheless, contained by the weekly celebration (DaMatta, 1997). The ritualistic temporality of repetition and transformation can be enacted as a collective or individual epiphany. Independently of the political atmosphere or the economic situation, carnival happens yearly and, since the 1980s, the aesthetic vocabularies of the samba school parades have welcomed innovation in themes, materials and choreographies. But they have also followed a repetitive recipe of grandiose glitter, stunning allegorical floats, technical displays and glamourized nudity.

Although wildly popular, carnival is not the only entertainment event that amasses crowds in the city. The yearly celebrations of the New Year, varied musical concerts, and a myriad of sporting events all contribute to the influx of people to the city. Even more relevantly, the carnival festivity no longer is – as was the case until the 1950s – such a crucial escape valve from the pressures and regulations of day-to-day life. Within the logic of the culture of consumption and given the democratic increase of social participation from all sectors of society, several forms of entertainment, even collective partying can be experienced, purchased and consumed all year round. Nevertheless, carnival still commands a heightened attention. Although the samba parade and street carnival are tourist, media and consumption events, the feast of Momo also re-enacts rituals of collective ecstasy where emotions, desires and bodily contact resurface in the midst of an increasingly virtual and disembodied media culture.

Aesthetically, carnival parades reveal their kinship with the baroque imaginary of monumental display and ornamentation; an imaginary that has deep roots in Brazilian culture ranging from colonial legacies to the inventions of contemporary culture. In its dichotomies, inversions and masquerades, carnival playfully evokes the baroque glorification of contrasts. Akin to the Baroque obsession with crowded surfaces, the carnivalesque aesthetic is also excessive and overflowing. Just as baroque architectural spaces are layered by ornaments and profusions of gold; in carnival, naked flesh is also masked in sequins, feathers, flounces and glitter. The sculpted figures and the grandiose allegorical floats are reminiscent of the Catholic pageantry of the holy procession of saints. Carnival's aesthetic sources are hybrid and combine popular culture, erudite references, and media myths where the influence of American pop and entertainment culture expressed by Las Vegas pastiche and Disneyland style dreamworlds are also featured. Enacted by dancing multitudes and performed for live audiences, the carnival parade is a popular opera cast for the camera eye. It is also the result of the variegated orchestrated efforts of choreographers, musicians, dancers, composers, sculptors, and a plethora of agents engaged in its gigantic production. If the carnival parade is manifestly feasible because of concerted efforts of multiple agents and organizations, the carnival crowds who gather in the streets of the city are also not just the product of a spontaneous *joie du vivre*. As mentioned, the sponsorship of different legal and illegal forms of commerce, the funds granted by the municipality, the hiring of professional musicians to participate in the percussion, the selling of T-shirts or costumes, are all aspects of a coordinated strategy of entertainment. Yet, the elaborate and gigantic carnival parade of the samba schools had its origins in popular carnival and the recent comeback of street carnival stems from multiple desires of regaining the streets for collective display.

Although carnival complies to the spectacularization of capitalist societies based on the repetition of the new in late modernity it also converses with collective energies that respond to both novel circumstances and traditional forms of belonging. Like the expectations roused by favela tours and any tourist enterprise, the mingling with the throng, the cheering of the samba schools, and the parading in the *sambódromo* itself are fuelled by previous cultural representations.

Finally, in Rio de Janeiro, the representations of the carnival crowd were largely coloured by the perspective of the intellectuals, artists, journalists and political authorities that either desired to polish the rowdy celebrations into a more 'refined' form of elite entertainment or saw the varied manifestations of the carnival event as a source of collective identity, a form of communitarian belonging, an expression of a national culture, and ultimately a local and global manifestation of the city's festive ethos. The recent comeback of the carnival crowd in Rio de Janeiro entailed not only the emergence of several new *blocos*. The presence of millions of partygoers decked in outlandish costumes, drinking alcohol, swaying to samba and funk-samba rhythms entailed a flurry of responses. How to deal with multitudes of partying drunken people? How to combat the thousands that urinate in the streets of Rio during the three-day festivity? How to ensure merriment without violence or repression?

Conclusion

Insofar as cultural legitimacy is concerned, the popular and media appeal of carnival has become consecrated. This not only entails that carnival culture from the popular classes has been both transformed and validated but also that it has become a source of considerable commercial profit that benefits specialized mediators and entrepreneurs.[17] But as mentioned before, carnival is not just media and commerce. There is something to be said about the desire to merge in the multitude (Canetti, 1978), about the freedom of the mask and the urgency of bodily contact in societies that are so saturated by vicarious media viewership and so conditioned by indirect experiences.

The suspension of normative patterns of work during carnival days, the presence of masqueraded multitudes boarding the suburban trains and the subways, the vision of exhausted revellers lying asleep in the streets in their bedraggled costumes at the closing of carnival, the heaps of debris, the broken carnival floats strewn at the end of the *sambódromo*, the stench of the urine soaked asphalt; all bring forth a sense of suspended quotidian life. From the day the mayor of Rio symbolically hands the keys of the city to King Momo, the city is caught in the frenzy of the festivity. Being caught in the carnival crowd, being pressed against masses of sweating bodies in the torrid temperatures of Rio's summer may not quite be an experience of delight, indeed, it may be a source of sheer torment or repulsion. But whether in ecstasy or dismay, the bodily contact of the crowd under the sway of music, the tactile rubbing of compressed bodies, the olfactory fumes of the sweat-drenched multitude all evoke a sensorial awakening far removed from the sanitized domains of modernity's non-places. In the thick of the carnival crowd it is almost impossible to even take a picture; to essay the quintessential contemporary gesture of seeing one's self living the instant through the mediation of the camera. It is almost impossible but not entirely. Carnival is not a breakthrough, it is not revolutionary, and it is not an inauguration of new worlds. Carnival can be the experience of the masked body dreaming its loss of self in the embrace of an ephemeral collectivity.

Notes

1 Within the considerable variation of the *blocos*, a core number of 12 *blocos* constitute the association called SEBASTIANA. The association was founded in 2000 and its components, the directors of 12 associated *blocos* have a common cultural agenda. According to the founders, the SEBASTIANA is 'an important agent for the recovery of the street carnival tradition in Rio and also a place for political and cultural discussions' (www.sebastiana.org.br, my translation). The SEBASTIANA ratified a phenomenon that had already been consolidated: the re-emergence of street carnival in the wake of the redemocratization processes of the mid 1980s. Teresa Guilhon, a researcher and also founding member of the bloco, Escravos da Mauá that belongs to SEBASTIANA argues that what distinguishes the *blocos* of the association is a connection between the revival of street carnival with notions of cultural identity forged by authenticity, affirmation of Brazilian cultural traits, and political extolment of freedom and spontaneity versus instrumental globalized agendas. Most of the founders of the *blocos* pertaining to the SEBASTIANA were engaged in political debates and had agendas of leftist politics. Although the carnival merry making in itself is not a political act, the programmed revival of street carnival by these *blocos* was nurtured by a desire to regain public space and to promote political causes.

2 According to the newspaper *O Globo*, in 2011: '7,400 chemical bathrooms and 40 containers with sanitary cabinets received 1.95 million litres of urine, the equivalent of three Olympic swimming pools filled with urine . . .'. Following the trail of the *blocos* and the Samba Schools, the municipal trash company (Comlurb) collected 1,304 tons of trash every single day of the carnival folly. (*O Globo*, 14 March 2011). One year later, in 2012, the city's biggest *bloco* continues to be the Cordão do Bola Preta. In the year 2012, 2.2 million people followed the Cordão do Bola Preta. Out of the nearly 5.5 million people in the streets, 32 per cent of the 1.2 million tourists were foreigners (*O Globo*, 27 February 2012) The urine issue was still one of the main problems addressed by the media and government authorities. Major efforts were undertaken in order to educate the population. The largest TV station, TV Globo, launched a public campaign featuring young pop music celebrities singing the 'piss samba', the lyrics alerted that 'pissing is meant for the toilet'. The song is entitled 'Do you feel like taking a piss?' and the music has a carnival samba rhythm. In 2012, despite the increase in the number of chemical bathrooms that numbered 15,000 disposed throughout the city, the difficult access to the spatially concentrated public toilets for the mass of revellers was criticized. (*Portal Terra*, 21 February 2012). Over 1,000 people – male and female – were arrested due to their inappropriate urinating in the streets of the city (*O Globo*, 27 February 2012). On the other hand, 23 per cent less trash was produced (1,000 tons, 300 less than in 2011). Unlike the daily routine concerning the news of the city, during carnival time crime is not a major concern and it remains fairly unmentioned by the mainstream commercial media which tends to praise the growing touristic – and hence financial – success of Rio's carnival.

The Sociological Review, 61:S1, pp. 69–88 (2013), DOI: 10.1111/1467-954X.12054
© 2013 The Author. Editorial organisation © 2013 The Editorial Board of the Sociological Review

3 The public responses to the comeback of street carnival have been usually favourable but neighbourhood associations and a number of disgruntled citizens have expressed their disapproval of the rowdy festivities through the press and other media (see *O Globo*, 25 September 2011, *O Globo*, 23 February 2012: http://oglobo.globo.com/blocos/moradores-comerciantes-dizem-que-lixo-ambulantes-mijoes-sao-problemas-nos-blocos-4053728).

4 For an overall discussion of the crowd in history, art and politics see the collection of essays edited by Schnapp and Tiews (2006).

5 See Hardt and Negri (2004). For an insightful discussion of Hardt and Negri's concept of multitude in relation to crowd theory see Mazarella (2010).

6 The word *carioca* refers to the inhabitants of the city of Rio de Janeiro.

7 In his classic study, *La ciudad letrada*, the critic Angel Rama proposes that cities in Latin America possessed a crucial core of administrators, civil servants and public intellectuals that constituted the 'lettered city'. The task of the lettered city was not only to uphold the status quo but also to imagine urban life and civil society. See *La ciudad letrada*, Hanover, Ediciones del Norte, 1984.

8 Aside from the references cited in this paper, see also Merquior (1972) and Vivieiros de Castro (1999).

9 As a figure of Greek mythology, Momo was the god of irreverence, satire and frolicking. Given his sarcastic wit towards the other gods, Momo was expelled from Olympus. In the Rio carnival the figure of Momo first appears as a giant paper effigy that was burned during the celebrations. But in 1933, journalists covering the carnival event elected a fellow colleague, Moraes Cardoso, a hefty jocose man to be crowned as King Momo, the ruler of the city during the days of carnival. The tradition of Momo continues until the present when the mayor of Rio symbolically hands the keys of the city to the elected figure of Momo. Momo's figure du role is of a very fat, jolly and festive man.

10 The term 'samba school' is credited to Ismael Silva (1905–1978), the legendary samba composer who was also the founder of the first samba school, *Deixa falar* in 1928. According to several interviews, Ismael Silva declared that he and his samba friends would gather together in a bar in a street in the neighbourhood of Estácio. In this street, there was a school who trained teachers and Ismael said that they, the samba musicians, were also teachers of samba. Whether these reminiscences are accurate or not is not truly relevant because the term samba 'school' denotes how humour was used to legitimate the cultural practices of popular sectors as they strove to gain respectability and municipal sponsorship for the samba parade. The *sambódromo* was inaugurated in 1984. Designed by the quintessential Brazilian modernist architect, Oscar Niemeyer, it was constructed in order to avoid the havoc and the expense of building yearly seats for the public beside the main avenue where the samba schools paraded. The *sambódromo* has often been criticized for having introduced the full commercialization of the samba festivities.

11 Felipe Ferreira in a text called 'Terra de samba e pandeiro' (2008/2009), comments that the *congos ou cucumbis* were ritual enactments of the battle between the catholic 'King of the Congo' and his rivals. After the battle where the King of Congo emerged triumphant, animal offerings of snakes, turtles and small alligators would be given to the king.

12 For a reading of João do Rio's story 'The Baby in Pink Tarlatan', see Antelo (1989).

13 In her book, *Ao som do samba: uma leitura do carnaval carioca*, Walnice Nogueira Galvão states the obligation to choreograph the parade according to nationalistic themes, which was adopted by the samba schools themselves in their efforts to gain support of the establishment. See Galvão (2009: 44).

14 See Bruno Cavalho's manuscript 'Porous City' where he discusses the symbolic and cultural trajectory of the neighbourhood of the Cidade Nova and the square of the Praça Onze where the carnival parades used to gather.

15 There is extensive bibliography on the significance of the *mulata* in Brazilian culture. Gilberto Freyre's seminal work in the 1930s examined the role of miscegenation and erotic interactions between slaves and masters in his classic study, *The Masters and the Slaves* (1986). See also Sandra Giacomini's (1992) discussion of the professional *mulata* dancer (Costa and Bruschini,

1992). Giacomini examines how samba dancers become professional *mulatas* independently of their skin colour. In interviews that I conducted with Coca, a professional samba dancer, for the film *Corpo do Rio*, directed by Izabel Jaguaribe and Olivia Guimarães, she confirmed Giacomini's thesis by explaining that to be a *mulata* in the samba context meant being able to execute the samba steps on a stage as well as in the carnival parade. In a recent film called *Mulatas: um tufão nos quadris* (2010) by the director Walmor Pamplona, the dancer Coca, now renamed Nilce Fran, again asserts that being a professional *mulata* is not related to skin colour. But the other interviewed women of the film affirm the erotic quality of being a *mulata* and the prejudice that envelops their colour.

16 The *sambódromo* was designed by the modernist architect Oscar Niemeyer and inaugurated in 1984. It consists of a large avenue framed by an arch and flanked by stadium seats. The sambódromo was built in order to curtail expenses of the yearly construction of seats for the carnival parade. But the transferral of the samba school parades to the sambódromo. For a reading of the *sambódromo* see Matos (2006). In this article, Matos details the shift as the samba parade moved from the Praça Onze, a celebrated space of Afro-Brazilian cultural exchange, to the Avenue Presidente Vargas, and finally to the Sambódromo in 1984.

17 In the year of 2012, Rio's carnival injected 1.5 billion reais (US\$850 million) into the city's economy, according to Reuters Brasil (27 February 2012).

References

Agamben, G., (2007), *Profanations*, New York: Zone Books.

Antelo, R., (1989), *O dândi e a especulação*, Rio de Janeiro: Taurus/Timbre.

Bilac, O., (1997), *Obra reunida*, Rio de Janeiro: Nova Aguilar.

Canetti, E., (1978), *Crowds and Power*, New York: Continuum.

Carvalho, J. M. de, (1987), *Os bestializados*, São Paulo: Companhia das Letras.

Costa, A. and Bruschini, C., (1992), *Entre a virtude e o pecado*, Rio de Janeiro: Editora Rosa dos Tempos.

Coutinho, E., (2006), *Os cronistas de Momo: imprensa e carnaval na Primeira República*, Rio de Janeiro: Editora UFRJ.

DaMatta, R., (1991), *Carnival, Rogues and Heroes,* trans. J. Drury, Notre Dame, IN: University of Notre Dame Press.

DaMatta, R., (1997), *Carnavais, malandros e heróis: para uma sociologia do dilema brasileiro*, Rio de Janeiro: Rocco.

Do Rio, J., (2001), 'O bebê da tarlatana rosa', in H. P. Cunha (ed.), *Melhores contos,* São Paulo: Global.

Do Rio, J., (2010), *A alma encantadora das ruas*, Rio de Janeiro: Cidade Viva.

Hardt, M. and Negri, A., (2004), *Multitude: War and Democracy in the Age of Empire*, New York: Penguin.

Ferreira, F., (2004), *O livro de ouro do carnaval brasileiro*, Rio de Janeiro: Ediouro.

Ferreira, F., Albin, R. C., Cabral, S., Kaz, L. and Loddi, N. P., (2008), *Meu carnaval Brasil*, Rio de Janeiro: Aprazível.

Freyre, G., (1986), *The Masters and the Slaves*, Berkeley, CA: University of California Press.

Galvão, W. N., (2009), *Ao som do samba: uma leitura do carnaval carioca*, São Paulo: Editorial Fundação Perseu Abramo.

Giacomini, S., (1992), 'Aprendendo a ser mulata: um estudo sobre a identidade da mulata profisional', in A. Costa and C. Bruschini (eds), *Entre a virtude e o pecado*, Rio de Janeiro: Editora Rosa dos Tempos.

Karasch, M. C., (1987), *Slave Life in Rio de Janeiro: 1808–1850*, Princeton, NJ: Princeton University Press.

Mazarella, W., (2010), 'Myth of the multitude, or, who's afraid of the crowd?', *Critical Inquiry*, 36: 697–727.

Matos, M. P., (2006), 'Da Praça Onze à Praça da Apoteose', *Contemporânea*, 6: 48–59.

Merquior, J. G., (1972), *Saudades do carnaval: introdução à crise da cultura*, Rio de Janeiro: Forense.

Moraes, E., (1958), *História do carnaval carioca*, Rio de Janeiro: Civilização Brasileira.

Pereira Cunha, M. C., (2001), *Ecos da folia: uma história social do carnaval carioca entre 1880 e 1920*, São Paulo: Companhia das Letras.

Pereira de Queiroz, M. I., (1992), *Carnaval brasileiro: o vivido e o mito*, São Paulo: Brasiliense.

Rama, A., (1984), *La ciudad letrada*, Hanover: Ediciones del Norte.

Schnapp, J. and Tiews, M., (2006), *Crowds*, Palo Alto, CA: Stanford University Press.

Soihet, R., (1998), *A subversão pelo riso*, Rio de Janeiro: Fundação Getúlio Vargas.

Vivieiros de Castro, M. L., (1999), *O rito e o tempo, ensaio sobre o carnaval*, Rio de Janeiro: Civilização Brasileira.

No time out: mobility, rhythmicity and urban patrol in the twenty-four hour city

Robin James Smith and Tom Hall

Abstract: This paper is about the twenty-four hour city and analyses this phenom-enon with the assistance of a case study dispersed across (temporally and spatially) twenty-four hours spent moving in, around and with the city centre of Cardiff, UK. Reporting from a continuous twenty-four hour period of fieldwork the paper describes the round-the-clock work of a range of urban patrols – street sweepers, Police Community Support Officers and outreach workers – who, in various ways, contribute to the maintenance of the social and physical fabric of the city centre. Describing the seemingly disparate activities of these patrols, we make an argument for an attention to the polychronic mobility practices in and through which the street-level politics of space, movement and time are produced and negotiated. Indeed, the circulations of these patrols throws up a supporting cast of vulnerable street-populations – the homeless, street drinkers and street-based sex workers. Here, then, we juxtapose our description of this quotidian city with the imagery and politics of the '24-Hour City' in pointing to a nuanced (rather than adversarial) and mobile (rather than static) relationship between need and vulnerability and the management of space, time and mobility in the city centre.

Keywords: mobility, homelessness, welfare, policing, 24-Hour City, patrol

Introduction

This paper is about the twenty-four hour city. In it, our aim is to take this subject both seriously and literally. We do so by way of description: an extended account of one full day's fieldwork spent with round-the-clock street-level pro-fessionals and practitioners: street sweepers, Police Community Support Offic-ers, a team of housing and homelessness outreach workers and a man called Mike. They appear, initially, an odd grouping, but they share two things. The first: they all spend a good deal of time moving around, and walking especially, in the centre of Cardiff, capital city of Wales. The second: they can all be said to attend and respond to the twenty-four hour demands of the 21st-century city. We begin with something of a contextualization in the form of a brief discussion of the processes currently rescoring city centre rhythms, the 24-Hour City

The Sociological Review, 61:S1, pp. 89–108 (2013), DOI: 10.1111/1467-954X.12055
© 2013 The Authors. Editorial organisation © 2013 The Editorial Board of the Sociological Review. Published by John Wiley & Sons Ltd, 9600 Garsington Road, Oxford OX4 2DQ, UK and 350 Main Street, Malden, MA 02148, USA

concept and night-time economy in particular, before moving to our account of a rather more pedestrian twenty-four hour city.

Rescoring urban rhythms

The stuttering coda of the industrial rhythms that underscored urban life in the UK for the greater part of the 20th century yielded a period of uncertainty and challenge for urban economies. Globally circulating strategies of regeneration couched in, and promoting, 'profit driven concerns of the entrepreneurial private sector and the lifestyle aspirations of its consumers' (Hetherington, 2007: 637) found opportunity in crisis for a reimaging of the city as a space of consumption rather than (only) dwelling and work (Harvey, 1989; Hall and Hubbard, 1998). Certainly in Cardiff, the response to the crises of industrial decline focused on a remaking of the city's docklands where rhythms of manufacture and shipping have been replaced with those of strolling, eating and drinking, and 'festival' events (see Smith, 2010). More recently still, as with other post-industrial cities with which Cardiff shares this pattern of decline and reinvention, efforts of regeneration have turned from former industrial sites toward the city centre. And the redevelopment of Cardiff's central spaces has been striking. Broadly circulated recommendations combining contradictory rhetoric and design strategies of inclusivity and segregation, freedom and surveillance, accessibility and restriction have produced a clean, safe and busy retail area. Incredibly detailed protocol for everything from types of paving stones and trees to the positioning and design of benches has seen the 'lonely walkways' and 'dead spaces' (Thomas and Bromley, 2000) of the city centre, along with places to stop or be in private, ironed out. Such strategies for the reconfiguration of city space also have a good deal to do with its temporality too. Regeneration, then, might well be thought of as the strategic reordering of the conditions of possibility of time and space – which is to say, urban rhythms – aimed at resolving interruptions and threats to the neo-liberal, post-industrial city. In this context, the city centre had long been a problem; a symbol of a failure of the urban economy to fully adapt from a producer to consumer orientated economy (Zukin, 1995). The neglect of the city centre, '5pm flight' (Thomas and Bromley, 2000), the enduring image of the night as dangerous frontierland (see Melbin, 1978 and Hadfield, 2006), combined with the moral fears of (potential) night-time city centre visitors and consumers (Oc and Tiesdell, 1997) was seen to be 'one of the most important problems facing cities at the end of the 20th century' (Heath, 1997: 193).

The response to the city centre 'crisis' of the mid 1990s came in the form of the '24-Hour City concept' (Bianchini, 1995; Heath and Stickland, 1997), an umbrella term for a series of planning initiatives aimed at changing patterns of city centre use and consumption. Relaxed licensing legislation, late-night retail initiatives, the development of themed leisure 'Quarters' (see Gottdiener, 2001), and public realm restructuring and renewal extended the active economic and social, *consuming*, hours of the city centre beyond the working day, into the early evening and through to the early hours. The imagery of the night-time city centre was shifted toward one of a thrilling yet safe site of consumption; retaining elements of the excitement found in 'braving' the night, whilst offering consumption and leisure in a setting of 'riskless risk' (Chatterton and Holland, 2003 and see Hannigan, 1998). This nocturnal 'economy of pleasure' (Lovatt and O'Connor, 1995) has, for some time now, been recognized as a key element of sustaining a vibrant post-industrial city. Yet, as observed by Jacobs (1961: 245), some time ago now, the cost of the successful attraction of such a high concentration of strangers 'all in too irresponsible a mood', is the requirement of 'unnatural' measures of control and regulation. Cardiff offers an example of this contradictory nature of the night-time economy. Praised for its realization of the 24-Hour City concept (Heath, 1997), Cardiff also provides something of a folk devil for the UK media – a site and symbol of the excesses of sex, drinking and violence. It has also, in consequence, become a site of innovation in technologies of surveillance, crowd control and governance (see Edwards, 2010). The night-time economy is thus characterized by a 'complex set of negotiations for a range of groups' (Chatterton and Holland, 2003: 10) taking place within a highly criminogenic environment framed and perpetuated by market forces and limited state social control (Hobbs *et al.*, 2000; Hadfield, 2006). At stake in these negotiations are the contradictions of simultaneously increasing deregulation and regulation, the politics, meaning and appropriation of the night-time city, the possibilities of diversity and the conditions of segregation. They are held between a number of public and (predominantly and increasingly powerful – see Chatterton and Holland, 2003) private stakeholders, competing social and cultural groups, between vast numbers of strangers; and between these strangers en masse and the city that must balance attraction, integration and regulation. Above all, the 24-Hour City concept and its Golem, the night-time economy, is a negotiation of space and time held in a far from neutral setting.

In a book concerned with urban rhythms there is, then, much to be learnt by attending to the 24-Hour City. Our concern, however, is that a focus on this 24-Hour City and the various issues associated with the spaces of the night-time economy for which it is shorthand, produces an ironically narrow view of the urban. A view which obscures the lived, street-level, politics revealed via a fuller engagement, spatially and temporally, with the quotidian city. We propose that an attention to rhythmicity, as suggested by Lefebvre (2004), offers an opportunity to glimpse, and retain, something of the complexity of the urban everyday. Doing so requires the spatial and temporal to be viewed in relation to each other; and this, we argue, requires an empirical attention to mobility. The paper thus seeks to reveal an urban politics of regulation and responsibility in public space by documenting the paths – as an entanglement of time, space, mobility and practice – along which such politics are realized (Hall and Smith, 2011).

As promised at the outset of the paper we intend to take the notion of a twenty-four hour city seriously and literally. Seriously, in that we are interested in exploring the ways in which negotiations of time and space occur around the clock, across in the city centre, and particularly at the margins of the city centre

from which the National Express coaches run (local bus services suspend at about midnight); at the far end one of Paul's dossers is sleeping on the floor, under blankets. Working his way up and down all the aisles, Paul moves slowly, eyes to the ground, casting about for scraps and remainders. The job is routine, though you never know what you might find: a dead swan, one day last week; some months ago one of the crew got a needle-stick injury and had to send away for tests to see if he'd got AIDS, so the story goes.

The two-bin truck has to be manoeuvred – up and down kerbs, round corners through gaps – and Paul is adept at this; also fluent in his juggling of brush and shovel and grabber, as required. Alongside the bus station, also on Central Square, is the train station forecourt. Paul's circuit takes him past this, but not inside. A line in the pavement marks the limit of his responsibility to clean. Other buildings he passes have small aprons of land outside that are not quite part of the street and so again not his responsibility (sometimes he will help out, if asked nicely; and sometimes not). Past the train station, plywood hoardings mask a proposed residential development (rubble, for now). Some larger items – crates and boxes – have been left here, which Paul cannot lift. He will arrange for collection later, on return to the depot. There is no sign of Ross this morning, a persistent beggar recently 'banned' from Central Square through the coordinated efforts of the police and city centre management – though only between 8 am and 8 pm, meaning that he is usually up and about early, putting in a couple of hours of hard work with the early commuter traffic before his curfew begins. The irony is not lost on Paul.

With Central Square finished, Paul turns down Wood Street as far as the river bridge and back and then down the lane behind, running by the Millennium Stadium and another building site, awaiting development. From there to Westgate Street, where he turns left and heads away from the centre. He has another hour to go before reporting back to base and a cup of tea.

Here the tail-end of the 24-Hour City overlaps with the beginnings of (just) another twenty-four hours in the city. The excitement and spectacle of a night out in Cardiff, followed by Paul's ordinary circuit of Central Square and the surrounding area. It is a circuit that captures something of what it is to be out on the street at this hour, the potential of repulsion alongside a certain romance of venturing out into the city in the liminal hours. Only, this kind work is intended to remove traces of the former in easing the prospect of the latter for workers and commuters at the start of the city day. In this sense, Paul's labour is a repeated act of quotidian regeneration. No grand-scale, eye-catching make-over, but, even so, a renewal of the city centre for the users yet to arrive on its streets. A small act of kindness, perhaps, by the city toward its public (Thrift, 2005; Graham and Thrift, 2007). There are, of course, members of the public to whom Paul's contribution is not directed toward and who do not necessarily stand to gain from a cleaner, renewed public realm. Spaces in which one might keep out of the way are being ironed out of the redeveloped centre of Cardiff and, more often than not, the homeless residents of the city centre have to make

The Sociological Review, 61:S1, pp. 89–108 (2013), DOI: 10.1111/1467-954X.12055

their arrangements for sleeping in increasingly public spaces. Out of place and in the way. Sleeping (if they actually manage to catch an hour or so) is not so much of a problem – so long as they are up early – but any detritus they leave behind, in a city centre where appearances are paramount, certainly is. Paul's work, in addition to a routine renewal, might be said to be managing the material evidence of an overlapping of rhythms and publics. Those who have slept soundly inside, arisen and are making their way in to work, coffee in hand, those already working and counting down to the end of the shift, and those who haven't been anywhere at all and barely slept. Producing and maintaining clean and safe streets, free from all kinds of rubbish, means work around the clock; the early morning shift ensures a head start.

06:50

Just across the river, to the east of Central Square, a van parks up on the kerb outside of an unremarkable end of terrace house. The only indication the house is the Night Shelter – a temporary accommodation project for Cardiff's homeless – is a security camera above the door. Traffic is sparse on the road in the pre-dawn light as Sue, a professional social worker and member of Cardiff Council's Housing and Neighbourhood Renewal outreach team, rings a buzzer and heads inside, through to the office at the back of the house. She is there to pick up supplies for the Breakfast Run; a daily, year round, patrol of Cardiff, started some fifteen years ago. The Breakfast Run operates before the city centre is in full swing, to check on the welfare of rough sleepers that might be found there on any given morning. With the offering of a hot drink and something warm to eat, it is intended to overcome many of the barriers which might otherwise prevent clients accessing the help they need. It is, essentially, about being out there, meeting clients on their own patch and terms, to build relationships and to try to encourage clients into suitable projects, such as the Night Shelter. Sue asks if they have any vacancies and is told no by the hostel staff, except that a resident didn't show up last night. Sue has another client in mind for the room and says she'll offer it to him, unless she sees the missing resident first and he has a good excuse. As the clock gets round to 07:00, Sue and Rob, the volunteer for that morning, load up the van with flasks of hot water, a bag of bacon and sausage rolls and boiled eggs, and a large box containing tea, coffee, fruit juice, fruit and yoghurts and head out.

First stop is Central Square. The van pulls up in a car park off to the side of the station building. Three men are already waiting. They approach the van, exchanging friendly greetings; Rob gets on with making coffee at the back of the van. Sue is talking to the men, asking if they're all right, if Ian made his appointment with the doctor yesterday, how Ron is managing sleeping on floor space at the city's principal homeless hostel. Sue then leaves to take a walk through the train station and around Central Square to see if anyone else is around, perhaps still asleep in one of the bus shelters. Rob had said he saw someone sleeping in the National Express stand on his way in. Sue returns, saying she didn't find anyone and Ron chips in, saying he saw someone sleeping under the railway bridge on his way to the van. Some speculation follows as to who it might be and whether it could be the same guy Rob saw, moved on from the relative shelter of the bus station.

After the van is packed up they continue making their way across the city, stopping en route to follow up on Ron's lead. Under the railway bridge, just around the corner from the central homeless hostel, Sue spots a pink blanket, the outline of a body huddled underneath it. She approaches, crouches down and says 'Morning. Are you all right there?' No response. Sue tries again, this time placing her hand where she figures his arm to be. Still no response. Sue glances at Rob, concerned. She tries again and this time elicits a mumbled response. She asks for a name and receives an answer that sounds like Kevin. 'Kevin' doesn't stir. Sue leaves him be and heads to the front of the hostel to see if they know anything about the man sleeping under the bridge. A discussion with the hostel staff follows; the police dropped someone here last night, too drunk to be let in and, besides, there were no spaces.

The patrol continues for the next hour and a half; moving, searching and stopping. In this time they visit the small space that a client, Philip, has claimed for himself, tucked away between the wall of a car park and the bank of a canal. They park the van in the car park and Philip makes his way up and along the bank to the back of the van. He has been there six months now, his appearance telling, hair matted and beard long. Philip is in good spirits today, chatting as his thermos flask is filled with hot water and he takes a vegetarian sausage roll, boiled egg, fruit and yoghurt. Any spares this morning guys?

Sue and Rob leave and spend time searching around and behind the buildings of the civic centre, where Harry Evans has been sleeping. Harry has had some trouble of late, moved on by security guards as a result of other rough sleepers moving into his space, messing things up for him by leaving rubbish, graffiti and shit behind. The team are worried about Harry and his health. He's in his early forties but looks at least fifteen years older. He walks with a stick and often has trouble getting up in the morning from the cold floor on which he has been sleeping. The search yields no trace of anyone having slept in the area and they move on, ending up back where they started, at the Night Shelter, where they record the names and location of the sixteen rough sleepers seen that morning.

Meeting up with regulars and searching out new clients, the Breakfast Run relies upon a particularly close knowledge of the city centre. Keeping up with changes in and amongst their client group, their preferred locations, and shifts in the terrain of the city centre itself, is a job of work. Numbers of rough sleepers seen on the Breakfast Run are resistant to pattern and hard to predict. Something that is consistent, however, is the timing of the Breakfast Run, in the early, liminal, hours, before the city, and the homeless, have got going for the day. And this creates a pressure on the patrol to complete a balanced tempo between searching, stopping and moving to meet those sleeping rough before they are up and away, by their own volition or otherwise. The work of

The Sociological Review, 61:S1, pp. 89–108 (2013), DOI: 10.1111/1467-954X.12055
© 2013 The Authors. Editorial organisation © 2013 The Editorial Board of the Sociological Review

the team is underpinned by a simple dichotomy of 'in' and 'out'; rhythmic in being intrinsically spatial and temporal. Clients out on the street, having, perhaps, arrived there after being in doors – or 'inside' – for a while need to be located and identified. The team spend a good deal of time out and about on the street, building trust and confidence in regular interactions such as those produced by the Breakfast Run. The repeated, careful and, at times, frustrating work is directed toward a longer-term aim of helping clients to get in somewhere, if possible. If that is the wider welfare and social care purpose of the team then a more immediate one is to get the rough sleepers up and away before other agents arrive to do so. The offer of breakfast is a tool for opening interactions but also encouraging people to get a move on in the morning. If street cleaning crews are involved in a quotidian regeneration of the material city each early morning, then the Breakfast Run could be said to operate as a social equivalent. They are moral street sweepers. So, whilst welfare is a priority for the team never in doubt, their work might also be seen to contribute to a politics of space and time in the city centre: the city and the outreach team each want the homeless off the streets, for good. Outreach work is, then, Janus faced (Rowe, 1999), playing a role in removing social matter out of place from the streets before the city begins the day proper and its other, less permanent but more welcome, publics arrive.

10:00

At Central Police Station the team of Police Community Support Officers (PCSOs) are preparing for the day shift. In a small briefing room with maps taped to a table demarcating the boundaries of the team's city centre area and its subdivision into various patrols, they don stab-jackets and high-visibility vests with the giveaway blue badges distinguishing the PCSOs from the Police Officers. Deb is talking to Sarah about their prospective patches for the day. Deb will patrol the central shopping area, including Central Square ('lucky you'). Sarah has the park ('that'll be exciting'). Deb talks to another officer, Gerry, about complaints regarding a rough sleeper who has made a spot for himself on the steps of the Cardiff International Arena. They haven't got there before he is up and away yet. Central Square is a well-known problem spot for the small team of PCSOs with various issues constantly arising that require management: taxis parking off rank and blocking access; drinking within and around the alcohol exclusion zone; and beggars targeting the more or less steady stream of people making their way to and from the train station and bus stands. Begging is a key issue for the city of late. It creates a bad image; especially right here on the welcome mat. Of the regular beggars in the city centre, it is spot beggars, like Ross Murphy, who are the biggest problem. The PCSOs and Neighbourhood Police Team know him well. Deb sees a cycle he has got himself trapped in. He has recently served time for breaching conditions of a previous Anti-Social Behaviour Order and is now banned from the city centre between 8 am and 8 pm. He is never inside long enough to really escape the problems he is caught up in on the outside, and so regularly finds himself back in the same loop upon being released. But you just can't have beggars approaching people in the street, especially when they are persistent and aggressive. It is intimidating.

Central Square is relatively quiet today. Deb notices that the gate to a building site abutting the train terminus is unlocked and takes the opportunity to investigate. Behind it is a large but secluded space, the ground strewn with rubble and litter, brick arches of the railway embankment making up one side and plywood hoardings the other three. The first archway contains three lots of bedding, bags and clothing – the occupants nowhere to be seen. Syringes lie on the ground along with 'those silver cup things they're giving out nowadays'. The next archway is also occupied; although this time the occupant – a man who looks in his forties – is still there, awake, sat up in a sleeping bag under piled blankets. Deb steps through a line of sparse bushes, and talks to him in a friendly manner, taking his details and asking if he knows the outreach team and where the homeless services in Cardiff are. Deb is concerned about the man; vulnerable there on his own, out of sight. Anything could happen to him. As such, Deb decides to visit the outreach team at their office, just across Central Square, to pass on the man's whereabouts and details. The site is visible from the team's office window and Deb and Sue look out whilst Deb explains that the police have been in touch with City Centre Management who have in turn been in touch with the construction firm about getting the entrance and perimeter secured properly. For everyone's sake.

PCSOs are the regular face of the police on the streets and in the public spaces of the city centre. Their patrol is tied to the hours of business and work in the city centre and, spatially, to the flows of pedestrians making their way around the central retail areas. Serving a community when one is working in the city centre is, of course, a distinct proposition from being based in the surrounding suburbs. In the centre, a remit of community support indicates a commitment to the retail and leisure establishments and residents of city centre apartment blocks, and close liaisons are thus maintained. Yet the PCSOs in the high-visibility foot patrol which accounts for 80 per cent of their time, also – and perhaps primarily so – tend to the looser, more transient community of pedestrians that at any one time make up a significant proportion of the city centre's population; walkers that the city centre is increasingly geared to attract, offering pleasurable, welcoming and secure public spaces. An ever-increasing visitor population arriving in the city centre exacerbates the visibility of begging and street drinking. Yet there exists a social ecology between the main stream of retail pedestrians and the homeless (who are the truly pedestrian), which finds these two groups sharing city centre space. Often the response is to enforce segregation by direct policing, bans and curfews. Sometimes it is a duty of care for the public which finds spaces like the building site secured, but removed as an available space for rough sleepers and others who want or need to escape from the public eye.

18:00

As one might expect at this time, Central Square is busy with people arriving in or leaving the city. Jeff, a senior outreach worker with the Housing and Neighbourhood Renewal (HANR) team is standing by the entrance to Marland House watching the passersby. The team's office is ideally located, right in the middle of things where a good number of its clients can be found throughout the day and on into the early evening. After a couple of minutes Jeff's colleague Dennis joins him on the steps. A group of young lads and two girls are hanging around in the alley next to the offices and by the public phone box on the street – being loud, squaring up to each other, making half-serious threats centred on debts for cigarettes and small amounts of money. This group are becoming known to the outreach workers. They have been turning up at the 'evening soup run', looking for trouble with the team's homeless clients who gather there. Jeff rolls his eyes at Dennis and they set off, walking slowly up St Mary's Street toward the civic centre.

There are still a good number of people on the main shopping streets, Queen Street in particular. On a corner, outside a convenience shop, Dennis stops to speak to a young man sat begging to the left of the doorway, blanket spread over his knees, hood up over his head. Dennis crouches down to talk to Dan; pedestrians have to make their way around the small, but now enhanced, obstruction that Dennis and Dan create together. Dennis asks him how it's going (the begging) and whether he's managed to sort out a place for the night. He tells Dan to get up to 'the bus' later, there are a few extra beds being made available and he might have a chance at one.

After walking the length of Queen Street, and back again, Jeff and Dennis arrive at the bus themselves. Parked up in front of the museum in the civic centre, a large purple double-decked bus – equipped with kitchen, washing facilities, and a TV and DVD player – makes for an unusual sight. It acts as a service point for the homeless of the city where they can get hot food, sometimes medical attention and register for a bed for the night in a hostel. The bus is tolerated in this central location because of its temporariness and mobility. It, and the particular crowd that the bus draws, never fails to attract the attention of early evening strollers heading toward Queen Street. There are probably twenty or so people there tonight, predominantly male and predominantly young, hanging around on the pavement and clustered at the hatch at the rear of the bus where the hot food is being served. To the front of the bus, the cab doubles as an office from which Jarek, a burly Polish man, coordinates available hostel bed spaces and emergency accommodation for those who 'present'. Jeff and Dennis separate, joining small groups and their conversations with ease. Everyone there knows and respects Jeff and Dennis. They spend an hour or so, listening to various complaints, receiving and dispensing light-hearted jibes and banter. Yet whilst the bus offers space and time to catch up with clients, this is outreach patrol; better to be moving, not stuck at the bus for too long, and so they say their goodbyes and walk back to Queen Street and on toward Charles

Street where the evening soup run will soon be setting up. On the way over they cut across a small grassed area behind the St David's 2 shopping centre and spot Harry Evans sitting on one of the concrete benches, on his own, staring into space. Jeff and Dennis both notice him and, knowing that he hadn't been seen by the Breakfast Run this morning, briefly glance at each other, making sure the other has seen, but carry on walking. No need to bother him just now, but good to see him all the same.

The soup run is organized by a cooperative of churches, and the team make a habit of arriving early, before the volunteers arrive to set up. This is a quiet time that the team and some of their most needy clients are pleased to share before the numbers swell and the scrum for the food and whatever other goods – clothes, toiletries and dog food – are available that night has formed. The soup run volunteers arrive and within half an hour have set up trestle tables from which to distribute the goods. A large crowd has formed which the volunteers try to organize into some sort of queue. First come first served, but beyond that no discrimination is made. Anyone who turns up can ask for food and will get it. Numbers can easily top forty. And this can complicate the work of outreach: 'sometimes it's like playing spot the homeless person'. Initially they stand back, observing. Dennis works the crowd from its fringe, leaning on a bin, smoking his pipe. A young man wearing a grey tracksuit comes over and they hold a private conversation out of earshot of the others. Jeff watches intently as the food is given out without incident. There are often times when outreach work at the soup run becomes a job of policing as much as anything else. In close proximity and in open competition for free food and goodies tensions accumulated over what, for some, has been a long day without much sleep the night before can boil over. But not tonight. The church volunteers circulate in the crowd offering the last of a packet of biscuits. Only now is the relative peace threatened as a string of obscenities and threats are directed by a man with long hair, wearing a leather jacket, toward another he is pursuing. Both are known to the outreach team who watch, but do nothing, as on this occasion the dispute rumbles on but without showing signs of escalating, continuing further down Charles Street.

Evening patrol with Cardiff City Council's HANR outreach team takes place in the crepuscular hours. It is no coincidence that these are also the liminal hours for the economy of the city centre. In this way evening outreach mirrors the Breakfast Run in slotting in to the marginal hours of the economy, operating in a small window of two hours or so in which people are busy making their way home after work or preparing to come back to the centre again. In taking place, as it does, at a later point in the day it is distinctive and brings different pressures. The morning patrol must manage the issues associated with the, sometimes daunting, prospect of the day ahead. The evening patrol is dealing with that day's accumulated troubles. Any leads must be followed, loose ends tied up. It presents a final chance for the team to contact and check up on clients before they have tucked themselves away for the night somewhere. The evening patrol – perhaps more so than the Breakfast Run – can thus be said to walk a

The Sociological Review, 61:S1, pp. 89–108 (2013), DOI: 10.1111/1467-954X.12055

line, literally and figuratively, which traces the complexities of welfare provision to and the management of their client group as an allocation of time and space.

20:30

Night-time outreach with the Streetlife project starts from the Salvation Army hostel, *Ty Gobaith*. The project was set up to protect young people and adults from prostitution, abuse and sexual exploitation and 'to help change the lives of those involved and affected by sex work'. During office hours, Streetlife project workers are available to meet with clients to provide mentoring and advocacy services. But the project also operates out of hours, at night – which is when (as with any other city) street-based sex work is at its busiest and most visible. Outreach is an important part of the project's remit and three times a week a service is delivered by van and on foot through the city's 'red light' areas. These areas are fairly well defined but not altogether stable and strung out along quite a swathe of city real estate, most of it running alongside the London to Cardiff railway line (the other side of the tracks from the hotspots of the night-time economy). A project van, stocked with hot drinks and snacks, needle exchange packs, condoms and assorted advice leaflets, is used to cover this area, parking up at regular intervals and whenever 'hailed' by any of the women out working. The van, though intentionally nondescript and unmarked, is well known to most of the regular street-based sex workers in Cardiff, many of whom are already in contact with the Streetlife project. But the population does shift and turn over, and one of the roles of night-time outreach is to identify and make contact with any 'new' women who may not have heard of the project.

Thursday evenings see staff from the HANR outreach team join Streetlife staff and/or volunteers, meeting up at *Ty Gobaith* to load up the van and head off for an hour or two driving up and down the same few streets and a familiar collection of industrial estates and business parks, all south of the city centre. It turns out to be a quiet night, as sometimes happens; demand for the service is uneven and can fluctuate considerably, even from one evening to the next, and certainly over longer periods. Tonight the police seem to be having something of a crackdown, and it is probably this more than any other single factor – the weather, the time of year, the shifting coalitions and rivalries of the woman involved – that has cleared the streets. There are police cars circling much the same route as the Streetlife van, and at least two police officers patrolling on foot.

The van stops for Wendy, a woman already in contact with the Streetlife service and well known to HANR outreach too. She is anxiously glancing round for police cars: 'If they stop me now, I'll say I was only waiting on outreach and then I'm going home. It's true. I'm only doing one more then I'm going home'. Condoms are handed over along with hot chocolate, cigarettes and details of a recently reported attack. Project workers routinely field and redistribute reports of 'dodgy' punters best avoided and cars – make, model, licence plate number – to keep away from. Incident reports like this one are also shared with the police, anonymously if requested by the women.

Ten minutes later another woman waves down the van. This is Heather, who starts up an urgent conversation about her Drug Rehabilitation Requirement (DRR).[3] 'I'm in such trouble', she begins, then launches into a confused account of why she has missed her latest supervision meeting. She is worried she will have triggered 'breach' proceedings and will soon be back in court. The outreach team take scribbled notes and Heather's mobile phone number; a Streetlife project worker will call her tomorrow in office hours to try and sort this out for her – if it can be sorted.

Then another, stood under the flyover. The van slows down on approach but then speeds up and drives by, warned off by a last-minute, covert flap of the hand: a punter has pulled over and the outreach team have learned to keep their distance on these occasions (the project van can be mistaken for an unmarked police vehicle). Then one more, who wants only condoms and doesn't have time to stop and chat (but notes the incident report). And then back to base. All agree it has been a quiet patrol – uneventful. A good thing?

These are core hours for the night-time economy and the vision of the 24-Hour City with which we began. Here, however, away from the crowds, music and neon we find an alternative night-time economy. Same times maybe, but found in the peripheral spaces of the city centre; industrial estates, distributor roads, outlying residential areas. To map the Streetlife patrol is to connect points of contact with Cardiff's street-based sex workers and their relationship to these outlying spaces. The patrol follows a fairly regular pattern; a pattern performed in part because both the outreach team and the clients with which it works must be locatable and visible. In this way the Streetlife patrol is less reliant on searching as mode of operation than patrols tending to the homeless. Like those other patrols with a social work remit, a locatable client group means the Streetlife project can build relationships in and through regular, and repeatable, interactions. If the women need to be visible to potential custom and are therefore visible to the Streetlife patrol, they are, of course, also visible to police patrol. And a crackdown by the police can have two outcomes. It can either keep the women out on the street for longer, as the presence of the police scares off what potential business there is – increasing the time it takes to make the money they came out to earn – or it drives the women off the street, making it harder still for the outreach team to locate them and keep in touch.

00:00

Mike Watkins has been helping Cardiff's homeless for twenty years, once a week every Thursday night. His operation is private and unfunded – his own car, time and donated goods from his church congregation. He is very well known, respected and relied upon by Cardiff's street population, but otherwise unsung and mostly unseen – he goes out at midnight, typically through to three or four in the morning.

The Sociological Review, 61:S1, pp. 89–108 (2013), DOI: 10.1111/1467-954X.12055

Mike climbs into his car which is tightly packed with thermos flasks and hot food, neatly folded piles of second-hand clothes, several pairs of new shoes, a dozen blankets and a couple of rucksacks. The first port of call is the civic centre, where Mike parks his car and steps out to organize the twenty or so assorted individuals waiting for him on the steps of the National Museum – not a few drunk, one or two of them known to be 'trouble'. This has become a regular stop over recent months and will remain so unless and until Mike feels it is getting too busy and difficult to manage, at which time he will start out again somewhere else. Those meeting up with Mike outnumber those sleeping out on any given night, and although Mike is pleased to spend time and share food and drink with anyone, he has his priorities. Those he is really here to help are those sleeping out – like Dave, stood apart from the more boisterous element, in his stained and greasily stiffened puffa jacket and full beard, muttering to himself.

Mike works the crowd, keeping order and making time for individual conversations. Stood at the rear of the car with the boot open he distributes hot drinks and snacks (holding back the hot food till later) and fields a steady stream of requests: a blanket, a jacket, socks, a rucksack, shoes, a sleeping bag. Some of these will have been logged last week, since when Mike has managed to secure whatever it was – size 9 boots, a sleeping bag. Some can't be met tonight: 'Next week. I'll see what I can do.' The gathering is mostly congenial. The weather is mild and there is no more than the usual irritation and difficulty. No one 'kicks off'. Slowly the crowd thins out, leaving only those who have nowhere else to go, at which point Mike breaks out the hot food he has kept out of sight behind a bin bag full of jumpers: baked potatoes, beans and cheese. Asked to do so, Mike says a short prayer.

After a good hour spent on the Museum steps, Mike begins to move around, beginning by circling the rest of the civic centre, where he finds several sleepers – asleep – under the portico of the Crown Courts. He tiptoes over, leaving food and drink and a scatter of cigarettes beside the lumpy bags and blankets. Next the back lanes running towards the city centre, looking in particular for a group who were at the Museum steps earlier but skipped out. Mike had arranged to meet up with this lot later, only now they are not where they said they would be; whatever plans they had have changed or been forgotten. Twenty minutes later Mike spots a young man he recognizes, stepping down from a police van with two large bags of what look to be hastily assembled belongings. It turns out he has been evicted, or at any rate removed – the details are unclear and no doubt contested – from the hostel he was staying at, and is now 'out' for what remains of the night. Mike fetches hot food and drinks and stays to talk for half an hour, mostly listening to the young man's grievances and regrets, delivered in a slurred monotone. He wants a job, more than anything. He repeats this like a mantra: if he only had a job, that would put things right.

Next is a visit to Philip's camp by the canal. Mike has wind of this location thanks to the HANR team, who first found Philip and passed the news along. A thin muddy path leads through bushes to Philip's remarkable abode. There is nothing as simple as a tent, rather the place has the look of a nest, woven together out of various scraps of available material, chief among which is a large sail of plastic sheeting that he has got from somewhere and somehow fixed to the wall against which he is lying. The sheeting hangs down at 45 degrees from about head height to the ground where it is presumably pinned. This makes for a triangular space: dirt floor, dank wall and overhead sloping plastic roof. Philip is inside, perfectly at ease it seems, and happy. He stays lying down, raised on one arm as he chats with Mike and gobbles down a baked potato.

After Philip, one last trip back into the centre, driving up Charles Street to park near the Ebenezer Church. Mike walks along Queen Street heading towards the Cardiff Castle, carrying flasks and bags of food. Halfway along he turns left to find two sleepers in a doorway close to Starbucks, and having left them with food and cigarettes he calls it a night and heads back to the car. It is close to three o'clock and the clubs on Queen Street are closed now or closing. Small pockets and throngs of partygoers are still about, though with the look of heading home.

Conclusion

A day and a night and the hours in between spent patrolling the city centre allows one to (begin to) appreciate the twenty-four hour city. A city quite distinct from the contradictory but popular imagery of bright lights, music and good times set against a backdrop of corporatization, violence and social control which the 24-Hour City concept conjures. The reader will have recognized the distinction in a series of connections strung throughout the day. The connections are not solely conceptual, but spatial and temporal too, made in the distribution, overlapping and intermeshing of the mobile practices described. The connections and distribution of practice are, then, rhythmic. And they are so in two senses. The first sense finds a given patrol operating within – constrained by – dominating rhythms, either circadian or those of capital and consumption. If the outreach team wants to locate, meet up with, and work with their homeless clients the times and spaces for this are (increasingly) peripheral. If the patrols of the PCSOs are to provide a reassuring presence and offer assistance to the public, then the inverse holds. The second sense finds the practice of urban patrol, in (at)tending to the physical and social fabric of the city centre, not only shaped by external rhythms of the city but also, and perhaps equally, shaping and (re)producing such rhythms in the management of space, time and mobility in the city centre.

The work undertaken in the course of these patrols is, despite our insistence upon its significance, modest, unremarkable; piecemeal, even. In much the same way that construction workers in high-visibility jackets blend into the background, the various practices of care and repair we document here are overlooked and under-observed (Graham and Thrift, 2007). This tinkering quality of patrol makes it a minority practice in the urban order (Hall, 2010), yet essential

The Sociological Review, 61:S1, pp. 89–108 (2013), DOI: 10.1111/1467-954X.12055

to the reproduction of that order from one day to the next. The contribution of the paper is, in part, to provide an empirical case as a basis from which to recognize the centrality of this work to the maintenance of the twenty-four hour city. Whilst this is contribution enough in its own right, we also intend this description as an argument for an attention to street-level, pedestrian practice (of street sweepers, PCSOs, welfare workers and independent volunteers in this case), as a means of tracing the lines along which a moral geography and timescape of the city is produced in everyday life. That our description is concerned not simply with the distribution of practice but with mobility practices proper finds the spatial and the temporal interwoven. And it is the centrality of mobility to our informants and, indeed, to our argument that leads us to our concluding commentary on the twenty-four hour city which we make by way of contrast with the 24-Hour City and its night-time economy.

Ranging across the city with the various patrols for an entire day was, of course, an immediate and obvious (if tiring) way of exploring the contrast between the two notions of what a twenty-four hour city might be. Having done so, a focus on mobile practices allows us – and now the reader – to see a contrast to the entrepreneurial, corporatized 24-Hour City which, we argue, offers an alternative understanding of the politics and management urban public space.

The first contrast is quantitative. At the outset of the paper we noted a concern with the ways in which the 24-Hour City, really, refers to a rather narrow segment of time and space, cut from a continuous urban rhythmicity. This view, of course, relates to an equally narrow segment of the population of the city centre, if not numerically then certainly in terms of diversity, which in turn comes to stand as symbol for the entire nocturnal urban population. As also noted at the outset of the paper, a directly proportionate relation exists between attraction and regulation in this condensed version of urban life; the more people an area is successful in attracting the more the area will require the 'unnatural' forms of regulation and intervention which provoked the scepticism of Jane Jacobs. As a consequence of the 'honey-pot effect' (Hadfield, 2006), the publics of the night-time economy are condensed, rather than dispersed. It follows, then, that the forms and strategies of control are essentially static in nature. CCTV, bouncers and a range of new additions (taxi marshals, street pastors and city ambassadors, for example) found in Cardiff and elsewhere operate from fixed positions, known trouble spots and high crime areas. Such static technologies point to a governance of flows and clots of publics in and out of a fixed site. The regulation of access, arrivals and departures, thresholds and comings together in public space is the stuff of night-time economy social control. There is, of course, much to be critical of regarding the proliferation of the technologies developed and deployed in these spaces; yet one might also consider the way in which the crowds of the night-time economy, once out of sight and site, are out of mind, bused out or put into taxis. A further critique lies in recognizing that over and above the issues within the spaces of the night-time economy, the 'conquering' of the night-time frontier by city planners and corporations has produced additional spaces and times in and during which the city is segregated and exclusory to a range of marginal social groups (Thomas and Bromley, 2000; Chatterton and Holland, 2003 *inter alia*); not least, the city centre homeless.

Moving out beyond the time and space of the night-time economy, and avoiding lazy juxtapositions between the nine-to-five city and the 'excitement' of nocturnal leisure, marginal yet essentially urban groups are made visible. Furthermore, one might consider how spending time moving, walking, in the city centre, rather than staying put, staring at space, has led us, perhaps inevitably, to the vulnerable, and most frequent, occupants of city centre streets. We note, again, that ours was not a study of need or vulnerability *per se* but, rather, of mobility and local knowledge in practice. What we find is that an attention to practitioners for whom moving and knowing come together in significant ways at street level, produces a supporting cast of rough sleepers, beggars, street drinkers and sex workers.[4] One might dismiss this as trivial happenstance. We think, however, that our description points to, and reveals, a relationship between (urban) vulnerability and mobility. In a city centre geared up for smooth and easy pedestrian circulation the problem for the street homeless is not so much that they have nowhere to go, but, rather, they have nowhere to stop, at least not for long (Hall and Smith, 2013). The real residents of the twenty-four hour city, those who variously *inhabit* rather than simply pass through the streets, experience mobility as a burden. They create an inconvenience for the image of a city going places in that they share public space with visitors, workers, tourists. They also inevitably come into contact or, better put, cross *paths* with patrols intended to maintain the city centre. Street sweepers and PCSOs fulfil a duty of care; a care sometimes directed to 'the city', sometimes to its public, sometimes to those at the margins, sometimes for their own good. The outreach teams and Mike are out in public space for different reasons; they operate with a more readily recognized care, for the vulnerable and those in need. Yet there is, as will have been recognized, an ambivalence in their practice too. The outreach team are also employees of the city. Their presence in the city centre is tolerated, for now, as they also perform a role of soft policing and monitoring, so long as they do not make too much of a scene in taking care of the homeless.[5] One might say that Mike, making his rounds in the hours after midnight, is a different case. But whilst the city might have anxieties about people heading out to feed and counsel the homeless in a wholly voluntary and 'unofficial' capacity, it still benefits from Mike's work. The intervention, no matter how small, contributes a mitigating effect upon urban inequalities which might otherwise become unmanageable.

In moving toward a conclusion it is possible to contrast the mundane twenty-four hour city with that of the 24-hour night-time economy in terms of the practices of care and welfare we have described here. There is, here, evidence of the exercise of a duty of care – of small acts of kindness within a wider infrastructure of support – by the city and its street-level practitioners for its most publically vulnerable citizens. Yet we do not offer this description as a simple

The Sociological Review, 61:S1, pp. 89–108 (2013), DOI: 10.1111/1467-954X.12055

counterpoint to the imagery of the night-time battlefield (Hadfield, 2006) where lines are drawn between the state, the private sector and various social groups excluded, made vulnerable or overly and overtly controlled in the nocturnal spaces of the city, by drawing another line of our own. We are not interested in reproducing an adversarial politics of the street but, rather, in pointing to a politics of urban public space which recognizes, in our description of urban patrol, a politics of negotiation running throughout practices of care, repair and maintenance, physical and social, in the city centre. And it is in urban patrol, that we find these negotiations traced in space in practices which combine in *managing* – through overlapping, polychronic modes of welfare and regulation – those that both threaten and pollute the vision of a sanitized, 'safe', and profitable city centre, whose presence in public space is directly linked to need and vulnerability. That is to say, in attending to the rhythmic and rhythmed practices of street sweepers, PCSOs, and welfare workers we hope to have captured something of the moral order of urban rhythmicity and perhaps offered a view of patrol as a process through which Lefebvre's dialectic of time and space and energy can be seen as negotiated, not statically *in* space, but on the move. In doing so, and perhaps above all, this description traces out across a single day, a relation between movement and need and care as found in an entanglement, a coming together of time, space, mobility and persons framed by, and producing, the rhythms of the twenty-four hour city, around the clock, with no time out.

Notes

1 Take paramedics, for example. For paramedics, movement is adjunct. Stuck with the difficulties of movement to a known destination in the urban environment, they must move as quickly and freely as possible to arrive somewhere in order to *begin* the work of a paramedic – informed by a knowledge of short cuts, the ability to drive through red lights and GPS navigation. In the extreme case emergency response cuts out the urban terrain completely. They use a helicopter. For outreach workers, moving in and with the urban environment is not adjunct nor inconvenience, but is central to, *is* outreach work. Rather than simply moving and arriving, our informants are, instead, searching, patrolling often with no fixed destination in mind.

2 There are a couple of exceptions, 'Mike Watkins' is one. Not so much as to protect his identity but to reflect his lack of interest in or need for publicity. Another is the various individuals encountered by our informants within the course of these twenty-four hours; the street homeless, and sex workers in particular. They were never our direct respondents, nor the focus of the research, and have been given pseudonyms.

3 The Drug Rehabilitation Requirement is a community-based penalty/programme offered in this case as an alternative to prison; Heather's DRR requirement includes a drug treatment package, regular supervision and mandatory drug testing.

4 That is not to say that we were surprised by this, only that the focus of the research on patrols was more profound than a means to 'get at' the city's vulnerable for research purposes.

5 At the time of writing, the Breakfast Run has received a sufficient number of complaints from various businesses and premises, who see them as 'attracting' the street homeless to the city centre, that they can no longer stop at Central Square, nor along the central shopping street. This further illustrates both the centrality of appearances in the centre of things and also the pressures that the rhythms of shoppers, tourists and workers arriving in the city in the morning exert.

References

Bianchini, F., (1995), 'Night cultures, night economies', *Planning and Practice Research*, 10 (2): 121–126.

Chatterton, P. and Holland, R., (2003), *Urban Nightscapes: Youth Cultures, Pleasure Spaces and Corporate Power*, London: Routledge.

Edwards, A., (2010), 'Evaluation of the Cardiff Night-Time Economy Co-ordinator (NTEC) post', Cardiff School of Social Sciences Working Paper Series, Paper 133.

Gottdiener, M., (2001), *The Themeing of America: American Dreams, Media Fantasies, and Themed Environment*, Boulder, CO: Westview Press.

Graham, S. and Thrift, N., (2007), 'Out of order: understanding repair and maintenance', *Theory, Culture and Society*, 24 (3): 1–25.

Hadfield, P., (2006), *Bar Wars: Contesting the Night in Contemporary British Cities*, Oxford: Oxford University Press.

Hall, T., (2010), 'Urban outreach in the polyrhythmic city', in T. Edensor (ed.), *Geographies of Rhythm: Nature, Place, Mobilities and Bodies*, 59–70, Farnham: Ashgate.

Hall, T. and Smith, R. J., (2011), 'Walking, welfare and the good city', *Anthropology in Action*, 18 (3): 33–44.

Hall, T. and Smith, R. J., (2013), 'Stop and go: a field study of pedestrian practice, immobility and urban outreach work', *Mobilities*, 8 (2): 272–292.

Hall, T. and Hubbard, P., (1998), 'The entrepreneurial city and the "new urban politics" ', in T. Hall and P. Hubbard (eds), *The Entrepreneurial City: Geographies of Politics, Regime and Representation*, Chichester: John Wiley & Sons.

Hannigan, M., (1998), *Fantasy City: Pleasure and Profit in the Postmodern Metropolis*, London: Routledge.

Harvey, D., (1989), 'From managerialism to entrepreneurialism: the transformation in urban governance in late capitalism', *Geografiska Annaler*, 71 (1): 3–17.

Heath, T., (1997), 'The twenty-four hour city concept – a review of initiatives in British cities', *Journal of Urban Design*, 2 (2): 139–204.

Heath, T. and Stickland, R., (1997), 'The twenty-four hour city concept', in T. Oc and S. Tiesdell (eds), *Safer City Centres: Reviving the Public Realm*, 170–183, London: Paul Chapman.

Hetherington, K., (2007), 'Manchester's Urbis', *Cultural Studies*, 21 (4): 630–649.

Hobbs, D., Lister, S., Hadfield, P., Winlow, S. and Hall, S., (2000), 'Receiving shadows: governance and liminality in the night-time economy', *British Journal of Sociology*, 51 (4): 701–717.

Jacobs, J., (1961), *The Death and Life of Great American Cities*, Harmondsworth: Penguin.

Lefebvre, H., (1990), *The Production of Space*, Oxford: Blackwell.

Lefebvre, H., (2004), *Rhythmanalysis: Space, Time and Everyday Life*, London: Continuum.

Lipsky, M., (1980), *Street-level Bureaucracy: Dilemmas of the Individual in Public Services*, New York: Russell Sage Foundation.

Lovatt, A. and O'Connor, J., (1995), 'Cities and the night-time economy', *Planning and Practice Research*, 10 (2): 127–134.

Melbin, M., (1978), 'Night as frontier', *American Sociological Review*, 43 (1): 3–22.

Oc, T. and Tiesdell, S. (eds), (1997), *Safer City Centres: Reviving the public realm*, London: Paul Chapman.

Rowe, M., (1999), *Crossing the Border: Encounters between Homeless People and Outreach Workers*, Berkeley, CA: University of California Press.

Smith, R. J., (2010), 'The social actor in the landscapes of regeneration', unpublished thesis, Cardiff University.

Solnit, R., (2001), *Wanderlust: A History of Walking*, London: Verso.

Thomas, C. J. and Bromley, R. D. F., (2000), 'City-centre revitalisation: problems of the fragmentation and fear in the evening and night time city', *Urban Studies*, 37: 1403–1429.

Thrift, N., (2005), 'But malice aforethought: cities and the natural history of hatred', *Transactions of the Institute of British Geographers*, 30 (2): 133–150.

Zukin, S., (1995), *The Cultures of Cities*, Oxford: Blackwell.

The Sociological Review, 61:S1, pp. 89–108 (2013), DOI: 10.1111/1467-954X.12055

Majority time: operations in the midst of Jakarta

AbdouMaliq Simone and Achmad Uzair Fauzan

Abstract: Across many cities of the so-called Global South, the primary responsibility for constructing spaces of inhabitation has fallen largely to residents themselves. Although these cities have been largely remade through the intensive segregations precipitated by property markets, many substantial traces of the continuous incremental renovations and readjustment of everyday life remain vital. It was not just a matter of households building their own homes. Affordability meant density. Densification was not just of bodies of techniques necessary to provide an array of affordances. This meant the intermixing of measures, angles, calculations, impulses, screens, surfaces, soundscapes, exposures, folds, circuitries, and layers, as instruments for associating things, bringing things into association, where things get their 'bearings' by having a 'bearing' on each other. But these associations required their own rhythm and time. Focusing on different heterogeneous districts in inner city Jakarta, the paper explores these mixtures of temporality and how they are materialized in local built and economic environments.

Keywords: Jakarta, local economy, incremental temporality, urban development, built environment, social infrastructure

The time that works

In the fields of urban development and change many assumptions are made about the capacities of residents to bring about improvements in the conditions of their lives. This is particularly the case for residents living in rapidly expanding urban mega-regions where complex rearrangements of life outpace the ability of policy-makers and institutions to always manage these transformations. The bulk of these assumptions centres on various organizational imaginaries – that is, the capacities of residents to organize in ways that identify and secure their collective interests and rights. If only residents were better able to pool their time, efforts and assets into more proficient investments and organizational capacities, then, the assumption goes, would they be better able to make the city something that works for them (Boonyabancha, 2009; Boudreau, 2007; Eckstein, 2000; Holston, 2008; Lindell, 2010; Walton, 1998).

The Sociological Review, 61:S1, pp. 109–123 (2013), DOI: 10.1111/1467-954X.12056
© 2013 The Authors. Editorial organisation © 2013 The Editorial Board of the Sociological Review. Published by John Wiley & Sons Ltd, 9600 Garsington Road, Oxford OX4 2DQ, UK and 350 Main Street, Malden, MA 02148, USA

But what are the criteria entailed in these notions of 'what works' and 'for them'? Additionally, given that the city is a constantly mutating intersection of materials, things, bodies and immaterialities only partially regulated or predictable, why don't residents take advantage of the multiplicity of collectivity possibilities embodied by urban life? Again, behind this question lurks some kind of optimal spatial solution, some format or calibration capable of generating synergistic effects that maximize the productivity of urban life (Elden, 2010; Gandy, 2006; McFarlane, 2009; Thrift, 2005).

We work in a lot of different districts in Jakarta, and mostly on issues of local urban economic development. People in these districts undertake a wide variety of different trades and livelihoods, largely outside of formal employment. The work that people do largely provides a basic income, but usually not much more. As a result, there is vast scepticism about the practices of local economy, and concern that people should be doing something different, more substantial and at larger scales. For example, there is a tendency to create employment opportunities only by subcontracting out to the lowest level of production activities and by creating 'firewalls' among activities rather than developing integrated approaches. New enterprises may be created, for example, in the textile sector, but usually these opportunities remain heavily dependent upon 'big players' who continue to dominate access to capital and machinery. This dependence is often reflected in very narrow market channels – in other words, the ability of new enterprises to explore various market opportunities is severely restricted because of these dependencies. Also, by separating out functions – such as the delivery of materials, the unloading of materials, and the retailing of these materials – each function develops into a specific zone of authority and pricing that often seeks to protect itself before thinking about the overall market of which it is a part.

Additionally, people within a trade are usually unable to put together new forms of economic association that cut across ethnic group or territorial affiliation. While, for example, ethnic-based developments of economic activities can be useful mechanisms to ensure inclusion of a wide range of people – both as workers and customers – they also reproduce the situation whereby certain actors continue to dominate the high end of each sector. It also limits the development of new practices and product lines, as well as the capacity of neighbourhood-based sectors to produce at scale. The expansion of investment savings and market share would seem to require new ways of explicitly articulating different businesses and facets of production activity within a sector.

A sense of timing and the becoming of an urban majority

What is often neglected in these discussions of urban movements and collective organization is a sense of timing – of what is the right time to do things, or how people pace themselves over time as a way of creating evidence for what they do or creating conditions that enable them to discern just how they affect the city and how the city affects them. These considerations go beyond calculations of

The Sociological Review, 61:S1, pp. 109–123 (2013), DOI: 10.1111/1467-954X.12056

risk – of just how much can be risked with what one has access to – or of savings, of deferring certain decisions or consumption to a future time in order to maximize abilities, impact or scale. Rather, they entail the very conditions of living in the city themselves.

The majority of urban residents in many cities of the postcolony remain outside of the 'count' – not in terms of their demography or occupations, but in terms of how little their lives and how they organize them have been taken into account. How much do we really know about the ways in which artisans, civil servants, storekeepers, drivers, market sellers, small-scale producers, teachers, service workers, repairers and police live their lives in today's megacities, and how they shape them? Yet, the capacities of such residents to operate as a majority – a site through which livelihoods could be constructed that simultaneously depended upon and circumvented wage labour, that con-solidated particular territorial and occupational identities in a specific place but yet largely used them as a platform from which to engage in highly flexible, provisional and mobile relations with many different 'walks of life' – also depended upon being kept out of the count. They depended upon circumvent-ing measurement and clear ascription or sites of political objective (Chatterjee, 2004; Fawaz, 2008).

The count is avoided precisely because the majority operates at those sites of urban life most maximally capable of facilitating the simultaneous negotiation of such different walks of life (Bayat, 2009; Benjamin, 2008; Elyachar, 2005; Goldstein, 2004; Haber, 2006; Konings *et al.*, 2006). Thus, they live in a time where their own consolidation as 'the majority' – a self-recognized cohesion of interests and practices aimed at taking power – is not the political ideal, not the objective of their efforts (Badiou, 2006). At the same time, while residents may seek to maximize their potentials to remake themselves in multiple ways along the ever-changing trajectories of urbanized interactions, they also know that eventually they must at least act accountable as 'one thing' – as a coherent, visibly self-managed entity.

Using Meillassoux's (2007) discussion of Bergson and Deleuze and the countervailing trajectories of becoming, we are reminded that living is not so much reflective of a process of interested choice but rather the mobilization of disinterest in the real. This disinterest constitutes the basis of perception. Here, only specific segments of what takes place, of what 'matters', constitutes the entirety of what is perceived. Choices are made among various options, but only following the action of the body which rules out the availability of an infinity of images; which has already screened out a wide range of images at various temporal and spatial scales. If reality and matter have 'all the rhythms of duration, then perception is the selection of one of the rhythms of a matter-image which contains each and every material quantity' (2007: 81). Matter is intercepted in that it becomes superficial as it is enveloped in perception. Within perception, matter does not cease to be itself but rather is subject to a 'detour', a 'break', a means through which a non-organic past is constituted for the procession of the living being.

For the living being to mobilize itself within a given environment, for it to act within it, requires what Deleuze (1986) calls a 'disinterested interest' – a way of engaging the world that has no recourse to 'step out' of the flow of events, and therefore must always be willing to affect and be affected by all that surrounds it; yet, at the same time, not to be 'carried away' with the flux of that environment. At the same time, something is always happening in a person's world; something is always interesting, always repositions all that exists in ever-changing relationships. Thus these trajectories of both active and reactive becoming are the conditions of any choice or calculation – that is, where do I put my body, who will I pay attention to, how will I use what resources I have? All of these dimensions have to be perceived and decided upon in city life.

Operating in the city requires a surfeit of affect to navigate the multiplicity of ways in which things, spirits, information, materials, bodies, spaces, techniques, forces and differentials pass through each other – come and go, circle and transverse, accumulate, dissipate and fold. To select, cut off, disconnect and screen out the reality that one is fully immersed in and constituted by does not in and of itself constitute spaces of refuge and withdrawal; for a person is fully within this complex concave reality at 'all times'. The question then becomes: how does one ward off being dissipated in the experiencing of all things 'at once' in the uninterrupted flood of communication (Terranova, 2004)? This is then a matter of timing, of time not 'all at once', but of breaks and detours, of disattention and disinterest, of looking here and not there, of orienting a body to a sense of 'here and there' that requires a 'passing away' from an incessant passing through (Meillassoux, 2007).

This time is not one of development stages, where momentary consolidation of self or collective then provides the 'answer' for what will come next. It is not the deployment of memory that contracts space by putting together images and precepts into story lines in order to constitute a present moment that can be managed. It is not the engineering of some 'critical distance' from the flow of events so that there might be time to read them as a certain progression embodying causation and meaning. Nor is it a process of time being 'bought' so that something more real or ideal can eventually emerge; where someone has in mind just what is to come or should come. Rather, the timing talked about here refers to a continuous process of becoming with and within the city, of living on the cusp of that difference – that is, moving with the city in all of its shifts and also organizing a means of inhabitation, something recognizable as a base within all of the flux (Latham and McCormack, 2004). A place, as Deleuze (1986) suggests, where one can 'set out again' – where the 'where' is not prescribed or always knowable, but where the uncertainty does not foreclose the capacity to act in new ways.

Taking on just enough: *tempeh* producers in Kampung Rawa

While there has much been discussion about how local economies need to 'scale up', it is not clear whether the benefits are unequivocal. In the sub-district of

The Sociological Review, 61:S1, pp. 109–123 (2013), DOI: 10.1111/1467-954X.12056

Kampung Rawa in central Jakarta, the artisanal production of bean curd *tempeh* has been key local economic activity for decades. It is a business that requires the continuous turnover of production given the value placed on keeping preservatives out of the mix. The vast majority of local producers, with some 80 of the city's 700 located in a contiguous series of small lanes in Kampung Rawa, come from a single city, Pekalongan. Production is usually sold in small neighbourhood markets and in street stands at various strategic locations, as well as in orders from caterers. A wide geographic region in the city is covered through this plurality of small producers, with profits accumulated by households concentrated near their workshops. These households are often related through kinship, at the same time that kinship in this sector is rarely a basis of entrepreneurial consolidation. Related small entrepreneurs pursue their businesses individually with little explicit coordination regarding market location or share.

Coverage, as a reference to both product distribution and the overall social welfare of producer households, is something more implicit in the entrepreneurial practices that are deployed. While producers are organized into sub-district and city wide cooperatives, the primary objective of this work is to secure inputs within an affordable price range. This means putting pressure on governmental bodies to curtail the power of a small number of importers who exert a de facto monopoly on the import of soybeans into the country. As there exists substantial price manipulation by the small number of soy wholesalers, cooperatives are engaged in the arduous process of attempting to politically curtail this power. The attitude on the part of cooperative leaders is that they will always have markets and the important thing is to guarantee the possibility of reproducing their present capacities.

Continuous turnover is not only a function of the short 'shelf-life' of the product but the dependence upon sales as usually the only capital available to keep the operations going. No matter how long the success of an individual producer, there is little investment capital available to upscale production and very little social or economic incentive for producers to work out standardized procedures that would be a key criterion for the agglomeration of enterprises. This is reflected in past temporary attempts to supply larger supermarkets or restaurant groups where supplies are paid for only thirty days after delivery and where a proportion of the costs entailed in unsold items have to be absorbed by the producers. Producers see the risks entailed in this jump in scale as excessive and prefer to carve out their own limited market niches, which usually also involve strong relationships with workers and retailers, often housed by the producers themselves.

So instead of an explicit and organized harmonization of quality, markets, production techniques, and business relations, a more implicit coordination occurs through the extensive circulation of information facilitated through kinship and the close proximity in which producers reside. At the same time, each producer operates with his or her own autonomy and sets their price. While many would not be adverse to securing larger market shares or expanding the scope of production, few are willing to relinquish their relative autonomy or to assume the risks or indebtedness that such expansion would entail. A limited sense of sufficiency thus prevails, with producers able to gradually improve their living conditions over time and use their long-term endurance as a platform on which to attain positions of local leadership that also are converted into various economic opportunities.

This sense of gradualism has been widespread across the districts of central Jakarta – the incremental improvement of living conditions, enterprises, individual capacities and status over time. Each attainment does not usually open exponentially a larger range of aspirations; residents expect to take their time over a long period of time to make modest changes. In part, this practice ensues from the absence of investment capital or its availability through participation in patronage systems which curtail individual or neighbourhood autonomy. But it also ensues from the evidence generated by others whose risks or naivety wiped out years of effort and available resources. The persistence of politics as essentially a game of money – a game accessible to only those with money and a game dedicated primarily to the extraction rents and payoffs – is reinforced by a widespread popular belief that personal efficacy has to be demonstrated through concrete works and that the safest, most assured way of accomplishing such works is one step at a time. While big political operators might construct fancy houses and throw money around in favours and charity, there are more numerous examples of those who have played the game and not accomplished anything. Evidence for this popular opinion is indeed widespread, but does not necessarily rule out some individual efforts to effect a more 'productive' engagement with local politics.

Knowing when to move and what to take on: the 'conductor' of Pasar Nangka

Abay is a 49-year-old father of two of the best heavy metal musicians in Indonesia and a guy who largely grew up on the streets cajoling and hustling for every little opportunity. The big payoff would come in his organizing a defence of local market, Pasar Nangka, with its highly strategic location straddling five different kinds of neighbourhoods. He expelled gangsters who were using the market to gamble and sell drugs. While the struggle was protracted, his key decision was to keep the market open around the clock, organize clear thoroughfares and generally make it a place where everyone could safely come at all hours. To keep the market open around the clock, Abay trained and organized a 'night staff' made up of some the most marginal 'losers' in the area, giving them a chance for steady employment, even if at a cut-rate wage. Widespread use of under-invoicing and direct contacts with farmers – avoiding the use of middlemen – ensured that prices were lower than any other market in the region, thus guaranteeing a high volume of turnover, a percentage of which he and his 'staff' extracted for various services, such as cleaning and security.

Instead of pocketing all of the proceeds he bought up property in the surrounding area for a variety of ancillary businesses to take advantage of proximity to the market and developed opportunities for the wholesaling of rice in a
partly successful effort to break the hold of long-established monopolies. Part of
these new expansions was used to house traders in the market, as well as his
staff. He also lobbied for the placement of an official police post at the entrance
of the market, literally subcontracting out security to those who are legally
culpable for enforcing it. All of these efforts cemented a great deal of loyalty,
and loyalty in turn generated financial rewards.

During the entirety of this process, Abay had no formally sanctioned role in
the market, which officially fell under the purview of a municipal association of
small enterprises and as such, was not even registered as a market. This manoeuvre which kept the official market authority, Pasar Jaya, out of administrative
control, and thus the extraction of service fees and taxes, entailed a modicum of
dissimulation on the part of both Abay and the traders as certain infrastructures
usually associated with markets had to be kept in abeyance and the general
appearance one of marked informality – even as trading and transportation
were highly organized.

Such success engenders jealousy and, therefore, Abay must always be conscious of protecting his position, which accounts for his involvement in party
politics – that is, to keep himself visible as a force to be reckoned with. While
Abay has over time acquired a cleaning service business and owns several
properties, he has no real political ambitions himself. He has his niche and has
used this niche to make steady but gradual improvements in his life conditions
and status. Rather politics, for Abay, is performance art – always making it
seem as if something is taking place, whether its alliances, conflicts, coalitions or
campaigns, when they are not yet in operation. It always seems that Abay
knows something that everyone else doesn't know but feels that they should
know and thus can't act as if they don't know it. Concretely, this ruse translates
into a game where Abay receives 'consultant fees' from various ministries for
bringing together different actors from his district of Kemayoran for workshops, capacity building sessions, and so forth, and where each participant
collects an honorarium for their participation – a process that further endears
Abay to a wider range of people. With wider connections and acquaintances,
Abay can also play as an intermediary for those who need masses in the can-
didacy for public office.

It also helps that Abay plays the part of a kind of gregarious 'fool'
who continuously disarms people by his 'ingenuous' forthrightness. But
Abay is certainly no fool, and part of this is that he has always been careful
never to overreach, never to take on too much, and thus not to owe anyone
anything. He talks about how many of his close peers he grew up with have
gone on to important positions in ministries and enterprises, but also indicates how obligated and thus confined they have become, always careful about
what they say and do, whereas he feels he is basically free to do what he
wants.

The Sociological Review, 61:S1, pp. 109–123 (2013), DOI: 10.1111/1467-954X.12056
© 2013 The Authors. Editorial organisation © 2013 The Editorial Board of the Sociological Review

The heterogeneity of time: managing lives as projects

What do urban residents experience as the heterogeneity of time? Increasingly, the operations of developers, attempting to maximize ground rent through the large-scale production of uniform living space, convey a message of equal access for residents to a 'larger world'. As more residents situate themselves in large-scale apartment blocks, serviced by shopping complexes with their array of conventional retailers and a standardized menu of amenities, the idea is that whatever histories residents may bring to the superblock, the scale offered has the capacity to absorb these diversities. Absorption in this instance becomes a modality of neutralization rather than a capacity to use these histories as a resource in unfolding particular economies and residential practices.

In cities like Jakarta, this promise of detachment can be attractive to an emerging or aspirant middle class that realizes that flexibility in affiliation, taste and commitment is necessary for successful careers. As the residential offerings of the superblock are tailored for nucleated families, residence within them also serves as a way to mitigate having to respond to kinship obligations, even if in many instances improvised adjustments are made to house multiple generations. The residential infrastructure, along with the emphasis on religious renewal, lifestyle and regimens of constant training and re-skilling across many cities, reiterates the message that for the individual to be eligible for success they must attenuate parochial orientations, family obligations and preoccupation with narrowly drawn social and personal identities. Superblocks thus become forms of erasure; they are not so much marketed in terms of what they are in and of themselves, but what they permit – that is, physical and social mobility, convenience, personal autonomy, security, managerial authority and proximity to critical resources.

Many residents who choose superblock residence have grown up in highly dense and mixed districts where former practices and institutions of social solidarity are waning and where local economies are increasingly overcrowded, resulting in the expansion of insecurity and illicit livelihoods. While having neighbours with different backgrounds, capacities and schedules may avail households to various supports and inexpensive services, the maintenance of functional relations may entail more frequent and arduous negotiations. Demands are increasingly viewed as excessive. Parents worry more about ensuring a 'good' environment for raising children. As more economically successful households move out of these districts, pressures are compounded by introducing new, more 'footloose' residents. These residents usually reside temporarily in houses that have been converted into short-term rental accommodation – most often by owners who have relocated elsewhere – or by wealthier residents who buy up property so as to construct new homes or businesses. In each case there is an infusion of residents who are usually less interested in participating in local solidarity practices and are only interested in the specificities of the district as being close to work, as an opportunity to construct at a scale not possible elsewhere, or for speculation.

Nevertheless, there remain significant areas in cities like Jakarta where a profusion of heterogeneity persists. The form of this persistence is probably less identifiable through forms of economic cooperation or social solidarity and more in the contiguities of scores of 'material projects' – from the maintenance and repair of existing infrastructure to new construction that proceeds at various speeds and scales. Districts may have specific genealogies. For example, they may have ensued from state initiated projects to allocate land to civil servants from particular ministries or have become the domain of workers in a particular industry or sector. Economic or residential corridors may have developed along specific transportation routes, public land, or at the periphery of planned developments. These genealogies may account for how households gained access to basic residential opportunities but often do not tell us much about what households eventually did with this access.

As such, districts which were founded with a certain commonality of population base, land certification and economic development 20–40 years ago usually undergo marked internal differentiation. They become replete with stories of accumulation and loss, of expansion and contraction. These stories are embodied in the shape of land disposition and the built environment. Households beginning with similar platforms of residency have pursued different forms of calculating and concretizing opportunity. For example, investments may have been made in consolidating contiguous plots into facilities which combine residential and economic activities. In other instances, plots may have been subdivided to accommodate expanding family size or sold off with residential expansion developed along a vertical trajectory. Original pavilions may not have been altered since their construction, while neighbouring plots have 'witnessed' several projects, owners and occupiers come and go. Single streets are often the inventories of discordant values embedded in the very selection of materials used to sustain or remake built projects. The selection of roofing, tiling or frontage – such as ceramics, wood, tin, steel, cinder block, aluminium – not only reflect differences in affordability and assessment of environmental conditions, but also social status and commitment.

Some residents aim for a 'summation' of their residence – that is, they wait until they have the financial resources, certification and permits to realize their project all at 'one go'. Others may 'take their time', construct things in stages, aiming to instantiate 'facts on the ground' – that is, additions that aim to secure a *fait accompli* in terms of particular claims to land use or economic activity. They may not have yet secured permission to build or operate but select ways of 'going ahead' that convey the sense that erasing what has been done will be too complicated for everyone involved. Yet if eviction does happen, the particular materials used and ways of trying to 'implant' these facts will not incur a debilitating financial loss or loss of prestige. Still others may simply build slowly over time, adding some increments to a basic frame or multiplying the use of particular asset or space.

While Jakarta law specifies that no substantial changes can be implemented to a resident's plot without the permission of neighbours living on both sides, this is rarely enforceable or even taken seriously by anyone. Thus, household projects are highly individuated and uncoordinated. Conflicts and negotiations may come from excessive consumption of collective resources, such as water, power and sanitation. But again, these projects are rarely elaborated at a scale that would register substantial disjunction in the resources consumed. While neighbourhoods will be full of talk about who is doing what and comparing resident access to money and opportunity, the most 'accomplished' of projects – in terms of the size or money spent – will not necessarily stand out, either as the concretization of what is to be aspired to or as the exemplar of efficacy. What is important is the sheer diversity of time-lines, that it is possible for so many different kinds of projects of the built environment to exist in close proximity to each other and that this diversity has been generated by people who still manage to know each other, and provide each other the basic elements of space and solidarity.

Whereas participation in specific sectors of the local economy, such as printing, textiles, furniture, automobile parts and repair may be largely a matter of ethnic affiliation, and whereas each household network, neighbourhood or ethnic group may aim to make sure that they are involved in each facet making up a sector, the shape of individual built environment projects seems to break with such patterns. A given ethnic group may prefer a certain style or organization of space, but there are no lesser or greater diversities in these projects when ethnic affiliation is factored into consideration.

This is heterogeneity that goes beyond negotiation and planning. As it reflects the diversity of individual narratives – of work, networks, personal decisions, institutional belongings – it shows just how the city opens up a plurality of life trajectories and that this plurality need not be an impediment to co-inhabitation in densely populated spaces. This is not to say that in such districts there are no conflicts or structural dynamics that disentangle long-term relationships of collaboration and solidarity. It is clear across cities everywhere that the forms through which we have relied upon in the past to think about collaboration are probably no longer salient or available. Instead of viewing the plurality of projects – often seemingly hodge-podge, without adequate planning or regulation – as a deficiency in need of better coordination, it may be the very evidence of a deepening of possibilities for livelihood within given spatial parameters, as well as a basis to think through new forms of economic cooperation and scale. Efficiencies in service provisioning systems do require forms of harmonization, but too often the language or coding systems through which harmonization is recognized as operative require excessive homogenization of the visual landscape. There is often limited appreciation as well for the ways in which very different looking built projects manage to adjust themselves to the lines of basic standards.

The Sociological Review, 61:S1, pp. 109–123 (2013), DOI: 10.1111/1467-954X.12056

Weighing confidence and caution: or how to operate under the radar

If stories are a particular spatialization of ways in which people connect to each other, then what kind of stories buy people time to attain some level of confidence in what they are doing? When do particular stories come to dominate collective imaginations in ways that seem to foreclose the possibilities of people doing different things with each other, of 'taking charge' of their lives in new ways? Do certain stories come to the fore that attribute histories and capacities to particular actors which may be a functional abbreviation of complex events but also leave many things out? Are the capacities and events left out – seemingly marginalized by these stories – at a disadvantage in terms of what they are able to actually do by virtue of being left out? Or, for the 'time being', is such occlusion a beneficial tactical manoeuvre? In other words, does everything that happens in a locality – whether it is a neighbourhood, economic sector or network of institutions – attain a wider range of possibilities by being included in the stories that come to represent it?

In the locality of Bungur in the Senen district of central Jakarta, just down the road from Kampung Rawa, the accelerated growth of the printing industry during the last ten years has substantially changed the character of the area. It has enfolded former residential areas as extensions of commerce and drawn in local households to the lowest level of subcontracting. While artisanal printing has existed in this area for a long time, in part due to its proximity to one of the city's major transportation hubs, the extensive agglomeration of designers, lithographers, cutters, finishers, maquette producers, plate makers and digital operators is a more recent phenomenon. The consolidation of a district that encompasses all facets of the printing industry, as well as its ability to service almost any customized order in a short period of time – given the wide range of artisanal production centres that co-exist with larger scale, but more standardized operations – enables it to dominate the printing market across the country. This is also made possible by its ability to peg pricing to its management of a broad range of trans-shipment opportunities, so that quick turnarounds can be actualized through linkage of the district to various air freight services. Economic efficiency is evidenced in the fact that yearly growth of the sector in the district has tripled the previous year's expansion in each of the past five years.

Still, local officials and residents widely bemoan the loss of their district. Perhaps more importantly, they feel that there is little they can do to either secure some benefit from the industry or to engage it as a mechanism to pursue their own particular development agendas in Bungur. To a large extent these concerns are completely legitimate. There are few environmental controls to deal with increased volumes of toxic waste and local authorities have few jurisdictional powers to enforce specific regulations dealing with commercial and employment practices. Local opportunities are largely defined in terms of hiring residents to manage parking or to perform low end tasks such as page compilation or binding. Most of those who populate the sector are designated as having come from the outside; many artisans indeed apprenticed with firms that were once located elsewhere and the printing business has integrated those having relevant skills, which in most cases have not included local residents whose primary economic activities were in other sectors.

But the key story told over and over again about changes in the district centres on almost absolute dominance of the printing industry by Indonesians of Chinese descent. Ten Indo-Chinese firms are seen as controlling almost every aspect of the industry, to the extent that their supposed control of market access, information, and orders gives them the capability to define how the hundreds of differentially scaled workshops and factories in the district are articulated. So even though the vast majority of actual producers may come from a broad range of Indonesian ethnic backgrounds, the ways in which they are connected along a series of forward and backward linkages – in terms of who gets orders in terms of volume, specialization and frequency – is represented as the purview of these ten firms.

It is true that the capital investments entailed in the technology of preparing photographic plates are usually only available to Chinese entrepreneurs, and thus their concomitant ability to control this essential aspect of the industry automatically propels them into a commanding position. This is often translated into an ability to function as the key intermediaries steering the sequence of the production process through artisans specializing in one or more aspects of it.

Still, anyone, no matter how big or small along the chain of the production process can serve as an intermediary. You can take a job to the smallest of artisans with the guarantee that he or she will steer the job through the system. Though it may be infrequent, each artisan maintains his or her own relationships across a wide network of others; they know what each is capable of doing; they know that they have considerable latitude in negotiating a final price or in delivering reciprocal favours so as to broaden their access to a potential market. While they may largely depend upon the capabilities of the Chinese firms to secure a steady market share for themselves, this does not foreclose their own abilities to map out and negotiate their own 'pathways' through the production process. Unlike the Chinese firms with their large sunk costs and their tendencies to transfer significant profit shares to larger ethnic-based entrepreneurial groupings, these artisans are not obligated to act as intermediaries and rather sometimes use the position as a means of 'experimenting' with different ways of articulating themselves to other actors in the printing sector.

While local residents rather than artisans are usually the ones responsible for the attributions of Chinese dominance, small artisans have little interest in making visible any countervailing evidence. While they may not doubt their potential ability to pool resources and organize to circumvent the power of the Chinese – as reflected in their control of essential yet expensive machinery – they also know that the risks incumbent in such a move are too great. The willingness to accede to these popular stories about the Chinese can thus act as a screen, not only to project the concerns and worries of a community in transition, but also as a means to be off the radar screen. In other words, they have the space to

The Sociological Review, 61:S1, pp. 109–123 (2013), DOI: 10.1111/1467-954X.12056
© 2013 The Authors. Editorial organisation © 2013 The Editorial Board of the Sociological Review

experiment as intermediaries in a highly competitive business where success at the top requires the ability to include a broad range of small artisan producers within a company's orbit and to find ways of setting them against each other so as to keep costs as low as possible.

When small artisans offer to play as intermediaries they usually have a different motivation in mind: to explore relationships that can find their own pace, that need not be reproduced time and time again as a means of protecting a high risk investment, and that potentially can lead to other things having little to do with the printing business per se and its schedules and exigencies. These efforts are not to be construed as a business challenge or a means of consolidating greater sectoral control. This is why the majority of such artisans tend to leave the Chinese alone and let them play the part of some essential overseer.

What is troubling in the use of this story line, however, is the apparent inability of the local residential community to 'see through it'; to see a way of getting through this story in order to take some greater advantage of the presence of this growing economic sector. Too often they seem to absolve their responsibility by turning themselves into victims. But given the dissatisfaction that many residents had in the character of their conditions separate from the growth of the printing business, even this performance of being victim may, as one *imam* at a local mosque told me, function as a kind of a ruse. According to him, community residents have been looking for ways out of the community for some time but were reluctant to make final decisions given the way in which land values were rising and felt that they should hold on a little longer. But with this story line of Chinese dominance and their own inability to do anything about it, residents can disentangle themselves from this dilemma, feel free to finally decide to leave, and with the increasing demands for commercial space, can sell and move on.

Conclusion: anticipating the common

Given the uncertainties and frequent hardships of city life, residents can be risk adverse and sometimes lack confidence in their abilities to create new opportunities. Sometimes it can seem as if entire districts are basically pursuing the same limited strategies of accumulation. Still, livelihood remains largely contingent upon a politics of anticipation – of not only canvassing the actual initiatives of others, but sensing what could have been done, what could have taken place. It isn't that what doesn't occur is necessarily ruled out, blocked or neglected, but is rather suggested, made possible by virtue of not having been decided, of being almost left to others. Anticipation may then 'traffic' in ways of doing things that may go unnoticed, provide cover for others, or provoke a wide range of varied responses. All of this buys time for residents trying on different initiatives for 'size', without having to make definitive commitments or to find ways to fit them into whatever is established.

Anticipation is not directed to a final known outcome or a specific objective, but rather a way of applying whatever is attained at a given moment to a set of different possibilities. Rather than working to coordinate a series of clear objectives and capacities, the practices of inhabitation in central Jakarta continue to emphasize the cultivation of ways of building, living, making money, calculating and deciding that do not necessarily fit well together or make explicit reference to each other. Nevertheless, they provide evidence of a certain efficacy for highly individuated practices of urban living. Thus the commonality of residents is not so much located in negotiated mutual understandings but in the stretching of the parameters of what can count as viable without having to assign any particular course of action with a counted value. New residents, money and ideas are pouring into these districts, just as long-term residents adamantly find ways to reiterate a sense of continuity. Time is then something that happens in between registration, between the count – that is, in between different trajectories of change and continuity, different experimentations and cautions, and where each singular path expands that which can be taken as common.

References

Badiou, A., (2006), *Theoretical Writings*, London: Continuum.
Bayat, A., (2009), *Life as Politics: How Ordinary People Change in the Middle East*, Stanford, CA: Stanford University Press.
Benjamin, S., (2008), 'Occupancy urbanism: radicalizing politics and economy beyond policy and programs', *International Journal of Urban and Regional Research*, 32: 719–729.
Boonyabancha, S., (2009), 'Land for housing the poor – by the poor: experiences from the Baan Mankong Network Slum Upgrading Project in Thailand', *Environment and Urbanization*, 21: 309–322.
Boudreau, J.-A., (2007), 'Making new political spaces: mobilizing spatial imaginaries, instrumentalizing spatial practices, and strategically using spatial tools', *Environment and Planning A*, 39: 2593–2611.
Chatterjee, P., (2004), *The Politics of the Governed: Popular Politics in Most of the World*, New York: Columbia University Press.
Deleuze, G., (1986), *Nietzsche and Philosophy*, New York: Columbia University Press.
Eckstein, S., (2000), 'Poor people versus the state: anatomy of a successful mobilization for housing in Mexico City', in S. Eckstein (ed.), *Power and Popular Protest: Latin American Social Movements*, 329–351, Berkeley, CA: University of California Press.
Elden, S., (2010), 'Land, terrain, territory', *Progress in Human Geography*, doi: 10.177/0309132510362603.
Elyachar, J., (2005), *Markets of Dispossession: NGOs, Economic Development and the State in Cairo*, Durham, NC and London: Duke University Press.
Fawaz, M., (2008), 'An unusual clique of city-makers: social networks in the production of a neighborhood in Beirut', *International Journal of Urban and Regional Research*, 32: 565–585.
Gandy, M., (2006), 'Zones of indistinction: biopolitical contestations in the urban arena', *Cultural Geographies*, 13: 497–516.
Goldstein, D., (2004), *The Spectacular City: Violence and Performance in Urban Bolivia*, Durham, NC and London: Duke University Press.
Haber, P., (2006), *Power from Experience: Urban Popular Movements in Late Twentieth-century Mexico*, University Park, PA: Penn State Press.

The Sociological Review, 61:S1, pp. 109–122 (2013), DOI: 10.1111/1467-954X.12056

Holston, J., (2008), *Insurgent Citizenship: Disjunctions of Democracy and Modernity in Brazil*, Princeton, NJ: Princeton University Press.

Konings, P., van Dijk, R. and Foeken, D., (2006), 'The African neighborhood: an introduction', in P. Konings and D. Foeken (eds), *Crisis and Creativity: Exploring the Wealth of the African Neighborhood*, Leiden: Brill.

Latham, A. and McCormack, D., (2004), 'Moving cities: rethinking the materialities of urban geographies', *Progress in Human Geography*, 28: 701–724.

Lindell, I., (2010), 'Informality and collective organizing: identities, alliances and transnational activism in Africa', *Third World Quarterly*, 31: 207–222.

McFarlane, C., (2009), 'Translocal assemblages: space, power and social movements', *Geoforum*, 40: 461–467.

Meillassoux, Q., (2007), 'Subtraction and contraction: Deleuze, immanence, and matter and memory', *Collapse III*: 63–107.

Terranova, T., (2004), *Network Cultures: Politics for the Information Age*, London: Pluto.

Thrift, N., (2005), 'But malice aforethought: cities and the natural history of hatred', *Transactions of the Institute of British Geographers*, 30: 133–150.

Walton, J., (1998), 'Urban conflict and social movements in poor countries: theory and evidence of collective action', *International Journal of Urban and Regional Research*, 22: 460–481.

From momentary to historic: rhythms in the social production of urban space, the case of Calçada de Sant'Ana, Lisbon

Panu Lehtovuori and Hille Koskela

Abstract: This paper presents a study of one street, Calçada de Sant'Ana in Lisbon, Portugal. In 2007, the authors lived on that street for a month. The stay facilitated observations that together help to understand how the social and the spatial are woven together, and how seemingly very different processes, time-scales and types of actor, such as momentary human encounters and slow decay of buildings, produce a specific socio-spatial continuum, a 'street-phenomenon'. Calçada de Sant'Ana can be characterized as a collective work, an *oeuvre*. Inspired by Henri Lefebvre's notion of rhythmanalysis, the paper explores how form, use and meaning are co-constitutive. Building on Doreen Massey's notion of urban places as specific articulations of both local and global, Gernot Böhme's idea that urban atmospheres concern the style and manner of the unfolding urban life, and Walter Benjamin's discussion of the porosity of space, we explore in detail a variety of moments in the social production of urban space. The study shows that an attention to urban rhythms provides important new insights in the analysis of public urban space. Calçada de Sant'Ana turns out to be a very positive example of open and inclusive contemporary public space, providing a counter-example to the dominant discourse of 'erosion' of its public character. Aspects of the case might be generalized as new tools of analysis and activism to create differential urban spaces elsewhere.

Keywords: public space, rhythmicity, inclusivity, *oeuvre*, encounter

Introduction

Within architectural theory and discourse, we can identify three main approaches to the analysis of urban space and processes: diachronic, synchronic and experiential. Diachronic analyses are historical, focusing on change and the evolution of urban form and its constituents. Typomorphology (Moudon, 1994; Rossi, 1982) is one important example of a diachronic approach. Synchronic analyses focus on the present situation, studying the qualities, performance and effects of spatial configuration across scales; a well-known example of such an approach being Space Syntax (see Hillier and Hanson, 1984; Hillier, 1996).

The Sociological Review, 61:S1, pp. 124–143 (2013), DOI: 10.1111/1467-954X.12057
© 2013 The Authors. Editorial organisation © 2013 The Editorial Board of the Sociological Review. Published by John Wiley & Sons Ltd, 9600 Garsington Road, Oxford OX4 2DQ, UK and 350 Main Street, Malden, MA 02148, USA

Experiential analyses explore the non-quantifiable and relational aspects of urban space focusing, for example, on users' preferences, feelings or affects. The experiential approach is, for example, currently exemplified by the study of urban atmospheres (Böhme, 1998, 2001). While the basic analytic categories of form, use and meaning are usually all present in architectural analyses of urban space, their relations are theorized in a variety of ways. The 'triad' of form, use and meaning has close resemblance to the 'instances' of social production of space as discussed by Henri Lefebvre in the opening chapter of *The Production of Space*. Schmid (2005) traces the origins of Lefebvre's concepts to the early 20th-century phenomenology and linguistics. The notion of 'the dialectic of space' is Lefebvre's genial proposal to create a dynamic relation between the conceived, perceived and lived instances in the production of space. Dialectics of space unearths the political significance of *urban* space, characterized by its centrality and understood as a site of resistance and creation of new urban life forms.

In this paper we focus on one case, that of Calçada de Sant'Ana in Lisbon, Portugal (Figure 1). We will explore, first, how form, use and meaning are co-constitutive (Massey, 2005) in producing a specific urban entity; secondly, we consider how the social organization of this setting has produced a very positive contemporary public urban space, unquestionably inclusive and with open parameters of the 'right to the city' (Lefebvre, 1991; Mitchell, 2003); and, thirdly, we make an argument for the way in which aspects of the case might be generalized as new tools of analysis and activism in creating inclusive and differential urban spaces elsewhere.

To choose a fairly unknown street as our case study is justified, first, by its positioning as a powerful counter-example to the dominant discourse on the erosion of public urban space. Calçada de Sant'Ana in Lisbon's inner city strikingly lacks the all-too-well-known signs of fear, control, commercialization and corporate power. It is a *different* contemporary space – even in the context of Lisbon. This difference raised our curiosity: there is something to learn and something to tell which is not limited to the geographic or climatic characteristics of the case. The case is justified, secondly, by its methodological links to a number of earlier detailed and specific studies on streets or neighbourhoods. We would like to mention Walter Benjamin's and Asja Lacis' work on Naples (1979 [1924]), Jane Jacobs' work on Greenwich Village (1961) and Edward Soja's work on Amsterdam city centre (1996). We are fully aware that at the moment of analysis, each of these places did belong to a set of larger systems or 'networks'. But, still, a creative focus on one place or one 'locality' did provide useful and interesting insights. We hope that the following pages show that this approach is still possible in this decade, in spite of intensified non-local connectivity and the technological mediation of experience. To show that focusing on one, seemingly small, case is not nostalgic or limiting, but rather forward-looking and inclusive, is one of our aims in this paper.

Our interest in rhythms as a tool of analysis is not external or theory-based. Rather, rhythms offered themselves as the first and most inviting access point

Figure 1

from which to start to observe, and make sense of, Calçada de Sant'Ana and its life. Despite the rather extensive academic work on production of space, both the *malleability* of urban space and its (relative) *stability* are still poorly theorized. Through our work on Calçada de Sant'Ana, we realized that an attention to urban rhythms provides important new insights into the social organization and production of space in general and, in particular, the analysis of public urban space.

The idea of rhythmanalysis in Lefebvre's late work can be seen as a direct continuation of his project to think spatiality and temporality together. Not to

The Sociological Review, 61:S1, pp. 124–143 (2013), DOI: 10.1111/1467-954X.12057

claim superiority for either of the two is a recurring methodological theme in the *Critique of Everyday Life, The Production of Space* and other texts (Lefebvre, 1991; Gottdiener, 1993, 1994; Elden, 2004). While Lefebvre does provide a general conceptual framework with which to grasp these dimensions, the empirical grounding of the discussion remains less than adequate; the ways in which small and mundane everyday acts simultaneously sustain urban space and are the 'site' of its change remains poorly developed. In this article, we wish to show the power of rhythms in exploring the two-way productive relations between people and space and in unearthing a dynamic co-constitution of elements that come together, juxtaposing themselves in urban space. Rhythms are not only 'movements and differences in repetition, as the interweaving of concrete times', but always also imply 'a relationship of time to space and place' (Nielsen and Simonsen, 2003: 917). In this theoretical frame, space is seen as a 'concrete abstraction' (Stanek, 2008), as a mental thing underpinned by real and material social practices. In the following pages we aim to demonstrate how rhythmanalysis opens new insights to social production of urban space and city understood as a collective and creative work, an *oeuvre* (Lefebvre, 1991).

1. Form, use and meaning

The butcher's cleaver

Calçada de Sant'Ana is a narrow, winding street, climbing uphill from the corner of Lisbon's main square Rossio (Praça dom Pedro IV). In 2007 our family – two adults, our twelve-year-old boy, and a puppy poodle – lived there for a month. Adjusting to the place, wondering where we actually were, and how to understand the place, we suddenly had a striking experience. One morning we woke to a repetitive sound: 'thup-thup-thup'. Realizing that it was the cleaver of the butcher a few buildings down the street, we started to listen. Soon we became immersed in that and other sounds, each with their own rhythm. Children, cars, neighbours in the hallway, birds on balconies, and again: animal bodies cut, 'thup-thup-thup' . . . Half-sleeping, half-awake, we were *grasped* by the rhythms of the street – our street – and became first curious, then intensely interested in it, in them.

At first sight, Calçada de Sant'Ana has many characteristic, even cliché, signs of a south European urban space: colourful buildings, laundry hanging over the street, old men chatting in bars, Catholic nuns on Sundays and, indeed, open butcher's shops. But very quickly we realized that in its ordinariness the street was unique. While it felt different from our previous urban experience and of our conventional academic understanding of 'contemporary cities', it was also different from most other streets in Lisbon's older neighbourhoods. Calçada de Sant'Ana seemed to have its own rhythm and logic. The street had a power, its own radiance, but at the same time was open and inviting. Even though we were outsiders or 'guests', we felt very strongly that we *partook in the production* of Calçada de Sant'Ana (Lehtovuori, 2008).

The butcher's cleaver awoke us to thinking of how rhythmanalysis, inspired by Lefebvre, might help us to understand the characteristics of the street and its public life. We wanted to make sense of this specific place. As Simpson (2008: 813) has argued, '[w]hilst many have called for or suggested the usefulness of rhythmanalysis in examining "the city", little work has appeared in print which engages in detail in actual, specific, everyday practices and performances in these cities through the lens of the Rhythmanalyst'. According to Cresswell (2010: 24), 'Lefebvre delineates how rhythms, such as those visible on any city square, are simultaneously organic, lived, and endogenous and exterior, imposed and mechanical. Frequently the exterior rhythm of rationalized time and space comes into contradiction with lived and embodied rhythm.' Specific places within cities can be 'perceived as temporally distinct' being 'characterized by a particular sense of flow and a soundscape' (Wunderlich, 2010: 45). In this spirit, we endeavoured to grasp the everyday rhythms and soundscapes which made Calçada de Sant'Ana so unique. We saw rhythmanalysis, following Edensor (2010: 2), as 'a useful tool with which to explore the everyday temporal structures and processes that (re)produce connections between the individual and the social'. Rhythms, as being 'a part of any social order or historical period' (Cresswell, 2010: 24), would further help to grasp the historicity of the momentary and local experience in Calçada de Sant'Ana.

An initial spatio-temporal analysis

As Edensor (2010: 1) points out, 'rhythmanalysis is particularly useful in investigating the patterning of a range of multiscalar temporalities – calendrical, diurnal and lunar, lifecycle, somatic and mechanical – whose rhythms provide an important constituent of the experience and organization of social time'. The body is the 'site' of rhythmanalysis, the starting point. Meyer (2008: 149) discusses the role of the body as 'metronome', a link between internal and external rhythms:

> The Rhythmanalyst is all ears. He listens not only to words, however, but to everything happening in the world. He hears things that are usually hardly noticed: noise and sound. He pays attention to the babble of voices, but also to silence. . . . His role as observer is that of one lost in thought. He is always listening to his body, to whatever it communicates to him. It is only then that he perceives rhythms coming from outside. The body is, so to speak, his metronome.

Lefebvre's word for the role of body is 'measure' [*mesure*], which, in French, has double meaning as 'meter' and 'moderation'. Bodily rhythms, such as hunger, sexual desire, sleep and awakening, menstruation, mid-winter depression and joy of spring, are cyclical and concrete. They provide an alternative 'measure' for the linear, repetitive rhythms of paid and regulated work and urban mobility. As Nielsen and Simonsen (2003: 918) note, '[t]he distinction

The Sociological Review, 61:S1, pp. 124–143 (2013), DOI: 10.1111/1467-954X.12057

and interaction between the cyclical and the linear manifests itself both in the body and in the city; both combine the cycle of day and night, need and desire with the linearity of gestures and manipulation of things – a measured, imposed and exterior time'. In Calçada de Sant'Ana, the cyclical rhythms were strong, if not dominant. Human gestures and voices, the cycle of morning, day, evening and night, as well as weekly and annual cycles characterized the experience of the street, while linear or repetitive rhythms remained in the background.

Calçada de Sant'Ana

Climbing uphill, Calçada de Sant'Ana has three distinct parts. Closest to Rossio, the street is very narrow. The hill is steep, and the street makes sharp turns, meandering uphill and branching to even smaller side-streets and urban stairs. After the labyrinthine first section, there is a straight but still rather steep section with one crossing, ending in a gentle turn to the left and another crossing. This is clearly the 'centre' of the street and the small neighbourhood defined by it: most shops, bars and restaurants are located in this central section. After the gentle turn, the street widens so that some cars can also park next to the one-way drive-lane. The top of the hill is closer, there is more light, and gradually some views start to open along the street to the sea and sideways to the neighbouring hills. Larger single concerns, such as Inatel, a public insurance and welfare agency,[1] an apartment-hotel and the local church, characterize the upper section. Life in the upper section becomes calmer and quieter. Also the socio-economic composition changes markedly: the lower part has a strong presence of immigrants, while the upper part is richer and more white in composition. Overall, the scale is very small: the width of the urban microcosm of Calçada de Sant'Ana varies between four and eight metres and its total length is less than half a kilometre.

In the upper part of the central section of the street, there is a place of specific interest. Exactly where the steep hill ends, turning to a gentler slope, there is a butcher's shop on the left side of the street. The butcher, a very talkative and social man, takes full opportunity of the moment when passers-by, and especially the elderly, are exhausted from climbing the hill and need a rest (the body, here, as a 'measure' of height and distance) exactly at this point. Standing in the doorway, the butcher waits for the clients, ready to start discussion. One after another, residents of the street stop there to exchange news and rumours, or just small talk, making the butcher's shop a real public exchange point. Between conversations, and often mixed with them, the butcher's cleaver makes its 'thup-thup-thup', following an organic, age-old dual rhythm of cutting meat and participation in street-sociality.

Gradually, encounters, observations, surprising findings and quiet reflections made us grasp concretely how the social and the spatial are woven together – how the performance of Calçada de Sant'Ana is structured. New perspectives and contacts were created by our child. Having a dog with us, gave further impulses. We learned how gestures, chance meetings, parties, rituals or the treatment of the homeless at night, as well as physical decay, vegetation, graffiti, Portugal's flags, canary birds on balconies, drying laundry or the rebuilding of a façade, all interactively produced this unique street, this unique socio-spatial continuum.

Atmosphere

The concept of *atmosphere* might help to analyse the street further. Gernot Böhme has developed atmosphere as a concept in aesthetics. For him, atmospheres do not exist outside (individual) perception but, nevertheless, are not subjective either. Atmospheres are '[s]omething *between* subject and object. They are not something relational, but the relation itself' (Böhme, 2001: 54). This linkage helps to conceptualize public spaces so that the users of the street partake in its production. Atmospheres are spatial and to an extent material, but they cannot be pinned down to positionable places (Schmitz, 1969; Isohanni, 2006). Twilight is an illustrative example: one perceives 'through' atmosphere, but it also has some objectual materiality as a 'half-thing' (Böhme, 1998: 19; 2001: 61–63). When discussing urban places, Böhme (1998: 53–55) proposes that the atmosphere of a city concerns the style and manner of its unfolding urban life.[2] Atmosphere is not primarily a question of built forms, colours or light, for example, but of citizens' activities and presence. *Atmosphere has to be lived* (Lehtovuori, 2012: 82).

Clearly, in Calçada de Sant'Ana the changing atmospheres of the street from the dense and labyrinthine lower section, to the calm and serene upper part were the experienced result of the mutual socio-spatial process, and thus rhythmic, not just a visual impression of the historico-architectural frame (Figure 2). Birds in their cages were brought out to the balcony in the morning and back inside at dusk. Colours were strong and distinguished, from the annual orange season to the weekly rhythm of different trash bags populating the street – one day black for bio-waste, one day yellow for plastic and metal, one day blue for paper – and to the ever-changing patterns of sunlight on buildings and ornaments. Plants in abandoned balconies and on rooftops of empty buildings were having their own vegetative life in the moist Atlantic air.

Semiotic balconies and doorways

> In order to *grasp* this fleeting object . . . it is necessary to situate oneself simultaneously inside and outside. A balcony does the job admirably, in relation to the street, and it is to this putting into perspective (of the street) that we owe the marvellous invention of balconies. (Lefebvre, 2004 [1992]: 27–28)

Calçada de Sant'Ana is an expressive or semiotic space. Windows, balconies, entrances and doorways are all used to make a mark, sometimes individual but often collective or communal. French balconies open the apartments – homes –

Figure 2

to the street. Portuguese flags are hung on many balconies, colouring the scene in red and green. Many residents of the street clearly share a national sentiment and pride, not least because of football. As we have argued above, the street is unique and 'local', but it would be a mistake to omit the contribution of non-local elements or *materiél* in its production. As Edensor (2006: 537) convincingly argues, 'local rhythms are often coordinated and synchronized with national rhythms, local customs are incorporated into the national cultural mosaic'. The habit of resting during the hottest hours of the day with family or friends is the prime example of such 'national synchronicities' or 'the time-space of national identity'. In the intimate microcosm of Calçada de Sant'Ana, this rest, resembling the Spanish siesta, is a very clear, visible and audible break in the active babble and hum of the street. Assistants, cooks and clerks, all the different people in different positions, partake in a process where '[t]he rhythmic structuring of the day is not merely individual but collective, and relies upon a synchronization of practices that become part of how "we" get things done' (Edensor, 2010: 8). Through their spatial practice they produce a national rhythm, 'a thick spatial intertextuality that stitches the local and national together' (Edensor, 2006: 537).

Besides flags in balconies, there is advertising and print media in many doorways, visible on the street. A stationer's pushes a selection of magazines and newspapers to its windows and to a stall on the sidewalk; a media or computer company has opened a tiny outlet, decorated with humorously space-age graphics; or the restaurants putting out their daily menus on small blackboards, adorned with a tiny colourful sunshade. Even though global brands are not visible, the street is connected and networked, opening to many non-local influences. But these influences unfold in a unique way. As Massey (2005: 183) puts it, '[o]ver and again, the counter-position of local and global resonates with an equation of the local with realness, with local place as earthly and meaningful, standing in opposition to a presumed abstraction of global space'.

Balconies and doorways are important places / moments in the social production of space in Calçada de Sant'Ana. Simmel famously discusses the bridge and the door as 'archetypal artefacts that concretize an essentially human act, the act to separate and connect simultaneously' (Stavrides, 2007: 175; Simmel, 1997). 'The doorway', as Stevens (2007a: 81) points out, 'frames a dialectical transition between the personal and the social'. 'Within the *threshold*, people are able to strike an acceptable balance between exposure to the unfamiliar and relative seclusion and safety' (Stevens, 2007a: 85, italics added). People in doorways include butchers, waiters, barmen, loiterers, as well as other public figures on balconies, on the vertical façade of the street. The built environment type (Moudon, 1994) common in Lisbon's old neighbourhoods – intimate street, small lots leading to many doorways as well as the outward oriented buildings with small rooms and many balconies – is simultaneously the condition and product of the thresholds and their meaning. Here the potential is rehearsed: 'At the moment when people cross thresholds between private and public space, they often make the most of the experiences which are possible there' (Stevens, 2007a: 81). During our study, we witnessed countless social scenarios, where the threshold was crossed, someone from a bar or shop joining discussions or games in the street.

2. Right to the city

Football on the street

Calçada de Sant'Ana is a 'shared space' *par excellence*. There are sidewalks, even though very narrow, but people use the whole street independent of them. One of the sharp curves at the lower part of the street is often taken over by a game of football: children, teenagers and men are immersed in the game. Sometimes the ball escapes to the side-streets or jumps to the doorsteps of a bar, causing action and giving cause for jokes and laughter. Passers-by cannot avoid becoming part of the game. As Stevens (2007a: 87) observes, this is an urban game situation where '[t]he barrier between watching and playing is highly permeable'. If a car or a delivery van drives down the street, the players sidestep, but return immediately. People walk on the drive-lane, during lunch-time construction workers sit on the kerbstones, while the homeless hang around, play with their dog or chat with bar-owners and passers-by.

In the crossing with the occasional football game, all the spatial underpinnings of playful behaviour – paths, intersections, boundaries, thresholds and props (Stevens, 2007b) – seem to come together. The game, its occasional cuts either by car passing by or the ball being temporarily lost, and the breathless shouts of boys and young men define another rather complex spatio-temporal rhythm. Nielsen and Simonsen (2003: 917–918) explain Lefebvre's distinction between 'rhythms of the self' and 'rhythms of the other': 'Rhythms of the self are deeply inscribed rhythms, performed by bodies themselves shaped in the conjunction of the two [self and other] and organizing a spatial temporality oriented towards private and intimate life, while rhythms of the other are rhythms turned outward towards and connecting in public life'. In our view, football on the street combines both.

Furthermore, the above-discussed semiotic elements, such as flags, posters and press, are an important part in the production of lively and open space. They are 'easily arranged and rearranged' so that they 'create visually complex and culturally specific streetscapes' and 'readily convey the cultural meanings associated with the specific uses' (Fernando, 2007: 69) Semiotic elements are additional 'props' for the multiplicity of uses, adding to the vitality and inviting quality of the street (Fernando, 2007: 71).

Walking

From the quick street-games of the teenagers to the slow ambulation of the elderly, from the wanderings of the tourists to the near-static stepping of waiters and shopkeepers at their doorsteps, the street encompasses a wide variety of walking practices. De Certeau (1984) has pointed to the power of individual users of public urban space in creating experiential and meaningful space through use, through walking. While hosting as many walking practices as almost any other street, Calçada de Sant'Ana's might be somewhat special in its ability to distinguish and stage each practice in a clear way. Students, tourists, nuns, night-hawks and early morning street-cleaners: all have their space and time. Discussing the links between time and place, Nielsen and Simonsen (2003: 919) state that 'walking practices cannot be seen only as simple movements in space, they spatialize' and 'weave places (and scales) together'. Wunderlich (2008: 134), furthermore, creates a link from the variety of walking practices to our perception of time, saying '[w]alking practices, with their pace and rhythm, together with the temporal character of places imposed by their place-rhythms, influence our perception of time, in terms of its experience and representation'. Indeed, Calçada de Sant'Ana had a strong presence of its own time, or place-rhythm.

Stavrides (2010: 25) sees that '[r]hythm seems to be a promising concept in an effort to connect a theory of practice as meaningful performance with the experience of time and space'. The polyrhythmia, or a certain distinctiveness of the different walking practices, is thus linked to their meaning and, collectively, to the performance of the street space as shared and open public urban space.

Public underwear

Calçada de Sant'Ana is a 'porous' space in the same sense Benjamin and Lacis (1979) describe Naples in their famous 1920s *Denkbild*. Laundry hanging over the street provides an illustrative example. In a few days people around us learned in which flat we were staying and, thus, what kind of underwear our family wears. Such blurring of private and public would be unimaginable in northern Europe, but in Calçada de Sant'Ana it was commonplace. This common practice, the rhythm of washing, drying and wearing clothes, coloured the street community. It gave a twist to sexualities, desires and identities. People on the street were seen and sensed in a different way, creating different kinds of social ties. It was about intimacy without blaming, about mutual care, which was warm and close to you, but still didn't break the civilized publicity of the street (Sennett, 1977). As Lefebvre sees no binary opposition between the private and the public, this separation 'is broken down with a starting point in the body and its senses, reaching out to the bustling world and linking the two' (Nielsen and Simonsen, 2003: 918).

Thresholds between public and private are also about change. Stepping in and stepping out always opens an opportunity to encounter something new. Imagine the most mundane visit to the shop of the talkative butcher: you may hear news that will change your day. 'Thresholds create or symbolically represent passages towards a possible future, already existing in the past' (Stavrides, 2007: 177). Indeed, 'both rhythm and exception are not only the means to establish a dominant spatial order but also forms through which spatialities of resistance are created ... a possible ground of encounter with otherness' (Stavrides, 2010: 19).

From a methodological point of view, our time in Calçada de Sant'Ana raises justified questions. The facts that we entered the street by chance (an empty flat found through the Internet) and lived there for a short period (almost as tourists) seems to suggest a weak position to conduct analysis; at best a fleeting and superficial outsider's view. Simultaneously, the production involved us. We were at a threshold, in an open situation of a two-way dynamic between people and space that our un-familiarity to the place made possible to study.

In *Attempt at the Rhythmanalysis of Mediterranean Cities*, Lefebvre and Régulier (2004: 88) discuss the position of the Rhythmanalyst: '[e]xternality is necessary; and yet in order to grasp a rhythm one must have been grasped by it, have given or abandoned oneself "inwardly" to the time that it rhythmed'. There might be a deep methodological point at hand here. If we understand correctly, Lefebvre and Régulier are saying that if you (as someone on the street) are fully immersed in your everyday routine, you are not able to analyse. But likewise, if you (as scientist) are too far in abstractions, you are not able to analyse, either.

A third position is needed. It might not be a coincidence that Benjamin and Lacis' classic rhythmanalysis of a Mediterranean city is a travel story. Their above-mentioned *Denkbild*, or impression, focuses on the 'porosity' and 'porous architecture' of Naples. They show the power of the ephemeral observer, someone who is capable of throwing oneself into urban life, grasping and being grasped, while remaining an outsider, a visitor, a guest. From this flickering vantage point, from a 'weak place' of re-thinking and re-imagining (Lehtovuori, 2000), something new could be said and written.

Tolerant and inclusive space

The clear positive qualities of Calçada de Sant'Ana seem to complement or counter the recent Anglo-American reasoning on urban change dominated by 'a notion of the crowd as a dangerous entity pregnant with collective hostility and loss of control' (Wilson, 1997: 134). In this reasoning, dominant discussions have focused the ways in which urban space is controlled and regulated, fortressed, and divided into privatized guarded zones and neglected areas. Public security, order and protection have become central issues, leading to the diffusion of insecurity, fear and phobia as influencing the use of space. In the name of fear, urban space is increasingly becoming a means of *exclusion* rather than supporting diversity and the positive notion of urbanity (Koskela, 2010). Unwanted behaviour is excluded, not tolerated; social integration and solidarity are replaced by segregation and zero tolerance. Bauman (2006: 130) talks about 'security obsession', referring to close connections between fear as an individual experience and fear as a transformation of political and normative dynamics within the socio-spatial order.

In Calçada de Sant'Ana, we could see and hear around us something very different: a compellingly positive exemplar of contemporary public urban space (Figure 3). We could hear, see and experience something which seemed to support diversity and positive urbanity, but not much that would allude to exclusion or obsession. In Calçada de Sant'Ana, discussions about insecurity were turned into discussions about a 'right to urban space' (Mitchell, 2003; cf. Lefebvre 1996), which seemed unquestionable. The street was tolerant and inclusive. Why?

The street is very short and we learned to know it house by house. Despite its intimate scale the street crystallized all signs of difference, discussed recently in the social sciences. Differences in gender, age, colour, sexual orientation and, to an extent, religion were visible and tolerated. Also the 'old-fashioned', but in the end, and possibly most importantly, class-difference was present in an amazing spectrum of professions and public roles. The intimate urban space of Calçada de Sant'Ana has several 'public figures' (Jacobs, 1961), people with a special role in the urban community. More 'eyes on the street' (Jacobs, 1961) are provided by people spending time on their balconies and sometimes at their windows, watching and listening to the unfolding everyday drama of the street.

Figure 3

The visible public figures led us to list all professions on the street. In a rough order of visibility, the street hosted shopkeepers (butcher, stationer, grocer, jeweller, etc.), bar owners, bartenders, waiters, sellers, barbers, shop assistants, printers, construction workers, the homeless, dustmen and trash collectors (many types), street sweepers, cooks of the institutional kitchen and drivers of *vehiculo electric* bringing supplies to the kitchen, clerks of the insurance company Inatel in their suits, office workers, taxi drivers, students of medicine, nuns, school children, doctors, priests, cantors, tourists, hipsters, a transient peddler, musicians (auditory observation), artists and even a Santa Claus (a plastic representation). The street as a socio-spatial phenomenon was formed by habits and traditions but also by differences, meetings and constant communication. The street was shared, and its uniqueness was built exactly on that sharing.

After some days of acquainting ourselves with the street, we realized the complete lack of formal and technical surveillance, such as police patrols, private guards, surveillance cameras, burglar alarms or door stickers of security patrols. There were no posters either claiming something as 'forbidden', asking people to take care of their property (wallets, cars etc.), or requesting the public to inform the authorities if they see something suspicious (unattended objects, dubious behaviour and so on). Also many other all-too-familiar elements of

The Sociological Review, 61:S1, pp. 124–143 (2013), DOI: 10.1111/1467-954X.12057

fortified and commercialized public urban space were non-existent. There were, for example, no big commercial units, no supermarkets, chain stores nor known brands.

Human keynote

When listening to the street, grasping its rhythms, we realized further two 'no's': there was no silence – but also *no noise*. Studying urban soundscapes, Schafer (1977) distinguishes three types of sound: the keynote, sound signals and soundmarks. The realization that there was no noise in Calçada de Sant'Ana, led us to think of the street in Schafer's terms. The keynote, the background against which other sounds are perceived, was a combination of human voices, canary birds and wind, a quiet and beautiful sound with its own rhythms and changes. Sound signals were always 'transparent': be it a loud car finding a parking space, a shout in the next corner, or the church bell, the source was understandable and easy to locate. Soundmarks, unique and a-typical sounds that characterize a community or place, might have not existed at all, underlining the everyday character of the street. It was unique in its ordinariness.

If the 'no list' was illustrative, the complementing 'yes list' became too long to be meaningful. Nevertheless, a certain bohemian character and indifference was very strong: dripping pipes, peeling paint, fallen mortar and political graffiti, related to squatting rights. The felt indifference is interesting in the light of the strong presence of public figures. Clearly, the street was self-organized and humanly regulated, so that formal rules and institutional violence were absent, creating simultaneously an indeterminate and safe situation. Discussing 'open streets', Fernando (2007: 67–68) suggests a range of public uses and behaviours, such as 'selling and buying, taking breaks from work, reading newspapers, sitting, walking, window-shopping, people-watching, meeting, socializing and waiting for transportation'. In Calçada de Sant'Ana, these were all present, and many more besides. Work itself, not only taking a break, was especially visible and audible. Printing and building but, just as much, homework: cooking, baking, making laundry. The street was also much about cycling, motorcycling, playing games, walking dogs – either on leash or loose, it did not matter – and even lifting groceries up with a rope to a friend upstairs on a balcony. Night-life was an integral part of the public life of the street: late night discussions between homeless and residents, sometimes leading to temporary sheltering; Sunday night's rock concerts in the local 'sports club'; dustmen removing the colourful bags at early hours.

3. Towards differential urban spaces

While the rhythmanalysis of Lisbon's Calçada de Sant'Ana may for its small part answer to the perceived lack of work on everyday practices in cities, it should be seen in a broader context. The important question is, if we can learn something about the future of cities, about social production of differential spaces and the potential of the 'urban continent' envisioned by Lefebvre in *La révolution urbaine* (Schmid, 2005: 330). In this broad perspective, the micro-case of Calçada de Sant'Ana opens a fresh, contemporary view to the links between past, present and future as well as between form, use and meaning. A detailed and grounded analysis of the dynamic between everyday use and the change (as well as stability) of urban space as its 'frame' helps to understand how the rhythms of producing urban space reach from momentary to historic, in other words, how the seemingly small and ephemeral everyday habits link together to a long-lasting, spatially anchored process that can sustain and adapt itself over years, decades and centuries.

We no longer live in an industrial society of organized collective consumption, but at a threshold of something new. Only a small proportion of the residents and visitors of Calçada de Sant'Ana were in traditional industrial jobs, even though they also were part of its social and economic fabric. It is as if the street had its own time, where 'all rhythms imply the relation of a time to a space, a localized time, or, if one prefers, a temporalised space' (Lefebvre and Régulier, 2004: 89) and where 'a sense of time as not only somewhat *intersubjective* but also *place-specific*' (Wunderlich, 2010: 45).

Calçada de Sant'Ana provides a luminous contemporary example of open and networked public space. The lack of noise, differential walking movements up and down the hill, missing signs of themeing, self-organized and governed security and tolerant nocturnal life, provide valuable insights into both how to defend differential spaces today and how to facilitate changes for the better in the future. As Bauman (2006: 133) notes, '[f]ear takes root in our motives and purposes, settles in our actions and saturates our daily routines'. New forms of vulnerability appear to be combined with moral ascendancy and fear of the Other which easily leads to different forms of exclusion of people regarded as outsiders. 'Meetings and encounters with different bodies of "strangers" and the emotions such meetings create' are, as Nielsen and Simonsen (2003: 918) argue, 'part of the construction of the city': these encounters can not only promote apprehension, but 'enjoyment and desire' as well. Fear easily provides a justification for behaving in a self-centred and family oriented way: instead of being devoted to taking care of others, people become committed to sustaining social control and spatial exclusion (Koskela, 2010).

In Calçada de Sant'Ana, the rhythms and their spatialization (Shields, 1999) provide a counter-example: instead of fear and vulnerability, its socio-spatial pattern promoted boldness and tolerance. Edensor's (2010: 16) suggestion of '*resistant* rhythms, which proffer alternative modes of spending time, different pacings and pulses which critique normative, disciplinary rhythms and offer unconventional, sometimes utopian visions of different temporalities', is very appropriate. The street – its space and people – was welcoming and tolerant, so that we could join its life in our way, but simultaneously it had power, so that our practices, roles in the family and even ideas changed. Evidently, as Massey (2005: 182) remarks, '[n]either a concept of the local as "only local" nor

The Sociological Review, 61:S1, pp. 124–143 (2013), DOI: 10.1111/1467-954X.12057
© 2013 The Authors. Editorial organisation © 2013 The Editorial Board of the Sociological Review

Figure 4

a romanticization of the local as bounded authenticity . . . offers much hope for a wider politics'. Nevertheless, our intention in pointing out the specific character of Calçada de Sant'Ana is not to despise or romanticize the place, but to present it as a 'counter story' for all-too common urban tendencies.

Conclusions: thresholds and cyclic rhythms

In Calçada de Sant'Ana the weaving together of social and spatial has produced a street-phenomenon, which can be characterized as a collective work, an *oeuvre*. This critical notion of Lefebvre's spatial thinking refers to both the process and result of an organic and rhythmic production of space, which has its own logic and time (Lehtovuori, 2008, 2010), uniqueness, radiance and style. A users' possibility to appropriate space, their freedom to do something meaningful and a certain indeterminacy of the space (Groth and Corijn, 2005) are important prerequisites for the process of *oeuvre*. Appropriation goes hand-in-hand with the notion of right to the city. In Calçada de Sant'Ana these rights were collectively held open in the tolerant but nevertheless structured urban life.

In the contemporary society, it is not necessarily easy to find *oeuvres,* as the dominant urban process is that of money and control (Figure 4). In Calçada de

The Sociological Review, 61:S1, pp. 124–143 (2013), DOI: 10.1111/1467-954X.12057

Sant'Ana, we found a counter-example, a contemporary, relatively central urban space that is sustaining a certain independence from the mechanical, repetitive rhythms of paid work as well as the boom-bust cycle of real estate and financial capitalism. The street is a pocket of local order (Ellegård and Vilhelmson, 2004), or a 'time-space'. Such places are, as Massey argues, 'open to the future; that makes them the ongoing constructions which are our continuing responsibility, the ongoing *event of place* which has to be addressed' (2005: 180, our italics).

Above, we described our experiences in Calçada de Sant'Ana, contextualizing them in selected theoretical perspectives. We listened to the street as external observers, and walked on the streets as part of its public life. In the spirit of Edensor (2006: 532), we painted a particular view to a general process where '[t]he repetition of daily, weekly and annual routines, how and when to eat, wash, move, work and play, constitutes a realm of "common sense", grounding culture and identity'. Besides 'how' and 'when', it is about 'where' and 'in connection to which'. Material urban space with buildings, pavements and trees, has its own rhythm, which is sometimes very slow, reaching from years to decades and centuries.

Calçada de Sant'Ana has been able to sustain itself, to keep a certain coherence, identity and distinctiveness. At the same time, the street has been able to adapt, to change and take in new people, new habits and new programmes. This dialectic of continuity and change, sameness and difference, or repetition and modulation is unfolding all the time in everyday events and the tiny details of spatial practice. The 'event of place' has been a miraculous success. Walking and stopping, mundane meetings, gestures, sudden laugh, and a loud Sunday night party are all part of the process of producing urban space. Likewise, spatial and material characteristics and nuances play a role: steepness of the hill, balconies, provisional structures, waste containers, banners, graffiti, decay.

From the perspective of producing differential urban futures, two points seem to be above others: cyclical rhythms and creative thresholds. We have to acknowledge that 'rhythm is not only a repetition of the same, but also the emergence of difference within that repetition' (Simpson, 2008: 814). According to Lefebvre, this creative potential is related, especially, to cyclical rhythms that are linked to becoming, while linear rhythms are mechanical (Lefebvre and Régulier, 2004: 90).

The bodily and traditional rhythms were quite strong in Calçada de Sant'Ana, characterized by a polyrhythmia of daily, weekly, lunatic, annual and historic cycles. While we can follow Lefebvre (2004: 48) and confirm that 'no genuine cycle returns exactly to its point of departure or reproduces itself exactly', we need a clearer spatial understanding of this statement. Here, the notion of threshold is very fruitful. Stavrides (2010: 20) defines threshold in an active way as 'a potential stage in which encountering otherness means visiting otherness, rehearsing, testing and exploring otherness.' Furthermore, '[r]ecognizing, opening, creating and inhabiting thresholds can become an important characteristic of emergent emancipatory spatialities' (Stavrides 2010: 41). The porous and closely knit *oeuvre* of Calçada de Sant'Ana was full of thresholds. It is not only about side-streets, balconies and doorways, but about the way these architectural elements are constantly *rehearsed*, so that their potentiality increases. At another level of abstraction, the whole street can be seen as a threshold between social groups, localized times and urban flows.

Is the character of Calçada de Sant'Ana an anomaly or a sign of a differential future? It is, of course, hard to say, but we hope that our observations help to find similar or related spatial and rhythmic characteristics elsewhere, to help in starting processes towards differential urban spaces, each of which might work as a test or pioneer of the 'urban continent' Lefebvre envisioned in *La révolution urbaine*. There also may be something specific in Lisbon. Referring to the *Attempt at the Rhythmanalysis of Mediterranean Cities*, Meyer (2008: 158) states that:

> [a]s in the case of most historic cities, the big cities of the Mediterranean are doomed by virtue of the proliferation of suburbs. And yet historic character seems able to survive better in the Mediterranean than elsewhere – this is Lefebvre and Régulier's cautiously worded thesis. A dogged power of resistance seems to emanate from the everyday lived rhythms and the organization of time.

While Lisbon shares a group resemblance with 'Mediterranean cities', the lessons from Calçada de Sant'Ana are not limited to any specific geographical area. 'As "the past continues in our present" so is also the distant implicated in our "here". Identities are relational in ways that are spatio-temporal' (Massey, 2005: 192).

We intend our case to provide concrete insights in sustaining differential spaces by keeping old (cyclical) rhythms and in producing new spaces by questioning current practices and providing alternative spatialities and time-patterns. We argue that it is precisely the character of the street as an *oeuvre* that explains its strong, radiating atmospheric quality – its 'presence' in Lefebvrean terms. Its atmosphere was not something to be enjoyed from a distance or like a tourist, but it was to be lived. In Calçada de Sant'Ana, history is exercised in every rhythm, in every moment so that 'past, present and future always occur and combine in unique ways to make new temporalities' (Edensor, 2010: 15). If we understand public space as an *oeuvre*, it becomes easier to value 'everything there is' – from feelings to chance encounters, from graffiti to carefully designed façade alterations, from temporary uses to big scale urban projects – as part of the *same* dynamic and meaningful space. Space, place, time, use and rhythms are not anymore seen abstractly as separate 'layers', but as an inter-woven socio-spatial process – how long has the butcher's cleaver been making its sound? How long will it continue?

Notes

1 In 2010, Inatel was re-organized as a private foundation.
2 *Die Atmosphäre einer Stadt ist eben die Art und Weise, wie sich das Leben in ihr vollzieht* (Böhme, 1998: 55).

References

Bauman, Z., (2006), *Liquid Fear*, Cambridge: Polity Press.

Benjamin, W. and Lacis, A., (1979 [1924]), 'Naples', in *One-Way Street and Other Writings*, 167–176, London: Verso.

Böhme, G., (1998), *Anmutungen. Über das Atmosphärische*, Stuttgart: Edition Tertium.

Böhme, G., (2001), *Aisthetik. Vorlesungen über Ästhetik als allgemeine Wahrnehmungslehre*, München: Wilhelm Fink Verlag.

Cresswell, T., (2010), 'Towards a politics of mobility', *Environment and Planning D: Society and Space*, 28 (1): 17–31.

de Certeau, M., (1984), *The Practice of Everyday Life*, Berkeley, CA: University of California Press.

Edensor, T., (2006), 'Reconsidering national temporalities: institutional times, everyday routines, serial spaces and synchronicities', *European Journal of Social Theory*, 9 (4): 525–545.

Edensor, T., (2010), 'Introduction: thinking about rhythm and space', in T. Edensor (ed.), *Geographies of Rhythm: Nature, Place, Mobilities and Bodies*, 1–18, Farnham: Ashgate.

Elden, S., (2004), *Understanding Henri Lefebvre: Theory and the Possible*, London: Continuum.

Ellegård, K. and Vilhelmson, B., (2004), 'Home as a pocket of local order: everyday activities and the friction of distance', *Geografiska Annaler: Series B, Human Geography*, 84 (4): 281–296.

Fernando, N. A., (2007), 'Open-ended space: urban streets in different cultural contexts', in K. A. Franck and Q. Stevens (eds), *Loose Space: Possibility and Diversity in Urban Life*, 54–72, London: Routledge.

Gottdiener, M., (1993), 'Henri Lefebvre and the production of space', *Sociological Theory*, 1 (11): 129–134.

Gottdiener, M. (1994) [1985], *The Social Production of Urban Space*, Austin: University of Texas Press.

Groth, J. and Corijn, E., (2005), 'Reclaiming urbanity: indeterminate spaces, informal actors and urban agenda setting', *Urban Studies*, 42 (3): 511–534.

Hillier, B., (1996), *Space Is the Machine: A Configurational Theory of Architecture*, Cambridge: Cambridge University Press.

Hillier, B. and Hanson, J., (1984), *The Social Logic of Space*, Cambridge: Cambridge University Press.

Isohanni, T., (2006), *Arabia, Arabia. Taiteellinen toiminta osana asuinalueen suunnittelua*, Helsinki: Taideteollinen korkeakoulu A 66.

Jacobs, J., (1961), *The Death and Life of American Cities*, New York: Vintage.

Koskela, H., (2010), 'Fear and its others', in S. J. Smith, R. Pain, S. Marsden and J. P. Jones III (eds), *Handbook of Social Geography*, 389–407, London: Sage.

Lefebvre, H., (1991 [1974]), *The Production of Space*, Oxford: Blackwell [*La production de l'espace*, English translation by Donald Nicholson-Smith].

Lefebvre, H., (1996 [1968]), 'Right to the city', in *Writings on Cities*, 61–181, Oxford: Blackwell [*Le droit à la ville*, English translation by E. Kofman and E. Lebas].

Lefebvre, H., (2004), *Rhythmanalysis: Space, Time and Everyday Life*, London: Continuum.

Lefebvre, H. and Régulier, C., (2004), 'Attempt at the rhythmanalysis of Mediterranean cities', in H. Lefebvre, *Rhythmanalysis: Space, Time and Everyday Life*, 85–100, London: Continuum.

Lehtovuori, P., (2000), 'Weak place: thoughts on strengthening soft phenomena', *City*, 4 (3): 398–415.

Lehtovuori, P., (2008), 'Artifacts, oeuvre and atmosphere: applying Lefebvre's spatial thinking in urban design', in T. Avermaete, K. Havik and H. Teerds (eds), *Oase 77: Into the Open*, 58–70, Rotterdam: NAI Publishers.

Lehtovuori, P., (2010), *Experience and Conflict: The Production of Urban Space*, Farnham: Ashgate.

Lehtovuori, P., (2012), 'Towards experiential urbanism', *Critical Sociology*, 38 (1): 71–87.

Massey, D. B., (2005), *For Space*, London: Sage.

The Sociological Review, 61:S1, pp. 124–143 (2013), DOI: 10.1111/1467-954X.12057

Meyer, K., (2008), 'Rhythms, streets, cities', in K. Goonewardena, S. Kipfer, R. Milgrom and C. Schmid (eds), *Space, Difference, Everyday Life: Reading Henri Lefebvre*, 147–160, New York: Routledge.

Mitchell, D., (2003), *The Right to the City: Social Justice and the Fight for Public Space*, New York: Guilford Press.

Moudon, A. V., (1994), 'Getting to know the built landscape: typomorphology', in K. A. Franck and L. Schneekloth (eds), *Ordering Space: Types in Architecture and Design*, 289–311, New York: Van Nostrand Reinhold.

Nielsen, E. H. and Simonsen, K., (2003), 'Scaling from "below": practices, strategies and urban spaces', *European Planning Studies*, 11 (8): 911–927.

Rossi, A., (1982), *The Architecture of the City*, Cambridge, MA: MIT Press.

Schafer, R. M., (1977), *The Tuning of the World* (republished in 1994 as *The Soundscape* [Rochester, VM: Destiny Books]).

Schmid, C., (2005), *Stadt, Raum und Gesellschaft. Henri Lefebvre und die Theorie der Produktion des Raumes*, München: Frank Steiner Verlag.

Schmitz, H., (1969), *Der Gefühlraum*, Bonn: Bouvier.

Sennett, R., (1977), *The Fall of Public Man*, Cambridge: Cambridge University Press.

Shields, R., (1999), *Lefebvre, Love and Struggle: Spatial Dialectics*, London: Routledge.

Simmel, G., (1997), 'Bridge and door', in N. Leach (ed.), *Rethinking Architecture: A Reader in Cultural Theory*, 66–68, London: Routledge.

Simpson, P., (2008), 'Chronic everyday life: rhythmanalysing street performance', *Social and Cultural Geography*, 9 (7): 807–829.

Soja, E., (1996), *Third Space: Journeys to Los Angeles and Other Real-and-imagined Places*, Cambridge, MA: Blackwell.

Stanek, L., (2008), 'Space as concrete abstraction: Hegel, Marx, and Modern Urbanism in Henri Lefebvre', in K. Goonewardena, S. Kipfer, R. Milgrom and C. Schmid (eds), *Space, Difference, Everyday Life: Reading Henri Lefebvre*, 62–79, London: Routledge.

Stavrides, S., (2007), 'Heterotopias and the experience of porous urban space', in K. A. Franck and Q. Stevens (eds), *Loose Space: Possibility and Diversity in Urban Life*, 174–192, London: Routledge.

Stavrides, S., (2010), *Towards the City of Thresholds*, professionaldreamers, Italy, www.professionaldreamers.net.

Stevens, Q., (2007a), 'Betwixt and between: building thresholds, liminality and public space', in K. A. Franck and Q. Stevens (eds), *Loose Space: Possibility and Diversity in Urban Life*, 73–92, London: Routledge.

Stevens, Q., (2007b), *The Ludic City: Exploring the Potential of Public Spaces*, New York: Routledge.

Wilson, E., (1997), 'Looking backward: nostalgia and the city', in S. Westwood and J. Williams (eds), *Imagining Cities: Scripts, Signs, Memory*, 127–139, London: Routledge.

Wunderlich, F. M., (2008), 'Walking and rhythmicity: sensing urban space', *Journal of Urban Design*, 13 (1): 125–139.

Wunderlich, F. M., (2010), 'The aesthetics of place-temporality in the everyday urban space: the case of Fitzroy Square', in T. Edensor (ed.), *Geographies of Rhythm: Nature, Place, Mobilities and Bodies*, 45–56, Farnham: Ashgate.

Communicating the rhythms of retromodernity: 'confused and mixed Shanghai'

Amanda Lagerkvist

Abstract: Visitors on sight-seeing tours in contemporary globalizing Shanghai observe the futuristic ambitions, exponential development and chaotic poly-rhythmicity of New Shanghai. The nostalgia industry simultaneously 'teleports' the tourists on tours back to a time when Shanghai was a legendary world metropolis; the Golden Age of the inter-war era. Inspired by Henri Lefebvre's critical rhythmanalysis, and by Jonathan Sterne's conceptualization of communication as organized movement and action, this paper explores bus tours by commission of the municipal government. Shanghai is the place where the movements of the buses, as well as the tourists on board, become part of communicating the place identity and multiple rhythms of the city. The buses are conceived as means of communication, in a twofold sense, and as both underscoring and binding together the many incommensurabilities of place: old and new, Western and Chinese, industrialism and post-industrialism, nationalism and globalism. The author argues that mobility, media modernity and a confounding mixture (reflexively manifested on the tour 'Confused and Mixed Shanghai') constitute a collective memory of the city, and that the buses in all their seeming banality, communicate Shanghai's particular rhythms of retromodernity.

Keywords: rhythmanalysis, memory, place identity, mobility, bus tours, Shanghai

Rhythmanalysis may seem elusive, scientifically 'unrigorous', perhaps even mysterious, yet, at once, tremendously apposite, both in commonsensical and scholarly approaches to urban spaces. From sleepy towns to bustling urban jungles, they all have their unswerving and sensuously felt rhythms. In a megalopolis like contemporary Shanghai, rhythmanalysis is almost too easy to invoke. For visitors, the city is, first and foremost, a multi-rhythmic experience in which rhythms and temporalities of globality, authoritarian state capitalism and those of the national techno-scientific bureaucracy clash and coalesce. I have elsewhere discussed how experiencing the city may be depicted as being in a temporal spiral that rotates backwards and forwards at the same time: a maelstrom that retroactively and self-reflexively copies and imitates fashion styles, themes, images and ideals, brazenly juxtaposing them into a rhythmic assemblage – all in

The Sociological Review, 61:S1, pp. 144–161 (2013), DOI: 10.1111/1467-954X.12058

a feverish movement toward the future (A. Lagerkvist, 2009). This Asian mega city is now reinventing itself by every means possible. Hence, rhythms of Shanghai are strange, multiple, 'heterotopian' and incongruous.[1] But this very heterogeneity also has a history in Shanghai. Adding to the picture is, in no small way, the sense in which the city is, through the memory industry, nostalgically returning to its pre-1949, mercantile, cosmopolitan, decadent and capitalistic past. It is, as Xudong Zhang (2000) has argued eloquently, narcissistically in love with its Golden Age and its stereotypical heterogeneity, thereby self-consciously promoting itself, as full of exciting and even befuddling contrasts and *rhythms* – now as in the past. One example of how this memory of the city is being reinvented exists on a tourist website, where Shanghai is described as related to other cities in the past. It appears as an amalgamation of East and West, and as a heterochrony of different epochs: 'Fortune Magazine, in 1935, called it the inheritor of ancient Baghdad, pre-War Constantinople, 19th century London and 20th century Manhattan'.[2]

The resurrection of Shanghai is part of the massive and rapid transformation of Chinese society and urban space in the past decades (Campanella, 2008). Shanghai is undergoing a programme of regeneration at a speed and to an extent that seem previously unknown to mankind. The development is exponential. The growth has been at double-digit figures, and with an average of 12 per cent between 1992 and 2008. Sublime architectonic structures, record visions and grand futuristic plans are part of the minutious and detailed planning of spatial production which involves all the 19 districts of the megacity. And the Master plan, covering 1999–2020, aims to develop Shanghai into a world centre for economy, trade and finance. Shanghai also sets itself on becoming both a green and digital space. The future is sculptured into being through a continuous interminable stream of demolished areas and newly projected sites.

Every inch of this city of 20 million inhabitants is fastidiously included in the masterplan. And still nothing seems to be in the right place here! Despite its rigorously planned future, there is a chaotic incompatibility to the rhythms of the city, a sense in which modernity and postmodernity, industrialization and post-industrialization, globalization and nationalism are fused and juxtaposed. This is reflected in the topologies of memory (Crang and Travlou, 2001) displayed in the city, where postmodern architecture, old Chinese alleys (Lilong och Shikumen), as well as Stalinist work units from the 1950s and colonial structures combine to produce the polyrhythmicity that is the primary sign of the city.

Rhythm, for Henri Lefebvre, unites the dimensions of time, space and the everyday (Lefebvre, 1996, 2004) while attesting to the multiplicity of spaces and the non-linearity of time, thus making apparent the heterogeneity, dynamism, multiplicity of time as a social and cultural experience (Edensor, 2010). For Lefebvre time is, in essence, diverse. Oddly, Shanghai seems to bear witness, both in a material and imaginary sense, to the simultaneity, the non-linearity and differentiality of time itself.[3] Shanghai is currently connecting with the temporality of global markets, delimited by financial flows, clock and digital time, whilst being under the influence of the inevitable forces of the state and national bureaucracy: 'Beijing Time' (Dutton, 2008).

Rhythmanalysis is above all a sensibility – here in relation to the urban – which enables registering the patterned particularities of place, indebted to the socio-economic order on which they rely, but through rhythm we may also perceive the integral changes, cracks and ripples in the official technocratic layout of cities (Lefebvre, 1996). But what do we make of these approaches in authoritarian ruled societies, and in places that seem very naturally 'postmodern' and ironically 'confused and mixed' (as one sightseeing tour in the city is named) in their visual make-up and communication? In other words, do the rhythmic discordances of Shanghai produce or contest its socio-economic and political order? How can we approach a place that, in effect, *celebrates its own arrhythmicity and polyrhythmicity*, while relying on a social and political order of authoritarian state capitalism currently in smooth partnership with the globalization process; a system that fails to deliver justice, political freedoms and human rights to its citizens?

In contrast with recent academic works that stress (and even praise) the economic, architectural and urban planning forces shaping the development of Shanghai (see, eg, Chen, 2009), I will here embody the position of a *critical rhythmanalyst*, following in Lefebvre's footsteps, in attempting to interrogate how the new geopolitical order and a new future in Asia, as the world seems to shift to the East, are felt and performed among Westerners through their participation in and potential rejection of the rhythms of the city. These elites constitute, through their own bodily movements and memory practices, parts of the transformations at hand. Lefebvre's thinking was 'differentialist', and strove to regroup separate elements into a unity of urban rhythms, in order to grasp the technocratic, capitalistic, uniform and quantifiable linearity of the city and its everyday life, as intertwined with the cyclical temporalities of disruption, or of people in movement in the streets (Kofman and Lebas, 1996). People moving about city spaces, including the tourists Lefebvre observed in Paris, are part of these cycles of time. He described them as: 'Incongruous crowds, yes. Tourists from faraway places, Finland, Sweden, Portugal . . . , buyers from afar, wholesalers, lovers of art or of novelties' (1996: xx). These crowds are involved in 'the interactions of various repetitive and different rhythms' as they 'animate the street and the neighbourhood'. While cities are full of repetitions, Lefebvre holds that these actually beget difference (cf. Highmore, 2005; Edensor, 2010). But how may these tourists on their beaten tracks, if at all, disrupt the linear and repetitive rhythms of the official spatial story of Shanghai, especially as the city is self-consciously thriving on being endlessly varied, assorted and in movement?

I tag along with Swedish tourists on sightseeing bus tours in the city, whose trips and physical and affectual movements are exposed to, while partaking in the production of, this space and its rhythms. Bodies are here conceived as involved in the making of timespace and place (Edensor, 2010: 5, see also May and Thrift, 2001; Crang, 2001; Grosz, 1992). In this essay, the transportation of two groups of Swedish tourists that visited Shanghai in 2006, travelling with the

The Sociological Review, 61:S1, pp. 144–161 (2013), DOI: 10.1111/1467-954X.12058

Swedish-Chinese Travel Agency, and with Lotus Travel, is triangulated with a thick contemporary and historical contextualization. Through fusing theoretical debates on media materialities, and the discourse on mobilities and memory studies, the additional objective here is to employ rhythm in order to *mobilize* the discourse on 'mediaspace' and 'media cities' (Couldry and McCarthy, 2004; McQuire, 2008). Scott McQuire's concept of *the media city* is a term that highlights 'the role of media technologies in the dynamic production of contemporary urban space in Lefebvre's sense of *binding affect and cognition to space*' (2008: vii, emphasis added). Sociospatial experience is, in McQuire's work, hardly approached as such but is grasped primarily through theorization, or through interpreting artistic representations of the urban experience. Here, instead, I hope to develop this approach by providing accounts of lived tourist practices *in relation to* scriptings of the city and the communicative movements of the buses. I will seek here, in addition, to accomplish a rhythmanalysis that may sensitize us to the rhythms of an urban space as experienced beyond the everyday (cf. Edensor, 2010), by short time sojourners and tourists.

Through a focus on rhythms in and through the movements and emotional reactions of visitors, in conjunction with a consideration of the official spatial story as communicated and conveyed on board tourist buses by commission of the municipal government, I am additionally tracing a memory of Shanghai. As I have argued at length elsewhere, a memory of futures past, of mobility and modernity, is a core aspect of Shanghai's spatial story (A. Lagerkvist, 2007, 2009, 2010, 2011 and forthcoming). A site that crystallizes this particularity of the city, its sense of *retromodernity* – of envisioning the new, and the future, through backward-looking practices (cf. Abbas, 2002; Lu, 2002) – is the Oriental Pearl TV Tower in Pudong New Area, the most iconic landmark structure in the city, and a place to where all sightseeing tourists go. This space age structure glows in the night sky with purple, green and red lights, embodying the medley of authoritarian state capitalism, nostalgia for the future of the 1960s, and globalization. The foremost challenge for rhythmanalysis in Shanghai, I suggest, is to conceive of the cracks in the crystal, the *fissures in the pearl* as it were; the punctum that interrupts and complicates the official discourses in the city (cf. Hetherington, this volume). In other words, to hear out those 'contrapuntal rhythms' of the city (Highmore, 2005: 150) beyond its themed sense of perplexity, through which Shanghai's alternative memories and futures may potentially be perceived.

Touring time

'Pinch my arm somebody', said Barbro, a 60-year-old pharmacist from Gothenburg, as we descended the tour bus on Nanjing Road East, close to the mythical Peace Hotel, in order to collectively cross the multi-lane avenue, the Bund, with the purpose of joining the densely frequented promenade along the *Huangpu* river with its view points across the water. She needed to be reminded that this was real, and that the stunning city centre was not a dream. The future had already arrived, she told me a couple of months later, and it was amazing!

For the mobile elites of the world, the mega-city of Shanghai has, during the past decade, reappeared on their itineraries. Tourist buses and sightseeing tours are as common here as in other metropolises. From the Shanghai Sightseeing Bus Center, which is situated in the southern part of the XuHui district, 400 buses leave daily on 108 different tours in the city, and it caters for around 5,000 tourists every 24 hours. It is a commercial venture, under the control of the municipal government. There are a number of different packages on offer, all with onboard guides, and including entrance tickets to all the sights. In addition to these tours, one has to take into account the hundreds of buses from foreign travel agencies and the thousands of tourists on board these. There is typically a Chinese guide, commissioned by the state, on board these tours.

The standard route of the tour seems to verify that Shanghai is 'very naturally postmodern'.[4] First, it runs to the China of a mythical past land of monks and Confucians and tea: the temple of the Jade Buddha on Anyuan Lu, which is one of Shanghai's most important Buddhist temples. Here one can observe the Burmese Sakyamuni, as well as other statues. The route then stretches to the East when the bus visits the legendary Bund (Waitan), a promenade along the riverside and the place where the cargo and passenger traffic moored in the past. Here a number of famous architectural structures from the colonial times can be found in neoclassical or Art Deco style, such as the Hong Kong Shanghai Bank Corporation Building, Peace Hotel, Customs House, Broadway Mansions and the Russian Consulate. Here you may gaze to the East across the Huangpu River, at the skyline of Pudong, to where the bus travels later across one of the newly built bridges to the other side of the river and into the future: to the Pudong New Area. This is the finance centre of the city, built in the past 20 years as a mini Manhattan with the famous Oriental Pearl TV tower which offers a magnificent view of the whole city, the Jin Mao Building, and Pudong World Finance Center, the highest building in Shanghai. Next the bus makes a stop at the Yuyuan Garden in the old Chinese City. The garden was built between 1559 and 1577 by the Pan Clan, a rich family of government officials, during the Ming Dynasty, but was demolished during the time of the Opium wars and the Boxer riots in 1919. From there a visit to People's Square, the previous race track in the international concession, which was rebuilt in 1949 by the Communists. Here one can visit the grandiose Shanghai Urban Planning Exhibition Centre to take part in the futuristic visions of the municipal government, the architects and urban planners for Shanghai 2020. The bus travels to the West, back in time, to the former French Concession where, apart from being able to consume the enormous range of food in restaurants from all corners of the earth, one may observe the Cathay Theatre (which is an old Art Deco Cinema Theatre,) shop on Huaihai Road (old Avenue Joffre) and visit the home of Sun Yatsen, the nation's Father. The French part of the city also contains the tourist area Xintiandi (New Heaven and Earth), a stop made almost exclusively by newly arrived foreigners and tourists. Here one finds a theme park simulation of the

The Sociological Review, 61:S1, pp. 144–161 (2013), DOI: 10.1111/1467-954X.12058
© 2013 The Author. Editorial organisation © 2013 The Editorial Board of the Sociological Review

Chinese-French architecture of Shikumen of the 1930s, a museum in the building where the Chinese Communist Party was founded in 1921 as well as all the exclusive global brands, restaurants, bars and a cinema theatre.

Communication, transportation and rhythm

An analysis of the movements of the bus and its passengers, and of the geography of the bus tour, can shed light on how they appropriate this kaleidoscopic landscape and its hyper- and retromodern rhythms. By interrogating the itinerary and running of the bus tour, I wish to sound out the orchestration of Shanghai's multiple rhythms of modernity. When the tour runs first to the recent past, then back in time several hundred years, and then on to a hypermodern skyline, which constitutes as well as points out the future, a pattern for perceiving Shanghai may become visible. Apart from being replete with contrasts, and the fact that these contrasts are visible in almost every corner of the city, you travel to different epochs in an 'uncoordinated' fashion, back and forth between different fragments and layers of time, to the colonial era and the legendary 1930s, old China, the hyper modern present, and into the future, and then back to the period of Communism (which is ideologically downplayed and reduced to a symbol for the independence of the nation and its grandeur).

A point of departure here is that the means of transportation are in themselves important for the rhythms of the city and how they are perceived, and this experience is multisensuous and emotional. This assumption is keyed in a theorization of communication as movement and action, and as a part of the social production of the rhythms of the city. How does this differ from more established notions of communication? Communication has traditionally been conceived of in two different ways, argues James Carey (1989). The classical *transmission model* is built on a geographical metaphor for the transportation of knowledge, ideas and information in space. The transportation of human beings, goods and information were identical processes until the invention of the telegraph, which separated communication as physical transportation from the mediation of symbolic messages. The spatial metaphor of transmission has continued to dominate the basic understanding of communication. Through the other model, *the ritual model*, Carey contributed to launching the critical study of communication as culture within Media Studies. Communication is here a process through which social reality is created symbolically and ritually. Carey stressed the clear etymological connections between communication and for example *communion* and *communitas*, that is, concepts that, in varying ways, describe human and social community. In challenging Carey's seminal work, Jonathan Sterne argues (2006: 118) that communication is best understood instead as organized movement and action. Sterne wants to open up the possibility of seeing communication as a process which sometimes involves meaning making processes, and sometimes not. Thinking about communication and transportation in conjunction is a way to regard them as a massive assemblage 'of organised movement in space' (2006: 119). Sterne emphasizes that many media scholars retain the notions of the message, meaning or information, as the only symbolic sides to communication, and as its only noteworthy aspects, but the supposedly non-symbolic aspects are reduced to background, infrastructure or enabling conditions (2006: 123). Social reality is not only shaped on symbolic levels, argues Sterne, and in turn we must acknowledge that some purely infrastructural aspects may contain symbolic dimensions. The bus is, in Mcluhanite terms, sometimes the message. His goal is to materialize mediation, while simultaneously teasing out the potential meaning making aspects of materiality.

The following discussion is inspired by Sterne's notion of communication for exploring the symbolic and, in effect, communicative dimensions of the materiality of the tours, conceived of here as bringing about and reflecting the rhythms of the city. I wish to explore how the buses may be understood as part of the reproduction and communication of the rhythmicity of urban space, through their involvement in the manuscript and rhythms of the city that tourists are obliged to follow, while they are simultaneously shaping it, in and through their movements.

Hijackings of modernity? Strange and uncanny

The Westerner who used to be very much at home in Shanghai has returned to take part in and observe Shanghai's resurgence. These are transnational elites, and apart from tourists and travellers, they are constituted by corporate migrants, architects, artists, students, journalists and English teachers. First time visitors are often taken aback by the city. It is an ecstatic and fascinating experience. The space traversed is, however, quite strange: few visitors possess the ability to navigate it. Many actually say they do not follow a script for Shanghai: 'I have no expectations whatsoever', said Anna-Stina, 63, when asked about this as we stood in line by the entrance to the Oriental Pearl TV tower. 'I've only just arrived'. When we ascended the observation deck in the middle section of the tower, where the endless forest of skyscrapers in all directions of the city are exposed to the eye, Peter, a well-travelled engineer from Stockholm, said (undeniably blowing my cover, once and for all): 'I understand why you feel we are interesting, because we're only here for such a short period of time, and still we construct images that we bring back home'.

Apart from this (self-reflexive) hesitation and wavering in foreigner's encounters with Shanghai, there is also, sometimes, an experience of uncanny resemblance of something already known or seen in all the awesome and partially foreign traits of the city. 'But this is America', said Moncia from Helsingborg, when she laid eyes on the modern architecture. This sensibility may be illustrated by the words of Rem Koolhaas:

[M]odernity is now a notion hijacked, appropriated, and claimed by Asia exactly at the moment when it seemed to be both depleted and discredited 'here.' Through this hijacking, modernity has been resemanticized and has acquired new meanings, which so far are least visible to us who have lived longest with its embers and don't believe they can ever be reignited. But what we think of as debased has become brand new. (Rajchman, 1994)

Koolhaas's choice of words, 'hijacking', is not innocent. Is there in fact something destabilizing and worrying, to encounter the known in the foreign – the old as new – the modern/the future in the guise of Asia? In this scenario of 'resemanticization', a logic for revitalization appears which, in resemblance with earlier scenarios, seems to be driven by the notion of the *other*, here in the shape of fantasies about Asian otherness,[5] with their distinct electronic exoticism (Todorov, 1993). The question is, of course, if tourists and visitors sense that they are witnessing a shift in Shanghai, which may seriously challenge the hegemony of Western culture and its politico-economic dominance for centuries?

From this geopolitical 'aerial shot', we may zoom in on the street level of Shanghai – where the tourist buses are now running on the road network system – in order to discuss to what extent the buses, together with a new infrastructure, architecture and new communication and information technologies, are a part of this recoding of modernity in Shanghai. The city may be depicted as a partially recoded and thereby new-and-old terrain for modernization. Here in post-Socialist China, Walter Benjamin's modern ruins of the bourgeoisie are, according to Xudong Zhang, symbolically and physically imitated and resurrected, in the renovated colonial architecture. And here, an old symbol of the new, the skyscraper, is towering in its reborn status as futurological marker. Research about the *new* (for example 'new media') has, according to Charles R. Acland, often ignored how older forms live on and coexist with new forms, or are resurrected; that is how both the old and the new depend on or are part of different dialectical processes, in relation to each other (Acland, 2007: xxiii–xxvii). These processes of repetition, exchange and cooperation have been highlighted by different scholars in terms of the remediation of media, space and mobility (Bolter and Grusin, 1999; Graham, 2004; Cresswell, 2010). What may we learn by encircling how the communicative role of the bus – that is, its role in shaping the urban rhythms of Shanghai – stands in a multidimensional relationship to earlier epochs, cultural practices and communication forms?

The tourist bus is a modern medium of transportation. In hyper- and retromodern Shanghai its presence testifies to the successful modernization and blooming tourism industry. But this space is much more than modern, in terms of 'new'. Old forms are lingering and here, as discussed above, a certain past is recreated and invented in a nostalgia for the 1920s and 30s. Residual historical forms – including the buses – exist alongside emergent forms such as digitalization and experimental architecture. What do the buses symbolize, within Raymond Williams' (1977) three-dimensional understanding of the dominant, emergent, residual cultural forms in modernity? According to Williams, cultural change is saturated by lags, and we are thereby faced with phenomena, artefacts, values and practices located within different places within their life cycles. Sometimes old forms are reborn as nostalgic cult objects (Acland, 2007: xxi). Of course there are residual functions and aspects of how the modern means of communication – buses – are used, and what they symbolize. The buses themselves – once very modern – are, however, neither spectacular nor nostalgic objects in Shanghai. After half a century of mass tourism in the West, the buses have lost all newfangledness, and modernity, and will not accomplish any shiverings in the heart and soul of the tourist. This tourism banality, as a means of communication and transportation, is appropriated through the natural attitude. First and foremost, the function of the buses is to make the tourist feel safe and at home whilst being taken around to observe all that is new and culturally different to him/her. Here, the tours generate, as elsewhere, a mobile and mediat(iz)ed gaze (Urry, 2002). Snapshots of historical landmarks and futuristic icons are presented but, and in a classic manner, we learn what is 'typically' Shanghaiese and how to read its signs (MacCannel, 1989). There is, of course, a growing tourism discourse about Shanghai – a script for the place, directing gazes, prescribing routes and promising experiences – that many have consumed before their journey. Its legendary reputation has been mediated innumerable times, as decadent, sinful, adventurous and entrepreneurial. It is also part of both a local and global production of nostalgia, in films, books, postcards, in cafes, restaurants and museums and renovated hotels. But the place itself affects visitors, sensuously and emotionally, in a way no script may ever exhaustively describe. Shanghai is the place where the Westerner perceives something partially known, where certain behaviours and certain attitudes are sanctioned, and certain experiences are guaranteed, but this is often a sundry and strange experience. This uncanny new-and-old, yet hyper-modern place is in equal proportion reinstating the primacy and sense of superiority of the Western visitor, as much as it confounds and unsettles him/her.

One rhythm of Shanghai is less perplexing, and for Westerners right up their alley: Shanghai's commercial imperative. Shanghai is where you are expected to max out your credit card and spend excessively without qualms. The bus tour will take you to one tourist shop, an outlet owned by the state where voluminous consumption of heritage artefacts or silk clothes, is expected: 'There are also sightseeing bus lines to prosperous commercial centers where are [*sic*] found commodities and specialities from different places in the country'.[6] The heart of the city is beating with a commercial ethos. Extravagant shopping is what most people have come to relate the city to. Rhythms of Shanghai that testify to its futurity are established in many different ways: through its commercial energy, thick air and hazy sci-fi night sky, spectacular architecture, new infrastructure, and through mediatization and digitalization. The transformation of Shanghai is a gigantic political project, a revelation about China's ambitions in our time. On the tours, the political dimensions of the apparently banal are visible, and they may be described as instating, carrying forward and communicating straightforward ideological messages – the linearity of rhythm – of the rise of China and its newly acquired economic role in the world markets. This story may also be recognized in other modernizing urban spaces. The 'harmonics' are

The Sociological Review, 61:S1, pp. 144–161 (2013), DOI: 10.1111/1467-954X.12058

utopian when the guide recounts the oft-told story about Pudong, built in only two decades, on land that was previously a muddy riverbed. On the tour, the tourist may encounter what Ving Travel, a Swedish travel organizer promises on their homepage: 'Arriving on Asia's Manhattan, is just like stepping into the future, with all the futuristic creations rising to the sky'.[7] The tours are not only evoking the technological sublime. The rhetoric echoes an old Communist beautifying propaganda on the part of the municipal government, stating the tour will take us to: 'gardens with beautiful, natural landscape, where tourists may breathe the fresh air of a modern metropolis'.[8] The dictatorship is here painting a deceiving picture of modern China, whose level of carbon emission is the highest in the world, and whose air is notoriously bad for your health. Despite the less than sustainable development of the country, officialdom stresses its unambiguous, self-sufficient and unbendable movement ahead. This is a story in which architecture, natural parks and technology become what Leo Marx has called a 'virtual embodiment – an ideal icon – for human progress' (Marx, 1997).

Futurity as natural tradition

The obsession with modernization, mobility and movement not only reflects the temporality of speed or advancement forward in the direction of the arrow of time. Backward-looking practices are equally important in the city resurrection. But these memory practices are intriguing since Shanghai's collective memory is pervaded precisely by eternal movement, futurity and regeneration (Lu, 2002). Movement is thus the spirit of Shanghai, its signified, its natural tradition. When it developed from a treaty port for the colonial powers, to a modern metropolis in the 1920s and 30s, mobilities were key in Shanghai's transformation. As historian Jeffrey Wasserstrom (2008) has shown, new means of transportation became pivotal for the pervasive transitions also during the decades before 1900. Trams then became as important and iconic in the city as the rickshaws. For foreign travel writers these technologies also contributed to the obscure sense in which Shanghai constituted a virtual West. For the natives, trams also became part of the everyday rhythms of the city. In his analysis of the Chinese author Zhang Ailing's novel, *Sealed Off* from 1943, Zhang (2000) describes how the author depicts modern Shanghai's sleepless energy, and eternal movement – allegorically represented by a mechanical-temporal order of the tram – through an interruption of the rhythms of the vehicle due to a distress signal for an air strike. The tram, whose movements could have gone on for ever, is at a standstill and throws its passengers into a vast empty timespace where the subsconsciousness of the modern – its ghostly dreamlife – is set loose when the passengers become exposed to one another, and try to ignore each other, by filling the eternal eventless waiting with something – anything. The tram is a quintessential sign for industrial modernity argues Zhang, and is transformed here from being a machine that enables an entrance into the city, into an apparatus for perceiving the basic temporal and psychological structures of the metropolis (2000: 352).

If mobility is Shanghai's natural tradition, then perhaps nothing may more accurately recount its key narrative, or embody its rhythms than the bus. Shanghai belongs to a group of cities displaying a particular need to (re)define themselves and their place identity in our global era, and to compete for an international audience. Reverberating with important aspects of Shanghai's identity, 'hypermodern' Singapore is characterized by idiosyncracies of constant movement and development (Phillips, 2005); Dubai may be depicted in terms of naturalized change as tradition (Devji, 2007) and Kuala Lumpur has been designated as a heterogenous laboratory of a heretofore unknown 'postmetropolitan' form that strangely repeats itself day by day (Kumar Biswas, 2005).

Shanghai seems to, in a similar vein, materialize flow and its specific signature is its continuing novelty. This also emphasizes that when these postcolonial spaces are reconquering their former modernity – which in itself has to be defined as a local, hybridized and vernacular variant of global patterns of modernization – then these are given new and not so new symbolic affordances (cf. Hansen, 1999; Zhang, 2005). But apart from mobility and newfangledness as tradition, as shown above in relation to the standard route in the city, a composition of heterotopian rhythms echo in Shanghai, reverberating also with the collective memory of the metropolis.

Confused and mixed

Through its name there is one tour in the city that is particularly conspicuous: 'Confused and nixed [*sic*. mixed] Shanghai'. The name discloses a kind of reflexivity surrounding the many confusing multiplicities of the city, and its bizarre temporal web. This also reflects that the city has always articulated its identity as a tension between East and West, Chinese and Western, migrants and traditions and cuisine from all the different provinces of China, old and new, tradition and modernity. The content of the tour is not, however, stranger than the others. It runs to People's Square, Shanghai Urban Planning Exhibition Centre, the Bund, the Bund Sightseeing Tunnel, Pudong New Area, Nanpu Bridge, YuYuan Garden and then on a River Cruise. The tour is an apparently unplanned, but in reality a highly conscious and organized, movement; an action that, in the words of Jonathan Sterne (2006), confirms that the transport itself is meaningful, constituting conditions for certain types of social action, and sometimes also their content.

On the 'Confused and mixed' tour, rhythms of Shanghai as diverse, exciting, rich, adventurous, electric and a little bit dangerous, are discernible. These facets of the city have a history in the cultural production of the past, argues Alexander Des Forges (2007). He emphasizes the role of texts for the formation of social reality and its ideology. In mediasphere Shanghai between 1890 and 1930, in

The Sociological Review, 61:S1, pp. 144–161 (2013), DOI: 10.1111/1467-954X.12058

guidebooks, novels, papers, illustrated books, films, a formal aesthetic was established. This covered core experiential fields in the city that were dominated by the features of simultaneity, interruption, mediation and excess. These features continue to shape how Shanghai is experienced today. One of the stops on this tour in time has more significance than the others. My central argument is that Shanghai celebrates its *future past* of the inter-war era. Among the many time periods that are traceable in Shanghai, it is in the modernity and mass culture of the 1920s and 1930s, as well as the famous architecture in the French concession and former international settlement in which the city has anchored its place identity. This way, imaginary time travel – also on board the buses – authenticates and naturalizes the futuristic claims of the city. The tour thereby assumes a teleporting function. Producing a nostalgia for the 1930s, is also part of producing a decadent time space, a particular romantic ideal about the Shanghai badlands, its media modernity, violence, gender politics and sinfulness, that have been reconquered by the municipal government in the past two decades. Shanghai has been re-established as a landscape of desire, a space for the 'last days' of long drinks and excessive consumption, arguably reinforcing the impulses to consume even more. It is through this mediated collective memory that people have also been convinced that Shanghai is this place of excess, and it is precisely through the physical return of the Westerners, that this memory has been brought to life, and has become significant. Here, linear and cyclical rhythms seem, in effect, to be effectively interwoven and merged.

Mediating rhythms

The words 'confused and mixed' allude to the cosmopolitan identity of the place. As discussed above, confusing multiplicity is at the heart of Shanghai's place myth. This discourse has a long history and is part of the collective memory of the city. Through the cultural industries, the image of this heterogeneity was produced, where the citizens had little or no contact or interaction. The distinctions were not as rigid in historical reality though (Lu, 2004: 25). Historical and biographical sources tell a story of division between rich and poor, Westerners and Chinese, but contacts and exchanges were common. Hanchao Lu has depicted how the foreign concession areas, from the beginning, expelled Chinese settlements but in the 1850s were obliged to allow an inflow of Chinese migrants escaping wars and social upheaval in different provinces. These people actually dominated the areas numerically, and within this group, rich and privileged Chinese were coexisting with less affluent migrants who were often employed in the households of the rich. These circumstances also contributed to making Shanghai the most cosmopolitan city in China.

In *Shanghai Boy, Shanghai Girl: Lives in Parallel*, two diametrically different lives in the city of the 1930s and 1940s are portrayed. One is about George Wang who came from a poor Chinese family a couple of kilometres to the south of the Chinese city, in an area called Kaochangmiao, and the other about the British

Betty Barr (later Wang's wife) who grew up on the other side, in the international settlement. That the city before 1943 was divided into three cities or even countries, is clear from Wang's description of the organizational independence and infrastructural differences on all levels:

> No wall separated one part from another, but each had its own city government, its own courts of justice, its own police force, and its own transport system. There were three different waterworks, run by the different owners, and there were three power companies. The light bulbs used in Frenchtown could not be used in the international settlement. (Wang and Barr, 2002: 9)

Wang and Barr testify to having been able to step onto the tram, and conduct a journey of 40 minutes through all the parts of the city; an account reflecting both the divides in a separated city and, perhaps, also the occasional possibility of bridging these:

> It was interesting to travel by tram all the way from Broadway Mansions in the north of the International settlement to Kaochangmiao in the south. Near Garden Bridge, across the Sochow creek near the Wangpoo River, you got on a tram made in Manchester England, and got off at the southern International settlement boundary. You then walked across the border street Avenue Edward VII, into Frenchtown and took the French made tram down to the border with Nanshih. After crossing that boundary you took a Chinese tram to the terminus in Kaochangmiao. Of course each time you got on a tram you had to pay a fare. (2002: 10)

The trams *mediated* between and connected the different concessional areas. Modern Shanghai of the 1920s and 30s, argues Zhang (2005: 50), was divided in 'a mixed spell of wonder and oppression', but the uneven urban geography was also encapsulated in this era, by a new infrastructure that saturated both the Chinese parts and the foreign concession areas. This period cannot be fully grasped without an understanding of its media culture, she argues. As Sterne (2006: 119) has argued, you may here trace how infrastructure and media culture constitute one another, as part of 'a particular social complex of communication'.

This aspect of mediation seems equally important today. Perhaps this feature is what the place requires? The final decade of the 20th century in Shanghai was a gigantic project to spatialize time and arrest the future, argues Zhang (2001: 134). The massive building of highways, airports, and bridges and railways became 'spatiotemporal passages a la Benjamin' (Zhang, 2001: 134), linking the old and the new and the rural and the urban. Can the bus tours be described in this way, as movements and media/communication forms that organize the clutter by connecting the time layers and by braiding the incommensurable into the *rhythms of Shanghai*?

The tram enabled the traveller to perceive a unity in all the separate and assorted aspects of the city's jurisdictions, and likewise, the movement aboard the buses may actually interweave the different sites. Here Shanghai's rhythms are composed; the voyager is participating in composing the globalizing city, as well as the nation and the one-party state. A marked sound of astonishment swept through the bus as the thousands of skyscrapers came into and filled our view: 'fantastic, awesome, very impressive', the group exclaimed. We were in Puxi, the district of Huangpu, and travelled on the elevated highway toward People's Square. Then on YanAn Road, the bus made a soft turn to the south west, onto the slightly curved promenade, the Bund, where we were simultaneously exposed to a magnificent view of Pudong, and the line of unrealistically high buildings of shimmering glass and steel on the eastern shore of the Huangpu River, and to the West we saw the Bund, with its line of restored Western colonial architecture. We stopped by the Bund for group photographs. First we gazed at Pudong, then, facing the camera, we turned our backs against the future while gazing at the future past – part of a ritual to be repeated by hundreds of thousands of people. The tour, and our bodies, thus binds the two parts of the city, Pudong och Puxi, the new and the old. The tram, as well as the infrastructure and communications at large in the past, constituted what the buses, bridges, road network and gazes do today: their movements mediate the city into a unitary experience. These tours in retromodernity, take us on time travel, back and forth, uniting and interweaving the fragments, and organizing a certain sense of order in this polyrhythmic space. But most importantly, the buses take the visitor on tours between now and then, which *trains her to perceive an endemic simultaneity between the different timespaces in the temporal braid.* Shanghai, argues Des Forges, is now an 'ideal laboratory for global modernity' posing itself as 'the best place in which to integrate globalization past and globalization future into a coherent narrative' (2007: 181). Shanghai's success in this endeavour is predicated upon, he suggests, the extent to which the city manages to mediate between old and new, straddle the past and future, in business ventures and at tourist attractions such as Shanghai Art Museum and the tourist enclave Xintiandi. In this essay I have approached a closely related aspect of this type of mediation, conducted by the bus tours for foreign visitors.

Rhythmic discordances: in conclusion

The tours represent while co-producing the heterogeneity of space. The city is confounding and the buses both confirm this and interweave its fragments and multiplicity into something unitary – not unlike how sociologists have described the role of tourism in modernity at large. The city has in several ways arrived at, I argue, an entanglement of the two modernities – into the rhythms of the city – something most succinctly expressed through the cult for the mass and media cultures of the 1930s. The rhythms of Shanghai invite the visitor to travel in time, and encourage her to get off and dwell in the golden interwar era and its combination of velvet and violence, opium dens and jazz, and to simultaneously partake in reproducing the complex temporal experience where the futuristic movement is also a movement into the past. On the tours it is almost mysterious and magical to see the many faces of the city. Its heterotopian boldness, and shameless chaos, as much as its architectural pluralism and beauty, contribute to the sense in which everything is possible, nothing is prohibited: '*Anything goes*'. *Utopia!* This very sense is also a core feature of how, according to Alexander Des Forges, the authorities in Shanghai expect its citizens to take control of their 'open future' (Des Forges, 2007: 183). But what is left out of this utopian fantasy, what significant silences are there in the official story of the city? And what evades the brief visitor? And can we capture how their impressions are perhaps compromising the official dogmatic linear rhythms of Shanghai?

I have, in this paper, discussed how the bus tours communicate a 'message' and 'make meaning', in line with Sterne, through their movements in the city, and through the official narratives and memories they convey. But the tour may also reveal something about the discordant rhythms and 'disorderly' aspects of sojourning in Shanghai. The divides in Chinese society are growing. Matti, aged 41, a local politician from small town Fagersta in Sweden, paid attention to this when we made a stop during the sightseeing tour in YuYuan Garden. He recalled his visual impression and the feelings evoked in the city:

> When I pulled aside the curtains in my hotel room and saw all the skyscrapers of Pudong, I thought that everything is just about to be torn down, and new highrises will be built here. Tear everything down, I thought. They will bring everything down, and build the largest metropolis in Asia, I thought. It is communism for the poor, and capitalism for the rich!

This account also reflects the complexities of the rhythms that mark this space, and how it may be felt on board the bus, through its movements: as a timespace saturated by an ambivalence that is prevalent throughout Chinese society. An important aspect of globalizing Shanghai is precisely this sense of combination between freedom and control, significantly present in China of today (J. Lagerkvist, 2010). Shanghai brings about this strange experience of a kind of utopian, borderless, nomadic, transnational and flowing condition (capitalism) simultaneously highly bounded, structured, nationalistic and controlled (the one party state). The capitalist emphasis on eternal exchange, and its unceasing hunger for the new, its transnational character is coexisting with the authoritarian social model stressing central governance, national stability and harmony through the party as final and capricious arbiter, in superior power. A tourist who travelled on a ferry along the Yangtze-river expressed in his travelblog his impressions of this tension inherent in the Chinese social transformation:

> China is still, officially, a Communist country, in a confused way. Mixed signals abound. There are old socialist touches. On top of the monumental dam is a monument to the dam. It's in the middle of a parking lot full of the Buicks, VWs and Audis of China's new capitalists. Next to that is a Buddhist garden, perfect for meditation, except loudspeakers in the shrubbery are playing pop songs.[9]

The hijacking of modernity, or its recoding, means that mutually exclusive social, cultural, temporal, economic and political forms are visible in the same timespace, in an even – by comparison with modernizing spaces in general – more accentuated manner. The buses are then underscoring the incomparable multiplicity in Shanghai's rhythmic composition, when they, as relics, circulate this futuristic yet retromodern space. These movements and the rhythms of Shanghai reproduce each other. But confusion may sometimes rise to levels beyond what the bus voyager can cognitively handle. In this circumstance, irony and humour is the last resort. In a sort of post-tourist irony, a blogger levels a comment about the 'Confused and mixed' tour, which also keeps those phantasmagorical self-representations of the city at bay:

> While we are on tours in China, I picked up a brochure from one of the tourist agents at the bus station last week that looks very interesting. It advertises a 'confused and nixed Shanghai' tour that promises to show the client an 'amazing Shanghai'. The brochure is skimpy on details of the tour but then why confuse people with the facts?[10]

The traveller wards off those aspects of the 'Confused and mixed' tour that stress Shanghai's idealized complexity. This is, arguably, the punctum, the moment when the linear rhythms are brought to a standstill, as tourists and travellers take a mental detour around them. Bus tours in Shanghai participate in stimulating genuine confoundedness in combination with fascination. This engenders a spatial practice of gawking, of excessively consuming this strange space, and all that it offers. But, I argue in conclusion, the tours cannot repress those non-themed and spontaneous rhythmic discordances, that evoke incompatible and uncanny feelings, as well as the sense of humour and even ironical social critique that travellers sometimes communicate – on their tours in retromodernity.

Acknowledgements

Parts of this article will appear in a different version as 'Confused and Mixed Shanghai: På turer i det retromoderna', in Lotten Gustafson Reinius, Ylva Habel and Solveig Jülich (eds), *Bussen är budskapet: materialitet, mobilitet och modernitet*, Stockholm: Mediehistoriskt Arkiv (forthcoming, 2013). The author wishes to thank Lotten Gustafson Reinius, Ylva Habel and Solveig Jülich as well as the other participants in the Bussen är budskapet-workshops for valuable comments on earlier drafts of this article.

Notes

1 Other post-Communist spaces have also been subject to similar analyses of their overlapping temporalities, for instance Talinn, Estonia. See Gustafsson Reinius (2002).
2 'Tales of Old Shanghai', http://www.earnshaw.com/shanghai-ed-india/tales/tales.htm (accessed 9 September 2010).
3 Understood phenomenologically time is a non-linear, social, lived and embodied experience (May and Thrift, 2001). Time is both holistic and fragmented at the same time, multiple and

heterogenous, structured, in turn, in both multiple and dynamic ways, shaping incompatible and contradictory, yet interrelated senses of time (Grosz, 1999). This suggests a radical unevenness in the nature and quality of social time itself.

4 Interview with Rachel, American playwright from LA, expatriate in Shanghai, Beijing, September 2009.

5 I am indebted to Ylva Habel for this astute point.

6 http://www.cityguideshanghai.com/.../shanghai-sightseeing-bus-center.html (accessed 4 June 2009).

7 http://www.ving.se/kina/shanghai (accessed 9 September 2010).

8 http://www.cityguideshanghai.com/.../shanghai-sightseeing-bus-center.html (accessed 4 June 2009).

9 'Yangtze Doodle Dandy', http://www.forbes.com, 13 November 2006 (accessed 9 September 2010).

10 http://peavine.blogspot.com/2007_05_01_archive.html (accessed 9 September 2010).

References

Abbas, A., (2002), 'Play it again Shanghai: urban preservation in the global era', in M. Gandelsonas (ed.), *Shanghai Reflections, Architecture, Urbanism, and the Search for Alternative Modernity*, 36–55. New York: Princeton Architectural Press.

Acland, C. R. (ed.), (2007), *Residual Media*, Minneapolis: University of Minnesota Press.

Bolter, J. D. and Grusin, R., (1999), *Remediation: Understanding New Media*, Boston: MIT Press.

Campanella, T. J., (2008), *The Concrete Dragon: China's Urban Revolution and What it Means for the World*, Princeton, NJ: Princeton Architectural Press.

Carey, J., (1989), *Communication as Culture: Essays in Media and Society*, New York: Routledge.

Chen, X. (ed.), (2009), *Shanghai Rising: State Power and Local Transformations in a Global Megacity*, Minneapolis: University of Minnesota Press.

Couldry, N. and McCarthy, A., (2004), *Mediaspace: Place, Scale and Culture in a Media Age*, London: Routledge.

Crang, M., (2001), 'Rhythms of the city: temporalised space and motion', in J. May and N. Thrift (eds), *Timespace: Geographies of Temporality*, London: Routledge.

Crang, M. and Travlou, P., (2001), 'The city and topologies of memory', *Environment and Planning D: Society and Space*, 19: 161–177.

Cresswell, T., (2010), 'Towards a politics of mobility', *Environment and Planning D: Society and Space*, 28: 17–31.

Des Forges, A., (2007), *Mediasphere Shanghai: The Aesthetics of Cultural Production*, Honolulu: University of Hawaii Press.

Devji, F., (2007), 'Dubai cosmopolis', www.openDemocracy.net (accessed 1 April 2007).

Dutton, M., (2008), *Beijing Time*, Cambridge, MA: Harvard University Press.

Edensor, T. (ed.), (2010), *Geographies of Rhythm: Nature, Place, Mobilities and Bodies*, Farnham: Ashgate.

Graham, S. (ed.), (2004), *The Cybercities Reader*, London: Routledge.

Grosz, E., (1992), 'Bodies/cities', in B. Colomina (ed.), *Sexuality and Space*, Princeton, NJ: Princeton Architectural Press.

Grosz, E., (1999), 'Thinking the new: of futures yet unthought', in E. Grosz (ed.), *Becomings: Explorations in Time, Memory and Futures*, Ithaca, NY: Cornell University Press.

Gustafsson Reinius, L., (2002), 'Medeltidskartor och minnespolitik', in A. Eriksen, J. Garnert and T. Selberg (eds), *Historien in på livet: Diskussioner om kulturarv och minnespolitik*, 31–45, Lund: Nordic Academic Press.

Hansen, M., (1999), 'The mass production of the senses: classical cinema as vernacular modernism', *Modernism/Modernity*, 6 (2): 59–77.

Highmore, B., (2005), *Cityscapes: Cultural Readings in the Material and Symbolic City*, London: Palgrave Macmillan.

Kofman, E. and Lebas, E., (1996), 'Lost in transposition – time, space and the city', in H. Lefebvre, *Writings on Cities*, Cambridge, MA: Blackwell.

Kumar Biswas, R., (2005), 'Kuala Lumpur: an allegorical postmetropolis', in S. Read, J. Rosemann and J. van Eldijk (eds), *Future City*, New York: Spon Press.

Lagerkvist, A., (2007), ' "Gazing at Pudong – with a drink in your hand": time travel, mediation, and multisensuous immersion in the future city of Shanghai', *Senses and Society*, 3 (2): 155–172.

Lagerkvist, A., (2009), 'La Villa Rouge: replaying decadence in Shanghai', in A. Jansson and A. Lagerkvist (eds), *Strange Spaces: Explorations into Mediated Obscurity*, Farnham: Ashgate.

Lagerkvist, A., (2010), 'The future is here: media, memory and futurity in Shanghai', *Space and Culture*, 13 (3): 220–238.

Lagerkvist, A., (2011), 'Velvet and violence: performing the mediatized memory of Shanghai's futurity', in P. P. Frassinelli, R. Frenkel and D. Watson (eds), *Traversing Transnationalism*, Amsterdam/New York: Rodopi.

Lagerkvist, A., (forthcoming), *Media and Memory in New Shanghai: Western Performances of Futures Past*, Basingstoke: Palgrave Macmillan.

Lagerkvist, J., (2010), *After the Internet, Before Democracy: Competing Norms in Chinese Media and Society*, New York: Peter Lang.

Lefebvre, H., (2004 [1992]), *Rhythmanalysis: Space, Time and Everyday Life*, London: Continuum.

Lefebvre, H., (1996), *Writings on Cities*, Cambridge, MA: Blackwell.

Lu, H., (2002), 'Nostalgia for the future: the resurgence of an alienated culture in China', *Pacific Affairs*, 75 (2): 169–186.

Lu, H., (2004), *Beyond the Neon Lights: Everyday Shanghai in the Early Twentieth Century*, Berkeley, CA: University of California Press.

MacCannel, D., (1989 [1976]), *The Tourist: A New Theory of the Leisure Class*, New York: Schocken Books.

Marx, L., (1997), 'Technology: the emergence of a hazardous concept', *Social Research*, 64 (3): 965–988.

May, J. and Thrift, N. (eds), (2001), *Timespace: Geographies of Temporality*, London: Routledge.

McQuire, S., (2008), *The Media City: Media, Architecture and Urban Space*, London: Sage.

Phillips, J., (2005), 'The future of the past: archiving Singapore', in Mark Crinson (ed.), *Urban Memory: History and Amnesia in the Modern City*, London: Routledge.

Rajchman, J., (1994), 'Thinking big: Dutch architect Rem Koolhaas (Interview)', *ArtForum*, December, http://www.highbeam.com/doc/1G1-16547724.html (accessed 16 May 2013).

Sterne, J., (2006), 'Transportation and communication: together as you've always wanted them', in C. Robertson and J. Packer, *Thinking with James Carey: Essays on Communications, Transportation, History*, New York: Peter Lang.

Todorov, T., (1993), *On Human Diversity. Nationalism, Racism, and Exoticism in French Thought*, Cambridge, MA: Harvard University Press.

Urry, J., (2002), *The Tourist Gaze*, London: Sage.

Wang, G. and Barr, B., (2002), *Shanghai Boy, Shanghai Girl: Lives in Parallel*, Hong Kong: Old China Hand Press.

Wasserstrom, J. N., (2008), *Global Shanghai, 1850–2010*, London: Routledge.

Williams, R., (1977), *Marxism and Literature*, Oxford: Oxford University Press.

Zhang, X., (2000), 'Shanghai nostalgia: postrevolutionary allegories in Wang Anyi's literary production in the 1990s', *positions*, 8 (2): 349–387.

Zhang, Z., (2001), 'Mediating time: the "rice bowl of youth" in fin de siècle China', in A. Appadurai (ed.), *Globalization*, Durham, NC: Duke University Press.

Zhang, Z., (2005), *An Amorous History of the Silver Screen*, Chicago: Chicago University Press.

Notes on contributors

Achmad Uzair Fauzan is a lecturer in the Faculty of Social Sciences and Humanities, State Islamic University of Sunan Kalijaga in Yogyakarta. Currently, he is a student at Flinders Asia Centre, School of International Studies, Flinders University, under the supervision of Dr Priyambudi Sulistiyanto. Among his primary research interests are resource politics, particularly at local level, and social movements. E-mail: achmad.fauzanuzair@flinders.edu.au

Tom Hall lectures in sociology and urban anthropology at the Cardiff University School of Social Sciences. He is interested in urban inequality and the politics of public space, waste and cleaning, and the street-level practices of urban care, repair and patrol. He is the author of *Better Times than This*, an ethnography of youth homelessness. E-mail: HallTA@cardiff.ac.uk

Kevin Hetherington is Professor of Geography at the Open University where he is currently Dean and Director of Studies in the Faculty of Social Sciences. He previously held a Chair in Cultural Sociology at Lancaster University and has worked across the boundary of both disciplines for most of his career. He currently researches on issues of museums, heritage and urban regeneration and social and spatial theory. His seven books include *The Badlands of Modernity* (1997), *Capitalism's Eye* (2007), and (with Anne Cronin) *Consuming the Entrepreneurial City* (2008). He is currently writing a book on museums. He is a member of several editorial boards including a recent reappointment to the board of *The Sociological Review* having been previously involved from 1994 to 2003. He was a founding co-editor of the journal *Museum and Society* (co-editor from 2003 to 2009) and currently co-edits the book series *Culture, Economy and the Social* for Routledge. E-mail: k.i.hetherington@open.ac.uk

Beatriz Jaguaribe teaches at the School of Communications of the Federal University of Rio de Janeiro. She has been a visiting professor at Dartmouth College, Stanford University, the New School of Social Research, Princeton University and New York University. In 2004 she was awarded a Guggenheim Fellowship and in 2009 she was nominated for the Andrés Bello Chair at the King Juan Carlos of Spain Center at NYU. Her research focuses on urban

The Sociological Review, 61:S1, pp. 162–164 (2013), DOI: 10.1111/1467-954X.12060
Editorial organisation © 2013 The Editorial Board of the Sociological Review. Published by John Wiley & Sons Ltd, 9600 Garsington Road, Oxford OX4 2DQ, UK and 350 Main Street, Malden, MA 02148, USA

cultures in Brazil, national imaginaries in Brazil and Argentina and the inventions of the self in literature and visual culture. Among her publications are *Fins de Século: Cidade e Cultura no Rio de Janeiro* (1998), *Mapa do Maravilhoso do Rio de Janeiro* (2001), *O choque do real* (2007), and the text written together with Mauricio Lissovsky for the photography book, *Só existe um Rio* (2008) Her forthcoming book *Rio de Janeiro: Urban Culture through the Eyes of the City* is due to be published by Routledge in 2014. E-mail: beajaguar@gmail.com

Hille Koskela is a Senior Lecturer in the Department of Geosciences and Geography, University of Helsinki, Finland. Her research interests include urban security politics, subcultures and the emotional experiences that relate to urban fear and danger. She has also conducted research on video surveillance and the responsibilization of the public to contribute in surveillance. She has published articles in journals such as *Surveillance and Society*, *Crime Media Culture* and *Theoretical Criminology*, and has contributed to several international anthologies. Her current research deals with surveillance-related uses of online webcams. E-mail: hille.koskela@helsinki.fi

Amanda Lagerkvist is an Associate Professor and Senior Lecturer in Media and Communication Studies at Södertörn University, Stockholm, Sweden. She is the author of *Media and Memory in New Shanghai: Western Performancs of Futures Past* (forthcoming with Palgrave Macmillan), the co-editor of *Strange Spaces: Explorations into Mediated Obscurity* (published by Ashgate, 2009) and the author of numerous articles on media space, mobilities and memory. Working from a socio-phenomenological theoretical framework, her research interests include relationships between urban space, mobilities and mediation, media and collective memory, digital memory cultures, and religion and the media. She is currently working on a project on the televisual memory of 9/11 in Sweden, and on the existential dimensions of the commemoration of mediated trauma. E-mail: amanda.lagerkvist@sh.se

Panu Lehtovuori works as Professor of Planning Theory at the School of Architecture, Tampere University of Technology, Finland. He is a partner of Livady Architects and acts as an associate in the Spatial Intelligence Unit (SPIN). Lehtovuori's current research interests are contemporary forms of public urban space and emerging spatial practices, such as temporary uses and digitally mediated services. Combining theory and practice, he aims at a critical rethinking of the foundations and tools of urban planning. His recent publications include articles in journals such as *Critical Sociology* and a monograph *Experience and Conflict: The Production of Urban Space* (Ashgate, 2010). E-mail: panu.lehtovuori@tut.fi

George Revill is a Senior Lecturer at the Open University. His research concerns issues of landscape, technology, culture and identity, and has included an analysis of the politics of landscape and national identity in music of the English musical renaissance (1880–1940). His current research interests centre on an attempt to bring issues of sound, mobility and landscape together. George has begun work on a book about the politics of landscape, music and environmental sound in the 20th century, *Britain Landscape, Music and the Politics of Sound*. His work is also concerned with landscape and the cultures of transport, mobility and technology; *Railway* (Reaktion Press, 2012) examines the role of the railway as a cultural icon of modernity. George was chair of the Landscape Research Group, 1999–2009 and a member of the newly formed Research Advisory Board to the National Museum of Science and Industry. E-mail: George.revill@open.ac.uk

AbdouMaliq Simone teaches at the University of South Australia. He is also Honorary Professor of Urban Studies at the African Centre for Cities, University of Cape Town. He is the author of *In Whose Image: Political Islam and Urbanization in Sudan; For the City Yet to Come: Urban Life in Four African Cities* and; *City Life from Jakarta to Dakar: Movements at the Crossroads.* E-mail: abdoumaliqsimone@gmail.com

Robin Smith teaches sociology and qualitative methodology at Cardiff University. His existing research has been broadly focused upon the interaction order of everyday urban public space. He is, in particular, interested in the street-level accomplishment and politics of encounter, mobility and territory. E-mail: Smithrj3@cardiff.ac.uk

Stavros Stavrides is Associate Professor at the School of Architecture, National Technical University of Athens Greece, where he teaches a graduate course on social housing, as well as a postgraduate course on the meaning of metropolitan experience. He has published five books (as well as numerous articles) on spatial theory: *The Symbolic Relation to Space* (Athens, 1990), *Advertising and the Meaning of Space* (Athens, 1996), *The Texture of Things* (Athens, 1996), *From the City-as-Screen to the City-as-Stage* (Athens, 2002; National Book Award), *Suspended Spaces of Alterity* (2010) and *Towards the City of Thresholds* (in English, 2010). His research is also focused on forms of emancipating spatial practices (characteristically developed in his contribution to K. Franck and Q. Stevens (eds), *Loose Space: Possibility and Diversity in Public Life* (Routledge, 2006), and to P. Barron and M. Mariani (eds) *Terrain Vague* (forthcoming). E-mail: zoesm@central.ntua.gr

Index

The Sociological Review, 61:S1, pp. 165–168 (2013), DOI: 10.1111/1467-954X.12073

The Sociological Review, 61:S1, pp. 165–168 (2013), DOI: 10.1111/1467-954X.12073
Editorial organisation © 2013 The Editorial Board of the Sociological Review